CASE STUDIES F

THE GOOD BOOK ON LEADERSHIP

JOHN BOREK

DANNY LOVETT

ELMER TOWNS

BROADMAN
&HOLMAN
PUBLISHERS

NASHVILLE, TENNESSEE

Ten-Digit ISBN: 0805431675
Eight-Digit ISBN: 9780805431674

Published by Broadman & Holman Publishers
Nashville, Tennessee

Dewey Decimal Classification: 303.3
Subject Heading: LEADERSHIP

Scripture quotations are from the New King James Version, copyright
© 1979, 1980, 1982, Thomas Nelson, Inc., Publishers.

1 2 3 4 5 6 7 8 9 10 10 09 08 07 06 05

Contents

Not Methods but Leadership

What is the greatest need in today's church? It is not more money, new buildings, bigger buildings, new workable methods, more workers, or any of the other "things" we throw at the church's problems. The greatest need of the church is leadership . . . biblical leadership . . . effective leadership . . . spiritual leadership. The right type of leadership can solve the church's problems.

The right leader can raise the needed money, build the necessary buildings, recruit willing workers, attract eager followers, and discover new methods to get the job done.

Successful ministry rises and falls on leadership.

This book is a case study of leadership in the Bible, considering people who used a variety of strengths and resources to accomplish the work of God. This book teaches there is no one leadership trait that can be used by all people, in all situations, to lead all groups. Leadership is always expressed differently because each leader has a different personality and different strengths, and each group of followers has different needs. Problems are different, as are customs, times, and motivations. But even though each of the leaders in the Bible is different, there tend to be clusters of traits evident with different leaders. This book will

1

examine twenty-three different expressions of leadership and how each leader in the Bible accomplished his or her task differently.

This book doesn't try to determine which leader type is best, or which is most effective, or even which has the most blessing of God. The reader will examine each leadership type—to see its strengths and weaknesses—to better learn leadership from these examples and case studies.

There is no perfect leader—except Jesus who was the God-man. All other leaders have human limitations. But human leaders who are called by God get the job done in a variety of ways. Since none of us has arrived, all of us should be growing leaders. We've written this book to help you apply these principles to your circumstances so you can become a better leader.

There is a subtheme in this book; it's the supernatural accomplishment that a leader can expect when empowered by God. The reader should sense a spirit of optimism while reading this book. What should be your expectations after finishing this book?

OPTIMISTIC BREAKTHROUGH

Getting the job done, in the face of insurmountable odds, with limited resources, in difficult circumstances to the glory of God.

We don't want you to apply just one chapter to your leadership skills. We say this because some will relate their strength or passion to the one chapter of this study that best reflects their abilities. We want you to apply all of these leadership traits to all the various tasks you face. Don't be a "narrow-focused" leader who reacts only one way. Be broad and learn as much as you can from each of these leadership traits.

While much of the world is searching for better tools and machines—while many in the church are searching for better methods—God is searching for better *people*. The answer to church renewal . . . growth in membership . . . and a return to renewed life is leadership.

Educated leadership
Prepared leadership
Spiritual leadership
Experienced leadership
Visionary leadership

Most books on leadership deal with theory, based on what the author has tried and used. Some theories are based on a study of one person, such as *Lincoln on Leadership* and *Jesus on Leadership*. A book that suggests a theoretical type of leadership is like the models that are built by automotive makers. They are snazzy but haven't proven themselves on the road. A model is how the engineers want it to run, and a leadership model is how the theorists want leadership to act. But life is not theoretical, life is encumbered with warts, memory lapses, sin, failure, and noncompliant followers. The leaders who are examined in this book are not perfect leaders, but they have strengths to excite us . . . victories to challenge us . . . traits to motivate us . . . and lessons to teach us. So let's learn from the total contribution of each trait; then let's become better leaders.

We give credit to many who have helped make this book a reality. Thanks to Douglas Porter for original research, and thanks to Linda Elliott for editing and proofreading. Thanks to Sharon Hartless, Linda Sweat, and Renee Grooms—our administrative assistants—the ones who help us get everything done. This book is the product of many who have taught us much about leadership, but in the final analysis, we the authors must shoulder the responsibility for all its weaknesses.

This book is dedicated to growing the leader in all of us. May we follow the lead of Jesus Christ to accomplish much for His glory.

John Borek, Ph.D., President, Liberty University
Danny Lovett, D.Min., Dean, Liberty Baptist Theological Seminary
Elmer Towns, D.Min., Dean, School of Religion, Liberty University

CHAPTER 1

The Nature of Leadership

*The hand of the diligent will rule, but the lazy man
will be put to forced labor.*

PROVERBS 12:24

Everything rises or falls on leadership." John Maxwell says this now!
Lee Roberson, pastor of one of the largest churches in America,
said it before him. And we forget who said it first.[1]

Counselors claim the presence of a strong and loving husband and
father can make all the difference in the world for the family. Recent
publications like *Daddy's Little Girl*,[2] *The Mom Factor*,[3] and *The
Blessing*[4] all report the significant impact parents have on children,
both positive and negative. Successful families rise or fall on leadership.

Some of America's finest schools are located in inner cities marked
by urban decay. They are the kind of institutions sociologists would
claim are destined for failure. Indeed, many were once an embarrassment to their state educational agency. But the vision of a new principal and the passion of dedicated teachers together with the
cooperation of parents and local community leaders have transformed
dying schools into model schools—schools that teach students who
learn and move on to institutions of higher education for further
training as they pursue lofty dreams. Schools rise or fall on leadership.

The best team in the league is not always the team with the best players. When National Hockey League players were first allowed to play in the Winter Olympics, everyone knew Team Canada had the gold medal sewn up. But the Gretzky gang was shut out of the medals completely and returned home empty-handed. In contrast, the Montreal Expos have consistently placed near the top of the standings throughout the last decade, despite having the second-lowest payroll in the major league. There are no superstars on the team, but great coaches on the bench. In every sport, teams rise or fall on leadership.

Great men of God build great churches. When people think of the world's largest churches, they usually think first of the pastor. To talk about Willow Creek Community Church is to talk about Bill Hybels. It is difficult to mention Saddleback Community Church without referring to Rick Warren. People are more likely to mention "Yonggi Cho's church" than to call it Yoido Full Gospel Church of Seoul, S. Korea, the largest local church in history with over 750,000 members. Mention a great church in your community, and someone is likely to say, "Isn't that where ____ is pastor?" Churches rise or fall on leadership.

Overwhelming force is not always the key to great military victories. Ever since David defeated Goliath, great military leaders have used limited resources to win great victories. Sir Francis Drake was clearly outnumbered when he defeated the Spanish Armada with his leadership skill and inspiration. Germany clearly had overwhelming air superiority in the Battle of Britain, but England was led by Sir Winston Churchill, the one man who put a steel backbone in England's resistance. George Washington's army wasn't much, but under his courage it was enough to defeat the largest empire in the world, the British, in the Revolutionary War. Great armies, navies, and air forces rise or fall on leadership.

Worthy causes depend on great leaders for success. Even when the cause is just, it is often neglected until embraced by a leader. Mother Teresa made people care about the poor of India. Elizabeth Fry embraced the cause of prison reform in her generation and transformed the character of Britain's penal institutions. Throughout the twentieth century, a host of national leaders rose in various European colonies worldwide to lead their nations to independence. When a popular leader takes up the cause of some dreaded disease, only then are the funds raised to finance the research needed to find a cure. Worthy causes rise or fall on leadership.

Leaders alone achieve success in business. Having a great product or service is not enough in today's competitive market. While having a loyal and committed team may help, they need a strong leader to show them the way. A strong leader can lead a team to overcome obstacles and accomplish their goals. It was obvious Microsoft would never amount to much in a market dominated by IBM, but Bill Gates gathered a team and made it happen. Today they know their greatest challenger may not be in an executive office in Silicon Valley. He may be struggling to make a new product or idea work in his garage, basement, or the spare room in his apartment. Businesses rise or fall on leadership.

Four Ways to Describe Leaders

Because we are so dependent on leaders for group success, it is not surprising that many have attempted to describe the essence of leadership. From the days of Nimrod, who led a group to establish a city and build a tower, people have tried to explain what makes a leader a leader. Often these definitions are like the blind man's description of an elephant. When touching it, the blind man determined an elephant was four pillars and a wall with a rope on one end and a hose on the other. He was able to discern the parts but unable to see the whole.

Leadership may be one of those things that is easier *caught* than *taught*. Despite our best efforts to the contrary, attempts at defining leadership tend to focus on the parts rather than the whole. Various leadership definitions tend to focus in four areas. Some definitions describe leadership in the context of the person who is leader. Others describe the process by which leaders lead. Still others tend to focus on the leader's ability to persuade others to follow. Then there are those who describe leaders in the context of the people being led.

Leadership does not exist without a leader. It has been said that leaders have two important characteristics: First, they are going somewhere; second, they are able to persuade other people to go with them. Tom Landry, long-time coach of the Dallas Cowboys, claimed, "Leadership is a matter of having people look at you and gain confidence, seeing how you react. If you are in control, they are in control."[5] If everything rises or falls on leadership, then it rises or falls on the one who is leader. Some students of leadership have even suggested it can be defined in the unique mix of certain personality traits.

Understanding the process by which leaders lead also provides insight into the nature of leadership. In one sense, leadership is the process of helping people do the worthwhile things they want to do. Good leadership has been described as the art of getting average people to do great work. At its highest, leadership consists of getting people to work for you when they are under no obligation to do so. That is why, according to Henry Cabot, "You lose leadership when you cease to lead."[6]

Perhaps the briefest definition of leadership states, "Leadership is influence." Ordway Tead described leadership as "the activity of influencing people to cooperate toward some goal, which they come to find desirable."[7] In a military context, it is the process by which one soldier influences others to accomplish the mission. Vance Packard called leadership "the art of getting another to want to do something that you are convinced should be done."[8] Apparently, Randy Houck agrees. He describes leadership as "getting people to do what they ordinarily wouldn't do on their own."[9]

It is virtually impossible to describe leadership without considering the group. According to the message in a Chinese fortune cookie, "He who thinks he leads when no one is following is just taking a walk." In this sense, leadership is the art of changing a group from what it is to what it ought to be. Leadership is in part a function of group dynamics.

The Eight Laws of Leadership

Like any other science, certain fundamental laws and principles govern the science of leadership. Various attempts have been made to identify and apply these principles to help leaders excel at what they do. Many successful leadership books tend to emphasize various expressions of a single law of leadership. These books appeal to leaders who are most comfortable applying that law of leadership. Also, certain laws of leadership tend to be more effective in some contexts. A more balanced approach to the science of leadership recognizes at least eight laws of leadership.

The first law of leadership is the Law of Dreams. People follow a leader who has a dream of a desirable objective. The Law of Dreams challenges the leader to direct followers to a desirable objective. When people buy into a leader's dreams, they buy into his/her leadership.

The second law of leadership is the Law of Rewards. People tend to follow a leader who rewards them when they accomplish their goals. Everyone wants or needs something in this life. This law states the leader who rewards his followers with the things they want ensures they will continue to follow him. In many organizations, things that get rewarded get done.

The Law of Credibility is the third law of leadership. People follow a leader when they have confidence in his plans. They not only follow; they work . . . they sacrifice . . . they won't give up, if their leader has a credible plan to reach the objective. The leader who believes in his followers usually has people who believe in him.

The fourth law of leadership is the Law of Communication. People follow a leader who effectively communicates his plan to reach the objective. Therefore, the successful leader must effectively communicate his ideas and plans to his followers if he hopes to motivate followers to reach the objective. People tend to follow a leader who gives clear directions. In contrast, as John Maxwell notes, "People are always down on what they are not up on."[10]

The Law of Accountability is the fifth law of leadership. Many people find it easier to follow a leader who gives them specific responsibilities to help them reach the objective. This means the leader must know the specific contribution his followers can make to help ensure the entire group reaches the goal. Then he must hold each group member accountable to do his part. People don't do what a leader expects, but what he or she inspects.

The sixth law of leadership is the Law of Motivation. Motivation is not stirring speeches, slogans, or threats. People tend to follow a leader who gives them compelling reasons to reach the objective. The primary task of the leader is to give his followers the best reasons to accomplish the objective. People follow you when you give them a reason to work.

The Law of Problem Solving is the seventh law of leadership. People follow a leader who gives solutions to problems that hinder them from reaching the objective. This means the leader must solve problems that hinder followers if he wishes to see his group move forward in reaching their objectives. The more barriers that frustrate your followers, the less likely your followers are to reach their goal.

The final law of leadership is the Law of Decision Making. People follow the leader who decides well when questions arise as the group moves toward accomplishing their objective. That means the leader must be a good decision maker. Leaders make good decisions on good information, bad decisions on bad information, and lucky decisions when they have no information.

Nine Spiritual Gifts that Influence Our Leadership Style

Every Christian is gifted with a spiritual gift that influences the way he thinks and acts. Because people are gifted differently, they think and act differently, which is why leaders usually lead differently.

Understanding our spiritual gifts will help us identify our potential leadership strengths. When various biblical lists of spiritual gifts are studied, there are usually nine task-oriented gifts that Christians use in effective ministry. These gifts include (1) evangelism (Eph. 4:11), (2) prophecy (Rom. 12:6), (3) teaching (Rom. 12:7), (4) exhortation (Rom. 12:8), (5) shepherding (Eph. 4:11), (6) empathy (Rom. 12:8), (7) serving (Rom. 12:7; 1 Cor. 12:28), (8) giving (Rom. 12:8), and (9) administration (Rom. 12:8; 1 Cor. 12:28).

Evangelism is communicating the gospel in the power of the Holy Spirit to unconverted persons at their point of need with the intent of effecting conversions. These conversions take place as people repent of their sin and put their trust in God through Jesus Christ, to accept Him as their Savior. Normally, those who are converted determine to serve the Lord in the fellowship of a local church. Those gifted in evangelism tend to lead by persuading followers of the validity of their plan and calling them to commitment.

The gift of *prophecy* is the creative application of a specific biblical truth to a particular problem, situation, or circumstance. The prophet "speaks edification and exhortation and comfort to men" (1 Cor. 14:3). Also, the gift of prophecy is strengthened by one's faith. Leaders who are gifted in prophecy tend to lead by attacking problems head-on. A prophet has negative motivation and will point out the injustice of the opposition, calling others to follow his plan to solve the problem and change the world.

The gift of *teaching* is the communication of biblical principles in the power of the Holy Spirit to others and demonstrating the relevance of those principles to the specific needs of their listeners. Those gifted in the area of teaching tend to be diligent students of Scripture who have accumulated a thorough understanding of biblical principles as a result of their consistent study habits. Those gifted in teaching tend to lead by collecting good data and communicating what they find to others who come to believe the teacher knows how to solve problems.

Leaders who are teachers tend to lead by their insight into what needs to be done to accomplish an objective.

The gift of *exhortation* is urging others to act on the basis of their faith in God, advising others how to accomplish specific goals in life and ministry, cautioning others against actions that are potentially dangerous, and motivating others in the Christian life and ministry. Those gifted in exhortation usually develop practical strategies to accomplish goals and effectively encourage and motivate others to remain faithful in their service for God. Leaders who are gifted in exhortation tend to lead through their practical strategies (transferable concepts) and their ability to motivate followers to action.

The gift of *shepherding* is compassionately caring for others in your sphere of influence through providing spiritual guidance, nourishment, and protection from potentially destructive individuals and influences. Those who have this gift readily express their concern for others and are often looked to for spiritual counsel and guidance. Leaders who are gifted in shepherding tend to lead through building healthy maturity into their followers.

The gift of *empathy* (showing mercy) is discovering emotionally stressed and distressed individuals and ministering to their emotional needs. This gift involves expressing sympathy, empathy, and spiritual ministry to help alleviate the inner pain that is causing a person's dysfunctional emotional response. Leaders who are gifted in empathy tend to attract hurting people and are somewhat effective in helping them rebuild their lives.

The gift of *serving* is discerning and meeting the spiritual and physical needs of individuals. Leaders who are gifted in this area tend to be supportive of others and concerned with helping them in any way possible. They often enjoy manual tasks. The leadership style of those gifted in serving is appropriately called "servant leadership."

The gift of *giving* is investing financial and other resources in ways that further the purposes of God through individuals and ministries. Leaders who have this gift are inclined to be effective in raising and using money or resources for a wide variety of ministry projects. It is not uncommon for them to develop financial expertise in the process of developing their gift. They lead through budgets and financial planning that ensure the project is adequately financed.

The gift of *administration* is the management of human, physical, and financial resources through planning, organizing, leading, and controlling. The planning leader projects the future; establishes objectives; develops policies, programs, procedures, and schedules for accomplishing those objectives; and budgets adequate resources for the task. Organization involves developing an organizational foundation, delegating responsibilities, and establishing interpersonal relationships. Leading involves making decisions; communicating ideas; and selecting, enlisting, training, and motivating people. Controlling involves establishing performance standards; then measuring, evaluating, and correcting performance on the basis of those standards. Although God has gifted various leaders in different ways, some writers describe the gift of administration as the gift of leadership.

Leaders who understand the influence of spiritual gifts on themselves and their followers will let that knowledge change the way they think about ministry. According to Carl F. George and Robert E. Logan, "Developing a gift-based ministry is a two-fold process, involving both education and organization. It requires helping people to discover their gifts and finding outlets to use their gifts. Simply teaching about gifts is not enough; you must organize a system to guide people into appropriate ministries. Structuring the church in a way that encourages people to discover, develop, and begin to use their gifts will help your church function as a healthy body."

Four Temperaments that Influence Your Leadership Style

In his book *Spirit-Controlled Temperament*,[11] Tim LaHaye described four basic personality types that he called "temperaments." LaHaye described these temperaments by using the language of ancient Greeks, calling them (1) sanguine, (2) choleric, (3) melancholic, and (4) phlegmatic. He was not the first to identify basic personality types or even the first to use these terms to identify them. His book was significant, however, in that it introduced the topic to a wide evangelical market and helped Christians begin to think of their own unique temperament. LaHaye developed an inventory to help people discover their temperament along with biblical guidelines to help them work through personal strengths while yielding themselves to God to minimize the effects of their natural weakness.

Sanguine leaders tend to have a lively outlook on life. They have the God-given ability to live in the present. They tend to be friendly and outgoing. They love people and have a tender and compassionate heart. They also can be restless. At times they are impractical and disorganized. They find it difficult to stay concentrated on reading the Word of God. Their basic problem is that they are weak-willed. They start many things but seldom finish them. They love to please everyone and talk about themselves (egotistical). Their warm nature can produce spontaneous anger, yet they never get ulcers; they just give them to everyone else. They are the type of people who repent for the same thing repeatedly. Their greatest needs in the filling of the Holy Spirit and Christian character are self-control, long-suffering, faith, peace, and goodness. The sanguine leader is a motivator and a people person who is genuinely liked by followers. However, the sanguine leader is not as reliable as leaders with other temperaments.

Choleric leaders are hot, quick, active, practical, and strong-willed. They are very independent. They make decisions easily for themselves and others. They thrive on activity and are prone to take a definite stand on issues. They are quick to recognize opportunities and push ahead. They have a well-organized mind and are often extroverted. On the negative side, they are often hot-tempered and may even be cruel at times. They do not show much compassion. They tend to be domineering and bossy. They find it hard to understand what Jesus meant when he said, "Without me you can do nothing" (John 15:5). They grieve the Holy Spirit through bitterness, wrath, and anger. It is very difficult for them to apologize when they are wrong. Their success often makes them very proud. They can be difficult to reach for Christ because they think they can do it on their own. Their greatest needs in the fullness of the Holy Spirit and Christian character are love, peace, gentleness, long-suffering, meekness, and goodness.

The leaders with a *melancholy* temperament are sometimes ones who are ruled by a black or dark impulse, but this can actually be the richest of all temperaments. The melancholy temperament is analytical, self-sacrificing, gifted, sensitive, and emotional. They may be somewhat of a perfectionist. It is not uncommon for these personality types to enjoy fine arts. They tend to be faithful friends and behind-the-scenes workers. The down side of this temperament is that they tend to be self-centered. Their tendency toward self-examination tends to paralyze their will and drain their energy. They also tend to be pessimistic, seeing many problems as larger problems than they really are. They are fearful about making decisions and moody with extreme highs and lows. Without proper discipline, they tend to be daydreamers and can be prone to seeking revenge. Their greatest needs in the fullness of the Holy Spirit and Christian character are love, joy, peace, faithfulness, and self-control.

The leaders with the fourth temperament, described as *phlegmatic,* are happy and pleasant people. They are cool, calm, easygoing, and well-balanced. They very seldom get ruffled. They have a very high boiling point, lots of friends, and a dry sense of humor. They are natural peacemakers. They are dependable, practical, and efficient— qualities that make them good diplomats, accountants, teachers, scientists, or counselors. The problem is they want to be spectators in life and try not to get involved with the activities of others. They usually do not take leadership on their own. They can be slow, lazy, and stubborn. They do not want to change. They usually lack motivation. When they think of projects, they are too unmotivated to do them. Their greatest needs in the fullness of the Holy Spirit and Christian character are love, goodness, faithfulness, meekness, and self-control.

The value in understanding your personal gifting and temperament relates to ergonomics. Knowing your natural strengths and weaknesses can be an important guide in determining how to do a particular task. When we work through our strengths, we achieve maximum results with minimum effort. In contrast, working through a weakness often results in fatigue. Carl F. George and Robert E. Logan advise, "Don't minister in your area of weakness or nonstrength any more than absolutely necessary. It's an open door to discouragement and often a waste of time."

Learning Leadership from Leaders

According to former U.S. president John F. Kennedy, "Leadership and learning are indispensable to each other."[12] Great leaders are students of leadership. A manual on military leadership claims, "Good leaders develop through a never-ending process of self-study, education, training, and experience."[13] The motto of Moores Mill School captures this theme well, "Learning Today: Leading Tomorrow."[14]

The focus of this book and the course based upon this text taught by the authors at Liberty University and elsewhere is to help you discover the principles of leadership and effectively develop methodologies to build leadership credibility. In the pages that follow, you will examine twenty-three approaches to building leadership. In the process, you will look at how each of these leadership styles fits into your own leadership kaleidoscope to enable you to become the kind of leader whom people follow. The study of leadership is the study of how men and women guide us through empty and frightening expanses of uncharted territory. Together, we will look at seventeen men and women in Scripture and the twenty-three ways they influenced those who followed them.

Abraham, *the entrepreneurial leader,* led his family and extended household through *vision.* He took significant risks when he left the security and familiarity of his homeland, leading his family from Ur to a promised land on the basis of God's vision for his life. Initially, he did not understand that vision completely, but he knew it well enough to know it was worth pursuing.

Jacob, the *pragmatic leader,* led his family through various conditions he faced in life. The way we lead most effectively is often tied to the context in which we are leading. As the father of Israel's patriarchs, Jacob modeled the principles of pragmatic leadership in a variety of situations with some success.

Joseph rose to a place of prominence in Egypt by leading through *problem solving* and *strategic planning.* In times of adversity, the key to leadership credibility is often how well the leader resolves problems. Joseph developed his leadership in the worst of conditions by using principles of decision making that later qualified him for greater leadership responsibilities. Many leaders who survive problems fail in times of prosperity because they lead without direction. Joseph modeled how to lead a country during an economic boom through developing a strategic plan that prepared the nation for the inevitable downturn in the economy.

Moses is among Israel's most admired leaders in history. At various times in his tenure, Moses was the *charismatic leader* with a unique call of God upon his life, an *administrative leader* who learned the principle of delegation, and a *people-management leader* with a plan for conflict resolution. In difficult times, people tend to be attracted to charismatic leadership that confidently communicates an appropriate vision with divine authority. Moses modeled charisma in leadership when he returned to Egypt to lead Israel to freedom.

Many leaders limit their leadership potential or quickly burn out because they fail to delegate. Moses learned this principle and appointed judges to do work he was doing that could be done as well or better by them. Sooner or later, every leader encounters pockets of resistance among his followers. Moses faced this problem with the strong *representative leadership* team that he developed to assist him in people management and conflict resolution.

Joshua was prepared by the mentoring leadership of Moses to become one of the most successful *military leaders* ever. In contemporary business culture, an executive M.B.A. opens doors that are closed to those who lack formal education. Part of Joshua's initial success as a leader is tied to his being mentored by Moses. The principles of mentoring in this relationship are key to effective mentoring today. But Joshua also modeled an important leadership principle in both the military and diplomatic phases of his leadership. Effective leadership leads from victory to victory.

Sometimes, important leadership principles can be learned from those who failed to live up to their potential. Research into the nature of *executive leadership* suggests the credibility factor in leadership is often closely tied to character. In his own lack of character, Samson demonstrated how a flawed character erodes one's leadership influence. Also, people follow leaders who look and act like leaders. Despite beginning his career with strong popular support, King Saul illustrates the importance of meeting expectations in his own long-term failure caused by constant wavering.

Sometimes timing is everything when it comes to leadership. David demonstrated the importance of timing in his waiting for the right time to become one of Israel's most successful leaders. His son, Solomon, faced the challenge of working through transitional times successfully. Solomon modeled the principles of *transitional leadership* when he assumed the throne of Israel from his father.

The greatest fear many leaders face is the fear of failure. Just as success gives leaders great credibility in the eyes of their followers, so failure creates a leadership crisis. Hezekiah modeled the principles of *crisis management leadership* when he faced failure and overcame defeat.

One of the greatest needs today is *spiritual leadership.* Leading people into a deeper relationship with and commitment to God requires a special kind of leader. Ezra was that kind of leader. His ministry among the Jewish remnant that returned to Jerusalem illustrates how leaders today can lead their people to experience God.

Motivational leadership accomplishes a task together, which none could do alone. Nowhere in Scripture is this better portrayed than in the rebuilding of Jerusalem's walls in fifty-two days. Nehemiah managed both the people and the project effectively to accomplish that goal.

Many of the world's most effective leaders remain relatively unknown because they never held an office of leadership. This is the challenge of *middle management leadership.* Daniel modeled how middle managers can lead effectively through influencing their superiors.

Sometimes, leaders are called to lead in times of hostility and crisis. Times of great uncertainty call for great leaders. When the genocide of her race had been planned and prescribed by law, Esther rose to the challenge of the hour and achieved both the defeat of those who planned the crime and the security of her people who had been threatened. In her actions, Esther demonstrated a courageous approach to *crisis leadership.*

While He is more than a leader to evangelical Christians, Jesus is undoubtedly one of history's most influential leaders. Jesus led through *serving leadership* and *mentoring leadership.* He proposed a view of leadership that differs significantly from the Machiavellian approach practiced by many political rulers. Rather, He taught how Christian leadership can find its credibility in ministry to others. He taught this principle to others and demonstrated it throughout His life. When He fulfilled His mandate as the Good Shepherd who gave His life for His sheep, Jesus laid the foundation for pastoral ministry today.

One of those mentored by Jesus was Peter, a disciple who seemed to struggle to apply consistently all he had learned. He learned *self-correcting leadership* in spite of his failures and uncertainties. Time and experiences shared by leaders and followers often result in a strengthened and expanded sphere of influence. This kind of leadership differs from other leadership styles in that followers follow the leader they have come to respect, not withstanding past failures.

Paul is the last of the leaders we will consider together. Described by some as the most effective Christian leader of all time, Paul led through *strategic planning leadership* and *disciple-making leadership*. When engaged in a significant project, a carefully planned strategy enables the leader to accomplish the task at hand with greater success. Paul developed various strategies to help him in one of history's most significant tasks—introducing Christianity to the Gentiles. Paul also understood that great leadership outlives the leader. He extended his leadership through the development of other leaders and the training of a new generation of leaders that would serve others when he was gone.

A Leadership Kaleidoscope

Many leadership books describe and promote a particular leadership style based on the premise that what worked for someone else in a particular situation will work for readers. Widely published testimonials used to market these leadership books demonstrate that this approach sometimes works. But beyond the marketing glitz is a lesser-known reality. Some leaders try to apply the principles as they read, yet achieve failure instead of success. At least four factors contribute to this phenomenon.

First, leadership styles grow out of the unique *personality* of leaders. Just as most personality-type indicators identify at least sixteen distinct personality types, so there must be at least that many effective leadership styles. The way an introvert leads effectively may not work for the extrovert.

Second, leadership styles are only as effective as they apply to the unique needs of the group that the leader is attempting to lead. Just as individuals are different, so groups also have unique personalities. Politicians lead differently than generals in part because they lead different groups marked by a different culture. Even among politicians, four congressmen, each representing constituents in their respective home states—Alabama, Iowa, Maine, and Oregon—are likely to have different leadership styles because they lead different people.

Leadership styles are also a response to *unique problems or situations* faced by the leader and his group. The strong leadership style of Churchill that gave England hope during World War II was so unattractive to the country a year later that the voters turned him out of office. Churchill's experience has also been that of other popular wartime presidents and prime ministers who failed in their reelection bids during a time of peace.

Finally, the effectiveness of a particular leadership style is linked to *timing.* Crisis management may work well for a leader initially, but if it continues too long, the leader may be suspected of manufacturing crises to continue his or her success. In contrast, servant leadership may be more effective in a longer-term situation. A business leader may need to refocus the vision of his company to turn things around, but once it begins turning a profit, he may want to deal in areas of customer relations and internal morale issues to ensure his company continues to remain profitable.

A Leadership Kaleidoscope suggests different approaches to leadership. Today's leaders need to be able to adapt quickly to the challenges they face in a changing world. It is not enough to create carbon-copy leaders based on the experiences of military, industrial, political, or social leaders of previous generations. Rather, today's leaders need to tap into the power of synergism and develop styles that are the convergence of many approaches welded together in the crucible of leadership itself.

The kaleidoscope was a popular children's toy in the midst of the twentieth century. Although the toy was mass-produced, the picture it produced when viewed by the child was always different. As the child turned the movable part of the toy, he could change the picture he viewed. The alignment of mirrors within the toy meant every picture created appeared to have perfect symmetry. *A Leadership Kaleidoscope* encourages a blending of different approaches to leadership in the balance needed in the particular context in which you lead.

The moral leadership crisis faced in the North American business community today is a reminder that enduring leadership must be more than a methodology. More than ever, character counts. Indeed, character is essential to the concept of a leadership kaleidoscope. The moral character of a leader is reflected through the various leadership styles that have been grafted into his personal paradigm. Without it, the symmetry is gone, and like the child's toy with a misaligned mirror, all that is left is confusion.

Leadership is more than a child's toy. It is who you are and how you influence others to be and accomplish more than they are or could do otherwise. Your future leadership success emerges from who you are and how you use the abilities you have acquired. As you read this book, you will not be asked to buy into a one-size-fits-all leadership style. Rather, you will be challenged to modify your personal leadership style by incorporating aspects of almost two dozen different approaches to leadership. You will be challenged by the examples of leaders who accomplished much and those who self-destructed. In the process, you will have the opportunity to add to your personal leadership kaleidoscope and equip yourself for long-term leadership that can adapt quickly to the changing world in which we live.

CHAPTER 2

Abraham

The Entrepreneurial Leader

I came. I saw. I conquered.

JULIUS CAESAR

When people were accustomed to hitching their horses to the wagon before taking a family trip, a horseless carriage sounded like something out of a science fiction novel. Even when a few brave entrepreneurial buggy manufacturers began modifying their designs to include a gas-powered engine, widespread skepticism remained.

Part of the problem early automobile manufacturers faced was the relatively high cost of their vehicles. The team of workers was building only one car at a time. Only the very rich could afford to purchase a car. Everyone else continued hitching their horses to their wagons. And when the rich in their horseless carriage drove down the same roads as those on horseback or in horse-drawn carriages, the noise of the new invention often spooked the animals, creating problems for the non-auto-riders.

Many communities decided the new invention was not worth the problems they caused. Some city councils decided to protect citizens from danger by banning automobiles, refusing them access to city streets. Others passed bylaws allowing the vehicles but only under strict conditions. A common regulation of the time required a person with a red flag to walk fifty feet before a horseless carriage warning people on the street of the danger that followed. It seemed like America would never embrace the automobile.

A young businessman became convinced the automobile was a good idea that could improve the quality of life for the average family. He believed the average working man would rather drive a car than walk or ride a horse, but the current price of a new vehicle was beyond his budget. In his opinion, the reason for the high cost of new automobiles was directly linked to the way cars were being made. At the time, each vehicle was being custom-made by a team of workers. Then Henry Ford came up with a better idea.

Instead of waiting for orders, Ford decided to design and build a general all-purpose vehicle for the working man. Further, he decided he could reduce costs if each worker in his factory assembled one part of the vehicle. The idea of an assembly line in manufacturing had never been tried before. It took time to organize the project, but it was an investment of time as Ford pursued his vision.

It was not long before notices began appearing in newspapers announcing an incredible offer. Henry Ford's assembly line increased production, lowering the cost of new cars to a mere $750. Company ads claimed, "Any working man can now afford a new Model A in any color he wants, as long as it is black." Within a generation, the new invention that the average person could not previously afford became a necessity for most American families.

Leading through Vision and Risk

One of the most dynamic approaches to leadership is that of the *entrepreneurial leader*. *The Random House Dictionary* defines the entrepreneur as "a person who organizes, manages, and assumes responsibility for a business or other enterprise." What is missing from this definition is that the entrepreneur usually does this long before the business or other enterprise exists. This approach to leadership usually begins with a vision of success, a glimmering intuition that solutions to problems are possible. Vince Lombardi was describing the entrepreneurial coach when he said, "The best coaches know what the end result looks like, whether it's an offensive play, a defensive play, or a defensive coverage. If you don't know what the end result is supposed to look like, you can't get there."[1]

Abraham modeled an entrepreneurial approach to leadership throughout much of his life. He took significant risks in leaving the security of his home. He led his family from Ur to Canaan on the basis of the promise of God. In pursuing God's vision for his life, he stepped out on faith and led his family not only to relocate, but to become a great and enduring nation.

Entrepreneurial leaders are the innovators of society, transforming the world as it is into a new world order as they perceive it. They are the pacesetters in culture. They are the first to introduce what later becomes a fad, then a trend, and ultimately an icon of the new culture. They are the men and women with dreams. Against all odds, they pursue those dreams to build new businesses, develop new technologies, and offer new products and services to the world in which they live. They are the inventors who see problems as a challenge and work hard to find the workable solution others failed to see. They are the pioneer church planters who go to a city and with limited resources in inadequate circumstances establish a new church in spite of insurmountable odds. They are the pioneer missionaries who devote their lives to reaching an unreached people group.

Entrepreneurial leaders march to the beat of a different drummer. They pursue a vision that others may find difficult to understand. If they move toward that vision faster than others can follow, they may leave their followers so far behind that they will just leave. Sometimes, the entrepreneurial leaders may be tempted to act in the absence of a clear vision, particularly in the details of implementing a plan. It is inevitable that those deeply committed to the status quo will find them easy targets to criticize. The late B. R. Lakin used to tell entrepreneurial pastors, "If you want to avoid criticism, just be nothing, say nothing, and do nothing." Then he would add, "As long as they are kicking you in the behind, you know you are still out in front."

Entrepreneurs face a variety of apparently insurmountable obstacles simply because they are the first ones to cut a path along the trail. They face the realization that no one else has ever done things that way before. As a result, they may experience the loneliness of leadership to a greater degree than other leaders and become overwhelmed by the immensity of their own vision.

Entrepreneurial leaders are often perceived as strong leaders, especially in the early phase of their business, organization, or movement. They tend to lead through their gift of evangelism, having a clear vision of recruiting followers to the objective. They may also lead through their gift of prophecy, having a clear view of things as they should be. Entrepreneurs gifted in exhortation may lead by equipping their followers with clear directions and a step-by-step strategy needed to pursue the vision and accomplish the goal. They tend to use the Law of Dreams to communicate their vision to motivate others to follow. They are often choleric in temperament.

Ironically, the very strengths of entrepreneurial leaders may also be their greatest weakness. If their vision is defective, everything about them is wrong. Also, because they are deeply committed to the pursuit of a vision, they may take unnecessary or extreme risks that others find unacceptable. The group culture they are trying to lead may not be receptive to their vision. When that happens, they will experience difficulty raising the resources necessary to accomplish the vision. They may also lack the skills needed to implement the vision. In their frustration, entrepreneurs may be tempted to pursue their vision without followers. Even if others follow them, conflicts will threaten their success when other group members propose alternate visions which appeal to a significant part of the group.

Despite the risks, it is imperative that leaders have vision. Vision is part of what it means to be a leader. In the Old Testament, one of the titles of the prophet was "seer" (1 Sam. 9:9). He must see before others do. He must see what others do not. He must see beyond the horizons of others. "Where there is no vision, the people perish" (Prov. 29:18, KJV). Jesus described leaders without vision and warned, "If the blind leads the blind, both will fall into a ditch" (Matt. 15:14).

Walt Disney, the founder of the Disney empire, dreamed of developing a family-oriented theme park based on the characters developed in his animated films. Although he led his company to begin the Disneyworld project, Disney himself died before this park was completed. At the opening of that park, a television commentator lamented to Mrs. Disney, "If only Walt could have seen this." The widow responded, "If he hadn't seen it first, you wouldn't see it today."

In describing those leaders who rose into the upper levels of management, Elliot Jacques wrote, "I have found that 'executive vision,' or the ability to view scenarios in terms of extended planning horizons, is an integral part of the upper management psyche. Some top executives, for instance, are capable of planning in twenty-year time spans." According to George Barna, "If you want to be a leader, vision is not an option; it is part of the standard equipment of a real leader. By definition, a leader has vision: what else would a leader lead people toward, if not to fulfill that vision?" Mark Leslie adds, "If there is no vision, there is no business."

"The leader's job is to create a vision," according to Robert L. Swiggett.[2] That vision gives the leader direction. The same vision gives followers a dream to adopt as their own. It motivates people out of complacency to achieve what otherwise might be beyond them. Vision stretches people to a greater faith in God. Also, it helps people endure the dark hours and difficult days they are bound to encounter in any leadership task.

Abraham: The Entrepreneurial Leader

Irish playwright George Bernard Shaw once observed, "Some men see things as they are and say, 'Why?' I dream of things that never were and say, 'Why not?' To a great extent, that also describes Abraham, the patriarch of Israel. Abraham had an encounter with God that launched him on a lifelong journey in pursuit of God's vision for his life. In that pursuit, Abraham modeled the entrepreneurial leader.

Abraham's growing vision grew out of his growing relationship with God. Stephen reminded the Sanhedrin, "The God of glory appeared to our father Abraham when he was in Mesopotamia, before he dwelt in Haran" (Acts 7:2). That encounter with God was the first of several in his life. In each meeting, God revealed a little more of His character to Abraham through various names. In the process, Abraham came to know God as "God Most High, Possessor of heaven and earth" (Gen. 14:19), his "shield" and "exceedingly great reward" (Gen. 15:1), the "Almighty [All-Sufficient] God" (Gen. 17:1), "the Judge of all the earth" (Gen. 18:25), "the Everlasting God" (Gen. 21:33), "the-LORD-Will-Provide" (Gen. 22:14) and "the LORD, the God of heaven and the God of the earth" (Gen. 24:3).

David was another man of faith in the Old Testament who understood the importance of pursuing God's vision in his life. In one of his psalms, he identified seven steps in discerning God's vision for your life and ministry (Ps. 37:3–8). The first step in this process is to "trust in the LORD" (Ps. 37:3). Step two involves doing what you know is right to do (Ps. 37:3). Third, count on the faithfulness of God in all that you do (Ps. 37:3). The Hebrew word for *faith* and *faithfulness* is the same, reminding us our faith in God is always based on His faithfulness toward us.

Fourth, "Delight yourself also in the LORD" (Ps. 37:4). This involves making Him the focus of your enjoyment in life. Next, "Commit your way to the LORD" (Ps. 37:5). This involves allowing Him the liberty to work in your life according to His agenda. The sixth step in this process is to "rest in the LORD, and wait patiently for Him" (Ps. 37:7). Solomon later noted God makes "everything beautiful in its time" (Eccl. 3:11). The final step in this process involves abandoning anger, wrath, and other attitudes that tend to distract you from God's vision (Ps. 37:8).

Abraham's vision of what God wanted to do in his life moved him out of his comfort zone to take risks others may not have understood. In His call to Abraham, God said, "Get out of your country and from your relatives, and come to a land that I will show you" (Acts 7:3). Abraham was being asked to leave behind all that was familiar for something he would only later learn about.

That vision required a long-term commitment to the cause, even when it seemed little progress was being made. "He came out of the land of the Chaldeans and dwelt in Haran. And from there, when his father was dead, He moved him to this land in which you now dwell" (Acts 7:4). Day after day, year after year, Abraham continued pursuing God's vision for his life in spite of mounting evidence it might never happen.

His vision called him to trust God's faithfulness to accomplish all He had promised. Abraham's faith was faith in spite of the circumstances. "And God gave him no inheritance in it, not even enough to set his foot on. But even when Abraham had no child, He promised to give it to him for a possession, and to his descendants after him" (Acts 7:5). When God confirmed His promise to Abraham late in life, Abraham continued to believe God. "Who, contrary to hope, in hope believed, so that he became the father of many nations, according to what was spoken, 'So shall your descendants be.' And not being weak in faith, he did not consider his own body, already dead (since he was about a hundred years old), and the deadness of Sarah's womb. He did not waver at the promise of God through unbelief, but was strengthened in faith, giving glory to God, and being fully convinced that what He had promised He was also able to perform" (Rom. 4:18–21).

God's vision for his life required trust and obedient response even when he had questions about the details of that vision. "By faith

Abraham obeyed when he was called to go out to the place which he would receive as an inheritance. And he went out, not knowing where he was going" (Heb. 11:8). Had he waited for all his questions to be answered before embarking on his journey of faith, Abraham might never have left Ur.

Abraham's vision called him to make significant lifestyle-related sacrifices as he pursued his goal. While others remained in comfortable homes and familiar surroundings, "he dwelt in the land of promise as in a foreign country, dwelling in tents" (Heb. 11:9). He continued trusting God as he waited "for the city which has foundations, whose builder and maker is God" (Heb. 11:10).

Knowing God's vision for his life strengthened both Abraham and Sarah to accomplish more than they could otherwise accomplish. "By faith Sarah herself also received strength to conceive seed, and she bore a child when she was past the age, because she judged Him faithful who had promised" (Heb. 11:11).

Solomon wrote, "Hope deferred makes the heart sick, but when the desire comes, it is a tree of life" (Prov. 13:12). It is easy to become discouraged in the pursuit of God's vision for your life. In Abraham's case, partial progress in the fulfillment of God's vision for his life energized the process by which the greater dreams were accomplished. "Therefore from one man, and him as good as dead, were born as many as the stars of the sky in multitude—innumerable as the sand which is by the seashore" (Heb. 11:12).

Abraham's vision enabled him to take significant risks with confidence, knowing the vision would be realized. This is the very heart of the entrepreneurial spirit. And there was no greater risk taken by Abraham than the day he climbed a mountain with Isaac to offer the sacrifice God had requested. "By faith Abraham, when he was tested, offered up Isaac, and he who had received the promises offered up his only begotten son . . . concluding that God was able to raise him up, even from the dead, from which he also received him in a figurative sense" (Heb. 11:17, 19).

The Nine Acts of Visionary Leadership

At the core of their being, entrepreneurial leaders are visionaries. God's vision for their lives is the foundation from which they lead. Those who would blend this leadership style into their own leadership kaleidoscope would be well-advised to begin with discerning God's vision for their life. George Barna has identified "The Nine Acts of Visionary Leadership" that are a helpful guide in this process.

The first act of visionary leadership involves understanding the basic concept of vision. Barna defines vision as "a clear mental portrait of a preferable future, communicated by God to His chosen servant-leaders, based upon an accurate understanding of God, self and circumstance." It is "seeing what others don't see," the possibilities instead of the problems. James M. Kouzes and Barry Z. Posner view vision as essential in any organization. "The most important role of visions in organizational life is to give focus to human energy. Visions are like lenses. They focus unrefracted rays of light. They enable everyone concerned with an enterprise to see more clearly what is ahead of them."

Leaders will not survive long without vision. According to Warren Bennis and Burt Nanus, "To choose a direction, a leader must first have developed a mental image of a possible and desirable future state of the organization. This image, which we call a vision, may be as vague as a dream or as precise as a goal or mission statement. The critical point is that a vision articulates a view of a realistic, credible, attractive future for the organization, a condition that is better in some important ways than what now exists."

Second, vision leaders not only understand the concept of vision; they understand the content of their personal vision. According to Newcomger, "It is more important to know where you are going, than to get there quickly." It is not uncommon for successful business executives, political leaders, or church leadership teams to set aside time periodically for vision setting. These sessions, which may last several days in some situations, tend to be focused times designed to identify and clarify exactly what the company, party, or church needs to be working toward.

Act three in this process involves owning the vision. The prophet Habakkuk wrote, "Write the vision and make it plain on tablets, that he may run who reads it. For the vision is yet for an appointed time; but at the end it will speak, and will not lie. Though it tarries, wait for it; because it will surely come, it it will not tarry" (Hab. 2:2–3). In this statement, Habakkuk identified six steps involved in committing oneself completely to God's vision for his life. These steps include: (1) recording God's vision for your life in a clear statement, (2) simplifying the statement of God's vision into an easy-to-remember maxim, (3) communicating that vision to others involved, (4) devoting significant energies to pursuing God's vision for your life, (5) continuing to believe in God's vision for your life, and (6) waiting on God's timing to accomplish all He intends to do for you.

The fourth act of visionary leadership is to make the vision realistic. Take time to write out your personal vision. Many leaders find it helpful to ask two questions to help them discern and express God's vision. If you could do anything at all for God, and there were no limitations on you, what would it be? This question helps you identify your God-given passion for ministry. How has God uniquely enabled you to accomplish that mission? As you consider your gifting, training, experiences, etc., you will gain insight into the way God is likely to use you to accomplish that vision.

Act five involves passing the vision around. David E. Berlew insists, "The executive must find a way to communicate the vision in a way that attracts and excites members of the organization." According to Kouzes and Posner, "In order to move others to share the vision, leaders (1) appeal to a common purpose, (2) communicate expressively, and (3) sincerely believe in what they are saying."

The sixth act of visionary leadership is selling that vision to followers. Kouzes and Posner note, "Leaders inspire a shared vision. They breathe life into what are the hopes and dreams of others and enable them to see the exciting possibilities that the future holds. Leaders get others to buy into their dreams by showing how all will be served by a common purpose." Before visionary leaders move forward to accomplish all they hope to accomplish, they must be certain their followers are on board, that their vision has become the vision of each follower.

Having accomplished the above, *the seventh step is to put the vision into action.* As Casey Stengel notes, "The main thing is to keep the main thing, the main thing." As leaders continue leading, this will be a constant struggle. Every organization has a tendency to drift from its vision if it is not constantly pursued. Robert H. Hayes observes, "Short-term goals also work to back companies into a mode of thinking that is based on forecasts (What do we think is going to happen?) rather than on vision (What do we want to happen?)." Visionary leaders need to be vigilant to ensure that subtle changes in thinking do not happen within their organization.

Act eight in this process involves refining the vision. According to Benjamin Disraeli, "If you want to be a leader of people, you must learn to watch events." This ongoing process of evaluation helps the entrepreneurial leader ensure his vision remains clear and focused in changing circumstances. His prayer is, "Lord, give me eyes that I may see the mistakes of the past and see the answers to the questions still future."

Finally, the vision needs to be reinforced. Barna suggests several ways this can be done. First, express appreciation to followers for their involvement in the project. Then second, take time to celebrate their successes. Third, constantly recommunicate the vision in unique new ways in relevant contexts. Fourth, provide your followers with insight into the progress being made toward your goal. Fifth, describe the growth of your movement and the effect your cause is having. Sixth, let them observe in unguarded moments your genuine and unbridled enthusiasm for the vision. Seventh, introduce them to the people who have caught and nurtured the vision and the forward movement that is evident. Finally, find new ways to motivate people who are on the verge of burnout or are beginning to lose their perspective.

CHAPTER 3

Jacob

The Pragmatic Leader

Do something . . . lead, follow, or get out of the way.

U.S. Army Slogan

When he died at age seventy-three, Louis Pasteur was a national hero in France and widely regarded around the world. It was not always like that. In the early years of his research, his ideas were ridiculed and he was discouraged from continuing his research because he was not trained in the field. Reflecting on the success he had experienced, he revealed his secret to all who would listen. "Let me tell you the secret that has led me to my goal," he said. "My strength lies solely in my tenacity."

Although he is credited with furthering medical progress more than any other man of his time, Pasteur was never a physician. He was trained as a chemist and devoted much time to laboratory research. When Pasteur postulated the existence of bacteria, those trained in medicine jeered at his theories. Yet he continued his research that eventually changed the way people live today.

Pasteur may be remembered by most people as inventing the process that bears his name, pasteurization. Based on the assumption that bacteria in milk was responsible for the spread of disease, he developed a process of heating milk to 140° F for thirty minutes, then cooling it rapidly in sealed sterile containers. This process is still used in much of Europe and North America today in the preparation of milk for the public.

But Pasteur's research in the field of bacteriology also led to cures for a silkworm disease, anthrax, and rabies. As a careful researcher, he sought to test his vaccines to prove his theory prior to making them available to the public. In the case of his rabies vaccine, he made an exception. When young Joseph Meister was bitten fourteen times by a rabid dog, his parents traveled from Germany to Pasteur's laboratory in Paris, France, and pleaded with the researcher to give their son the unproved vaccine. Pasteur agreed only after two doctors urged him to do so, noting the boy would certainly die without the vaccine. Pasteur's vaccine worked, and the Pasteur Institute became known worldwide as a cutting-edge medical research center. Meister later became a gatekeeper at that institute and remained loyal to Pasteur for the rest of his life.

Pasteur himself never did understand what all the fuss was about when he was warmly greeted at international medical conferences. He simply had an idea and pursued it until he could figure out how to make it work for others. Although he died in 1895, medical researchers today still use his ideas to create vaccines for new diseases and vaccinate people at risk against them.

Making Things Happen

People can be divided into three groups: those who make things happen; those who watch things happen; and those who wonder what happened. The pragmatic leader ignores those who watch things happen and does whatever he can to make things happen. Sometimes, his followers may be among those left wondering what happened.

Our approach to leadership is often tied to the context in which we are leading. As the father of Israel's tribal patriarchs, Jacob modeled the

CANADA'S NATIONAL HERO

When most countries talk about their national heroes, they are often great political or military heroes who shaped the character of their nation. Sometimes, they are great athletes responsible for scoring the winning goal in an international competition. But when Canadians are polled to identify a national hero, their overwhelming first choice is a young man who died at age twenty-nine. Further, he is remembered for running a marathon he never completed.

Terry Fox was born in Winnipeg, Manitoba, and moved to Port Coquitlam, British Columbia, with his family when he was ten years old. His mother remembers him as "average in everything but determination." His passion in life was basketball, and as a student at Simon Fraser University, he tried out for the junior basketball team and made it by sheer desire.

During the year, Terry noticed a pain in his right knee but decided not to tell anyone until the season was over. In March, he was diagnosed with osteosarcoma, a rare form of bone cancer. Three days later, his right leg was amputated above the knee. Rather than wallowing in sorrow, Terry shocked family and friends by maintaining a positive attitude. When he read a story about Dick Traum, a one-legged man who had run the New York Marathon, Terry began talking about running his own "Marathon of Hope."

principles of pragmatic leadership in a variety of situations with some success. This is especially evident in the account of how he acquired his wealth during his sojourn in Haran.

Pragmatic leaders emerge in every sphere of life. In business, they are the troubleshooters called in to resolve a problem and resolve it quickly. In cultural institutions, pragmatic leaders are often involved in the marketing aspects of the institutions. Church leaders may use pragmatic leadership when rebuilding declining ministries or establishing new ministries.

Terry had been deeply moved by the suffering and courage of other cancer patients he met in the hospital. He set a goal to run across Canada from coast to coast raising money for cancer research. He dreamed big, hoping to raise one dollar from every Canadian in the nation.

After years of preparation, Terry began his run in St. John's, Newfoundland, on April 12, 1980. Although it began without much media attention, he received much more coverage as he ran through Quebec and Ontario. But as he left Thunder Bay, Ontario, and began running toward Manitoba, doctors who were monitoring his progress discovered the cancer had not only returned but had spread throughout his body. The run ended just west of Thunder Bay and Terry returned home and died within months.

News of the end of his marathon sparked a spontaneous outpouring of support for Terry's cause. When a national television network encouraged people to contribute to the Cancer Society in Terry's honor, the two million dollars he had raised swelled to twenty-five million within days. Though the "Marathon of Hope" ended early, the goal of raising one dollar for every Canadian in the nation was reached. More than two decades later, many Canadian communities continue organizing local runs to raise money for cancer research in honor of a young man who defied odds and did what he could for a cause in which he believed.

Those who adopt this leadership style face their own unique problems and challenges. They may feel boxed in by existing policies and procedures within the institution. Sometimes, they are so project-oriented they fail to recognize the value of the people they need to accomplish the task at hand. They may be frustrated by those committed to existing processes within the organization. Sometimes they find existing committees hard to work with. The task of maintaining an existing ministry may be frustrating because it lacks challenge. They may even create problems as they try to force previous solutions on new problems, even when they don't fit well. A pastor who saw three previous churches revitalized in a building program may lead a church that does not need a new building into a building project and not experience the hoped-for results.

Notwithstanding the problems faced by pragmatic leaders, they can be strong leaders. They lead best through their gifts of exhortation or serving. They may be skilled at applying the Law of Motivation to mobilize their followers to action. They also are likely to consistently apply the Law of Accountability to ensure assigned work gets done and gets done right. Their leadership credibility is often enhanced as they apply the Law of Problem Solving to various challenges that arise as they lead followers to accomplish a specific task. It is not uncommon for pragmatic leaders to be choleric in temperament.

Those who use this leadership style need to be cautious of the dangers inherent in pragmatic leadership. Pragmatic leaders tend to justify the means used by the end result. In their zeal to get the job done right and on time, pragmatic leaders often step on people's feelings. They run a significant risk of losing followers by not involving them in the process. They are prone to make unacceptable compromises to achieve an immediate goal. Sometimes, their pragmatism may hide a serious character flaw. Often, they tend to sacrifice excellence by accepting interim solutions to long-term problems. Pragmatic leaders have a tendency to act too quickly without first taking time to evaluate a strategy. Because they fail to see the bigger picture, they may win a battle at the risk of losing the larger war. They may be manipulative, successful in getting an initial response but unsuccessful in building strong loyalty among their followers.

There are several things leaders need to learn to embrace pragmatic leadership into the leadership kaleidoscope. First, they need to know how to get things done. Second, they need to make healthy compromises to achieve noble goals without sacrificing their integrity. Third, pragmatic leaders need to be able to fix some problems quickly. Fourth, these kinds of leaders need to appreciate the ability of others to accomplish tasks that challenge them. Finally, they need to be able to spot those who are pragmatic in a negative sense and protect their followers from manipulative people.

Jacob: The Pragmatic Leader

Throughout his life, Jacob took a pragmatic approach to dealing with the circumstances he encountered. When Esau came in from the field hungry, wanting some of the stew Jacob had been cooking, Jacob seized the opportunity to purchase the birthright from his brother. Later, he aligned himself with his mother to steal his father's blessing when the opportunity arose. When he arrived in Haran and met Rebecca, he once again negotiated a deal to earn the right to marry her. When he returned home and heard his brother was coming to meet him, he rearranged his camp to ensure his safety and appease his brother's wrath.

As noted above, there were times when Jacob's approach to problems earned him the reputation of being manipulative. Yet there were other times when Jacob's pragmatism was exercised with character. One example of this was his attempt to provide financial security for his growing family in Haran. Jacob's actions on that occasion illustrate pragmatic leadership that produces good results.

On that occasion, Jacob began by identifying a problem that needed to be resolved in his own life. Jacob's problem was that he had invested his life creating prosperity for Laban while neglecting his own need to establish economic stability for his own family. In a conversation with his uncle, he commented, "For what you had before I came was little, and it has increased to a great amount; the LORD has blessed you since my coming. And now, when shall I also provide for my own house?" (Gen. 30:30).

Sometimes, the way to evaluate leaders is to find out what it takes to stop them. For many people, any problem will do. They travel the path of least resistance and fail to accomplish much of lasting value. But others, like Emerson, understand "difficulties exist to be surmounted."

DO IT ANYWAY!

Leaders looking for reasons to quit usually do not have to look far. Ironically, when understood correctly, many reasons why leaders might quit are really reasons why people need leaders to keep at it. In an article entitled, "Paradoxical Commandments of Leadership," an unknown writer made the following observations.

People are illogical, unreasonable, and self-centered. Love them anyway.

If you do good, people will accuse you of selfish ulterior motives. Do good anyway.

If you are successful, you will win false friends and true enemies. Succeed anyway.

The good you do today will be forgotten tomorrow. Do good anyway.

Honesty and frankness make you vulnerable. Be honest and frank anyway.

The biggest men with the biggest ideas can be shot down by the smallest men with the smallest minds. Think big anyway.

People favor underdogs but follow only top dogs. Fight for a few underdogs anyway.

What you spend years building may be destroyed overnight. Build anyway.

People really need help but may attack you if you do help them. Help them anyway.

Give the best you have and you may still get kicked in the teeth. Give the world the best you have anyway.

According to Thomas Fuller, "All things are difficult before they are easy." Even their vocabulary tends to betray their attitude. For them, problems are challenges, opportunities to do something bigger than the apparent difficulty before them. One of them put it in perspective when he said, "Be thankful for problems. If they were less difficult, someone with less ability might have your job."

When faced with a problem, pragmatic leaders develop a plan to resolve the problem. Teddy Roosevelt advised others, "Do what you can, with what you have, where you are." Jacob developed a plan that would provide the assets he needed to resolve his own problem. He appealed to Laban, "Let me pass through all your flock today, removing from there all the speckled and spotted sheep, and all the brown ones among the lambs, and the spotted and speckled among the goats; and these shall be my wages" (Gen. 30:32).

Because both Jacob and Laban would be raising livestock under Jacob's proposal, he understood Laban would need a means by which the herds could be inspected to ensure the security of his own flock. Jacob was prepared to address this situation. "So my righteousness will answer for me in time to come, when the subject of my wages comes before you: every one that is not speckled and spotted among the goats, and brown among the lambs, will be considered stolen, if it is with me" (Gen. 30:33).

The real strength of Jacob's proposal was that it appeared viable from Laban's perspective. Anyone looking at Jacob's herd would see livestock that appeared to have defects. Even those taking a quick glance could see they were spotted, speckled, and brown. In contrast, Laban's herd would be composed of livestock that appeared to be more pure. The deal was struck when Laban agreed, "Oh, that it were according to your word!" (Gen. 30:34).

With the deal struck, Jacob separated the herds to protect the integrity of his assets. His sons had learned shepherding from their father and had matured enough to be responsible for the care of the family flock. He entrusted the family assets to their care and "put three days' journey between" the two flocks (Gen. 30:36). Then he engaged in selective breeding to ensure a significant increase in his asset base (Gen. 30:39). Using his knowledge of the herd, Jacob ensured stronger livestock was bred into his herd and weaker livestock was bred into Laban's herd (Gen. 30:41–42).

Other shepherds may have thought Jacob was lucky to have his herd grow so fast, but Jacob knew otherwise. He would have agreed with Stephen Leacock when he claimed, "I am a firm believer in luck and find the harder I work, the more I have of it." He had the wisdom to keep back part of his plan from the negotiating process, giving him an advantage Laban had not considered. According to Charles de Gaulle, "A true leader always keeps an element of surprise up his sleeve, which others cannot grasp, but keeps his public excited and breathless."

Jacob's plan was successful. It resolved his problem and reversed his fortune. As the size of his herd continued growing, he apparently traded part of his herd for other assets. In the process, he acquired servants, camels, and donkeys. No doubt these also enabled him to build further assets. "Thus the man became exceedingly prosperous, and had large flocks, female and male servants, and camels and donkeys" (Gen. 30:43).

While Jacob's plan was effective in resolving the problem it was designed to address, Jacob knew problems would continually be part of life. He remained vigilant and quickly recognized new problems growing out of his success. In the process, "Jacob saw the countenance of Laban, and indeed it was not favorable toward him as before" (Gen. 31:2). In the face of a new problem, the pragmatic Jacob developed a new plan and began putting it to work as he had done when facing problems in the past.

Taking a Pragmatic Look at Leadership

Some people have a personality type that naturally inclines them to look at life pragmatically. For others, this is definitely not part of their natural approach to doing things. Yet all leaders will encounter situations that require a "hard-nosed" approach. As leaders develop their personal leadership kaleidoscope, there are specific actions they can take to blend pragmatic leadership into the way they influence others.

Begin by recognizing the wrong in your world and committing yourself to do right anyway. Douglas MacArthur once observed, "There is no security on the earth. There is only opportunity." Learn to look beyond the problems before you to the opportunity they offer.

Next, learn to discern the right things to do, then do them. Successful leaders know what to do, how to do it, and when to do it. Beyond that, they do it. Anthony T. Dadovano claimed, "A good leader is not the person who does things right, but the person who finds the right things to do." He is an ordinary person with extraordinary determination and confidence in his ultimate destination. According to Dr. James Louis Bledsoe, "It is imperative that the leader leads in the right direction."

Third, build your credibility as a leader by convincing others you know how to solve the problem. Leaders must not only know where they are going; they must also make others glad to go with them. They have been described as "the ones who know the way, go the way, and show the way." It is not enough that leaders know what they are doing. They must know that they know, and be able to make it abundantly clear to those around them that they know.

Part of building that credibility involves solving problems by implementing your problem-solving solution to situations you face in the context in which you lead. According to Henry Ford, "You cannot build a reputation on what you are going to do." People judge leaders by what they complete, not by what they start.

As you lead, measure and report on your progress to strengthen the resolve of your followers. A. Whitney Griswold was right when he warned, "Loyalty cannot be coerced or compelled. It must be won." Some leaders believe they have converted followers to the cause simply because they have silenced the opposition. But that is not enough. The pragmatic leaders realize people are not really following until they are involved in making something happen.

Always be willing to make adjustments as necessary to resolve the problem more completely. Dr. Lynn Fanning advises, "Leaders should plan for the best, but prepare for the worst." Understanding the worst-case scenario and being prepared for it should it arrive ensures you will not be blindsided by minor hiccups in the process of resolving problems. Someone observed, "Success is never final, nor is failure ever fatal." Pragmatic leaders who recognize the problem know its potential for disaster, and have a plan to deal with that situation should it develop, will have the courage needed to lead in the most difficult contexts.

Part of being a pragmatic leader involves remembering life is a journey, not a destination. There will always be problems to deal with, even when you resolve the problem you currently face. Be alert to new problems that may grow out of your success. Leadership involves remembering past mistakes, an analysis of today's achievements, and a well-grounded imagination in visualizing the problems yet future.

CHAPTER 4

Joseph
The Decision-Making Leader

You can judge a leader by the size of problem he tackles.
People nearly always pick a problem their own size, and
ignore or leave to others the bigger or smaller ones.

ANTHONY JAY

As he stood in Buckingham Palace in May 1996, Prince Philip placed the silver medallion around his neck. The man being honored was not an international statesman in the normal sense of the word, even though he was among those who had made the greatest impact on the world in the last half of the twentieth century. Nor was he a great military leader or athlete, although outstanding members of both professions looked to him as a mentor. He perceived himself as simply an American businessman on a mission for God.

As the author of more than a hundred books and booklets and thousands of articles and pamphlets that have been widely distributed in most of the world's major languages, Bill Bright was certainly one of the most influential Christian leaders at the dawn of the twenty-first century. More than 2.5 billion copies of his booklet, "Have You Heard of the Four Spiritual Laws?"[1] have been distributed in more than 200 languages.

Fifty years after Bill and his wife founded Campus Crusade to reach students on the campus of UCLA, that ministry had more than 25,000 full-time staff serving with over a half-million trained volunteer staff in 196 countries representing 99.6 percent of the world's population. The campus ministry has expanded to include more than seventy special ministries and projects to target and reach various people with the gospel.

One of the many ministries designed to help fulfill Christ's command to take the gospel to the entire world is the *Jesus* film. Based on the Gospel of Luke, it has been translated into more than 730 languages. More than 4.5 billion people have viewed the film in 234 countries with more than 148 million people having indicated they trusted Christ as Savior after seeing it. Those figures do not include the estimated millions who are believed to have made similar decisions after viewing the film on television or hearing a radio version of the movie. Campus Crusade reports that the film is currently being translated into three hundred additional languages.

How does one explain the impact of a life like that of Bill Bright? Michael Richardson, Bright's biographer, hinted at part of the answer when he gave the biography the title, *Amazing Faith*. Without question, Bill Bright is an amazing man of faith, but faith alone does not explain this phenomenon. In response to the question, "How'd he do all that?" Richardson answered, "As best I can tell, the answer has to do with the following key decisions Bill made in life, the same choices any of us can make."[2] He then listed seventy-seven key decisions that shaped Bill's life.

Near the top of the list was a decision Bright made as a young man in the spring of 1945. Although quite comfortable with the life that was his as a successful small businessman, the gentle witness of several Christians in his life brought him to the realization that "the happy pagan" really lacked that inner happiness that could only be his if he yielded his life to Christ. After hearing Henrietta Mears explain the gospel and challenge the group of which he was a part to make a decision about what they were hearing within the next few days, Bright realized he was ready to receive Christ as Savior that night. His life has never been the same since.

Decision number ten on Richardson's list took place in 1951. Becoming convinced God's vision for his life was to fulfill the Great Commission, Bill and his wife wrote and signed a literal contract with God, relinquishing ownership of all they had. Together they purposed to live their lives in submission to God as their "full and major partner." From that point on, they would always think of God as their Master and themselves as his slaves. Campus Crusade was born out of that commitment.

The list goes on, listing various specific commitments concluding with a most unusual statement considering all he had accomplished for God during his life. "And he concluded that he is not at all special but rather ordinary, and only microscopic in comparison to an infinite but loving God."[3] Author Richardson adds, "Because of that last conclusion, to Bill Bright's way of thinking, anyone else who happens to be willing to live like this can have the same degree of impact Bill has had."[4]

Leaders Who Make Decisions

One of the prime responsibilities of leaders is decision making. Decision-making leaders are leaders who solve problems by making good decisions that result in lasting solutions. Often, the key to leadership credibility is how well the leaders resolve problems, especially in times of adversity. The Scriptures describe Joseph as one who developed his leadership credibility in the worst of conditions by making good decisions. The skills he developed in less-than-favorable conditions qualified him for the significant leadership responsibilities entrusted to him later.

Decision-making leaders are widely used in business at every level of management. In a "bottom-up" approach to management, many businesses attempt to move decision making and problem solving to the lowest possible point in the organizational hierarchy. In those same businesses, those who consistently make good decisions and resolve problems are often those who are promoted to increased responsibility.

While many social and cultural institutions make major decisions by committee consensus, the larger and more successful of these institutions entrust decision making to their staff. They expect them to make good decisions that are compatible with the general governance principles and policies of their organization.

Church leaders are called upon to make decisions in every aspect of ministry. While the nature of some decisions may require wide consultation with others, even the involvement of the whole church, many other decisions can and should be made by those given specific responsibility for ministry. It should not require a committee decision to direct the janitor about the color of toilet paper to be purchased for the church washrooms.

Decision-making leaders face a unique set of problems as they attempt to use this skill in leadership. Sometimes, their decision making may be impacted by a perception of what is expected by others. They may also be influenced by previous commitments made by or on behalf of the leader. Often, other principles by which the leaders live tend to color the decisions they make. One of their greatest challenges may be gathering the reliable data they need to make a good decision. Even when decision-making leaders make a good decision, they must always be careful to get the timing right in implementing that decision.

Decision-making leaders are often gifted with the spiritual gift of administration. They tend to be most effective in their work when they apply the laws of decision making and problem solving to the context in which they find themselves. It is not uncommon for a decision-making leader to be choleric in temperament.

As with other leadership styles you may incorporate into your personal leadership kaleidoscope, there are inherent dangers commonly faced by decision-making leaders. Often, they tend to be blamed for failure, even when others supported their decision at the time it was made. Sometimes, the situation in which they find themselves requires them to make decisions with inadequate or wrong information. Every time decision-making leaders make decisions, they run the risk of alienating some of their followers who oppose the decision made. They may be pressured into making a decision at the wrong time or hindered by the failures of others who preceded them. Sometimes, even the best decision makers make wrong decisions. They just get it wrong.

Still, leaders need to learn how to make decisions. They are often responsible to lead a group through the decision-making process when that group needs to make a major decision. By definition, leaders are decision makers. You cannot lead if you will not decide. People expect their leaders to make decisions. Failure to make decisions tends to erode the credibility of the leader.

Often the success of leaders is measured by the success of the decisions they make. Great leaders make great decisions to accomplish great feats. Average leaders make average decisions and have maintenance tenure. Poor leaders make poor decisions that hurt the cause and harm their followers.

Joseph: Leading through Decision Making

As the prime minister of Egypt responsible for preparing for and managing the country through a severe famine, Joseph's life was given over to making decisions. During those fourteen years in office, he led Egypt through a complete restructuring of the economy and society that made them the dominant world power of that day. But Joseph did not learn to make decisions the day he was appointed to office by Pharaoh. He led by decision making through the varied experiences of his earlier life.

Joseph recognized God was at work in his life through situations over which he had no control. Further, he understood God used those situations to shape him into what God wanted him to be, regardless of the motives of others. In a meeting with his brothers following his father's death, he explained, "But as for you, you meant evil against me; but God meant it for good, in order to bring it about as it is this day, to save many people alive" (Gen. 50:20).

Life began tough for Joseph and remained that way for a long time. His father was married to two sisters jealous of each other for his affection (Gen. 30:15). As one might expect, this resulted in the development of a severely dysfunctional family. When God began giving Joseph dreams as a young man, others refused to buy into those dreams. His brothers responded by calling him the "dreamer" (Gen. 37:19) and making plans to kill him (Gen. 37:20). Even when he pled for his own life in anguish, they ignored his cry for help (Gen. 42:21). His life was apparently preserved only when some of his brothers realized they could turn a profit by selling him as a slave to a group of Midianite traders (Gen. 37:28).

Although Joseph's life was preserved, the quality of his life did not improve. He went from being the favorite son of his father to being auctioned off as a common slave. Against his will, he was compelled to live in and adapt to a foreign culture. He worked hard and was given increased responsibilities by his new master, but ended up being falsely accused and thrown into prison (Gen. 39:13–20). He continued helping people in prison, but those he helped who promised to help him failed to remember his name for two years (Gen. 40:23).

Joseph recognized that his dreams and the ability to interpret them came from God alone. When Pharaoh's officers were troubled over dreams they had, Joseph asked them, "Do not interpretations belong to God?" (Gen. 40:8). Later, when he was called on to interpret Pharaoh's dreams, Joseph confessed, "It is not in me; God will give Pharaoh an answer of peace" (Gen. 41:16). When we dream dreams that come from God, we dream beyond our circumstances and present situation. We focus on God "who is able to do exceedingly abundantly above all that we ask or think, according to the power that works in us" (Eph. 3:20).

The Scriptures attribute Joseph's personal success to the blessing of God. As a slave in Potiphar's house, "the LORD was with Joseph, and he was a successful man" (Gen. 39:2). Later, when he was falsely accused and imprisoned, "the keeper of the prison did not look into anything that was under Joseph's authority, because the LORD was with him; and whatever he did, the LORD made it prosper" (Gen. 39:23). Joseph was productive in life because he was connected to the source of life. Jesus later taught His disciples, "As the branch cannot bear fruit of itself, unless it abides in the vine, neither can you, unless you abide in Me" (John 15:4).

The "Doctrine of Blessability" teaches that God chooses to bless the faith and faithfulness He sees in our lives rather than to withhold His blessing because of our inconsistencies. Throughout the Scriptures, the blessing of God is tied to several conditions. One of these conditions involves living a life separated to God and from the world. David wrote, "Blessed is the man who walks not in the counsel of the ungodly, nor stands in the path of sinners, nor sits in the seat of the scornful" (Ps. 1:1). Later, he also tied the blessing of God to dealing with personal sin. "Blessed is he whose transgression is forgiven, whose sin is covered. Blessed is the man to whom the LORD does not impute iniquity, and in whose spirit there is no deceit" (Ps. 32:1–2). These conditions assume the blessed person is also a person of faith, which is another condition tied to the blessing of God. "Blessed is the man who trusts in the LORD, and whose hope is the LORD" (Jer. 17:7).

The blessing of God is also tied to our attitude toward God and others. The blessed person has a sincere reverence for God and His Word. "Blessed is the man who fears the LORD, who delights greatly in His commandments" (Ps. 112:1). That reverence for God is reflected in the way a person lives. "Blessed is every one who fears the LORD, who walks in His ways" (Ps. 128:1). Also, the person who has a right attitude toward God will also be concerned for others, especially those in need. "Blessed is he who considers the poor; the LORD will deliver him in time of trouble" (Ps. 41:1).

The blessing of God is also tied to the pursuit of wisdom. In his discussion of the value of wisdom, Solomon wrote, "Blessed is the man who listens to me, watching daily at my gates, waiting at the posts of my doors. For whoever finds me finds life, and obtains favor from the LORD" (Prov. 8:34–35). In the New Testament, James linked the blessing of God to enduring trials or temptation. "Blessed is the man who endures temptation; for when he has been approved, he will receive the crown of life which the Lord has promised to those who love Him" (James 1:12).

The blessing of God is often tied to the Scriptures themselves. John began the final book of the New Testament with the promise, "Blessed is he who reads and those who hear the words of this prophecy, and keeps those things which are written in it; for the time is near" (Rev. 1:3). The book ends with a similar promise from the lips of Jesus: "Behold, I am coming quickly! Blessed is he who keeps the words of the prophecy of this book" (Rev. 22:7). God expects us not only to read and hear the Scriptures, but also to put them into practice. The psalmist wrote, "Blessed are the undefiled in the way, who walk in the law of the LORD! Blessed are those who keep His testimonies, who seek Him with the whole heart!" (Ps. 119:1–2). Jesus emphasized this same principle when He said, "More than that, blessed are those who hear the word of God and keep it!" (Luke 11:28).

Joseph's activities in the dark hours and dungeons of his life demonstrate his servant's heart. Even though he had been sold into slavery against his will, he served Potiphar with a pure heart. As Potiphar recognized Joseph was trustworthy, he gave him increased responsibility. "So it was, from the time that he had made him overseer of his house and all that he had, that the LORD blessed the Egyptian's house for Joseph's sake; and the blessing of the LORD was on all that he had in the house and in the field" (Gen. 39:5). Joseph understood, "He who is greatest among you, let him be as the younger, and he who governs as he who serves" (Luke 22:26).

Throughout his life, Joseph was willing to assume new responsibilities and take on new challenges in his pursuit of God's vision for his life. He learned about and practiced animal husbandry as a shepherd in his father's home. As a slave in Potiphar's household, he eventually practiced resource management in caring for his master's affairs. As a prisoner, Joseph was entrusted with responsibility over part of the prison. In that situation, Joseph practiced people management with some of the most difficult people in the world. These experiences prepared him for his role as prime minister where he was involved in the economic restructuring of the nation.

Former U.S. President Richard Nixon had good advice for decision-making leaders—advice he would have been wise to heed. "I have an absolute rule. I refuse to make a decision that somebody else can make. The first rule of leadership is to save yourself for the big decision. Don't allow your mind to become cluttered with the trivia. Don't let yourself become the issue."[5]

Joseph proved himself to be a man committed to certain unalterable core values in life. These values guided him and helped him make wise and healthy decisions. In seeking to live by the principles of God, he found sufficient reason to avoid becoming involved in an immoral relationship with Potiphar's wife (Gen. 39:9). His faith in God enabled him to see God at work in a variety of situations throughout his life (Gen. 50:20). Throughout all these experiences, Joseph made the kind of decisions that shaped who he became.

Someone once said, "The man who follows the crowd will never be followed by a crowd." Jesus warned His disciples to build their lives on the bedrock of His principles rather than the shifting sands of public opinion. "Therefore whoever hears these sayings of Mine, and does them, I will liken him to a wise man who built his house on the rock" (Matt. 7:24). Those eternal principles of God are revealed in Scripture for our benefit. According to Moses, "The secret things belong to the LORD our God, but those things which are revealed belong to us and to our children forever, that we may do all the words of this law" (Deut. 29:29).

Developing a Personal Decision-Making Strategy

There is a widely reported story of a conversation between a retiring banker and a young man just beginning his career in finance. As the young man saw his elder emptying the contents of his desk into a box, he realized this would be his final chance to glean wisdom from this source. Eventually, he summoned the courage to approach his senior.

"Excuse me," he began. "I was wondering if you could help me. With all your years of experience, could you tell me what it takes to be successful in this business?" he asked.

The retiring banker paused to think and then answered, "Two words. Good decisions."

The young man wanted more. "Can you tell me how I can learn to make good decisions?" he asked.

The older man must have been expecting the second question. Without hesitation he answered, "Two words. Bad decisions."

While it is true many great decision makers have their share of bad decisions on their record, part of learning to make good decisions involves having a good decision-making strategy. Sometimes a leader can "guess lucky" and make a good decision, but knowing how to consistently make good decisions is an important skill long-term leaders need to blend into their leadership kaleidoscope.

Making good decisions is a process that begins with an awareness of the problem. Great leaders develop a keen sense of awareness to detect problems early, before they get too big. Unfortunately, as organizations grow, leaders are often distanced from the places problems are likely to begin. Some leaders seek to minimize the effect of this trend by practicing MBWA, "management by walking around." Even though they may not be involved in the minute details of their business, school, or church, they routinely walk around and talk to people at random, gaining important information that is unlikely to be communicated to them otherwise. Often, they learn of potential problems as they begin and can make decisions that will prevent them from becoming unmanageable.

Once problems have been identified, it is important to take time to define the problem, issue, or question. Former U.S. President Woodrow Wilson observed, "One cool judgment is worth a thousand hasty counsels." The ancient Greek philosopher Euripides cautioned, "Second thoughts are wisest." Taking time to define the problem helps prevent offering immediate answers that might create bigger problems down the road. Gilbert Keith Chesterton warned, "Don't take the fence down until you know the reason it was put up."[6]

Good decision making always involves an analysis of the problem. According to Peter Drucker, "The knowledge society will inevitably become far more competitive than any society we have yet known for the simple reason that with knowledge being universally accessible, there will be no excuses for nonperformance." The more a leader knows about a problem, the more likely he will be able to resolve that problem. Napoleon claimed, "The first quality of the commander-in-chief is a cool head to receive a correct impression of things. He should not allow himself to be confused by either good or bad news."

In gathering the facts about a particular problem, there are several things to look for and questions to ask. First, what factors caused this problem? While one cause may quickly come to mind, it is not uncommon for several factors to be involved in a problematic situation. Second, how could this problem be redefined? Asking this question helps leaders gain a broader perspective of the situation with which they are dealing. Third, what assumptions are at work in this situation? Expectations that have not been communicated are often an important part of interpersonal conflict. On other occasions, an individual may be frustrated with the failure of someone to take action on something never assigned to him or her. It is often better to ask questions than to know all the answers. And as you listen to the response, remember strong words often betray a weak argument.

Those who make good decisions have learned to look for the best decision rather than the right decision. There are usually many ways to deal with a problem. As you look for the best response, take time to identify and evaluate those alternatives. In doing so, remember the counsel of the retiring banker. Good judgment is the result of experience, experience that is gained through bad judgment. While leaders need to think rationally as they evaluate the alternatives, don't discount feelings entirely as you make decisions. Sometimes emotions are as important as logic in making the right choice.

After careful consideration of your options, it is time to choose the best potential solution to the problem from the various creative options available. Usually, the larger the number of people involved in any decision, the greater the pressure on the entire group for conformity. Still, someone needs to lead through this process. Left to itself, the democratic process usually lowers the standard to the least common denominator.

Once the decision has been made, implement it and make it work. John Hancock Field observed, "All worthwhile men have good thoughts, good ideas, and good intentions, but precious few of them ever translate those into actions." Leaders do not second-guess themselves and hesitate once the decision has been made. According to Will Rogers, "Even if you are on the right track, you will get run over if you just sit there."

As you make decisions, remember the "Maxwell Rule of Timing." According to John C. Maxwell, "The wrong decision at the wrong time is a disaster. The wrong decision at the right time is a mistake. The right decision at the wrong time is not acceptable. The right decision at the right time leads to success."[7]

CHAPTER 5

Joseph
The Strategic Leader

*One reason why things aren't going according to plan is because
there never was a plan.*

ASHLEIGH BRILLIANT

Napoleon was born into an Italian family of minor nobility in which no Bonaparte had ever engaged in military service. His education began with a focus on the "gentleman subjects" of his day, but that changed when Napoleon attended military schools in France. While there, he devoted much of his time to reading military history. By the time he graduated from the academy in Paris at age sixteen, he sought a military commission and joined the artillery as second lieutenant.

During the French Revolution, Napoleon joined the Jacobins and advanced rapidly in both rank and responsibility within the army. He joined the siege of British forces at Toulon. He assumed command of the French artillery after its commander was seriously wounded, and despite his own bayonet wound, he led the unit to a victory for France that resulted in widespread fame and a promotion to the rank of brigadier general.

On October 5, 1795, he fired his famous "whiff of grapeshot," a single artillery volley in Paris that suppressed the Royalist uprising. His actions resulted in his first field command that he used to continue building his reputation as a leader. At the battle of Lodi, Napoleon displayed his personal bravery by leading a bayonet charge across a bridge to overcome the Austrian rear guard. Unaccustomed to seeing such actions by high-ranking officers, his soldiers began referring to him as "the Little Corporal."

Although his bravery as a military leader is beyond dispute, Napoleon was also an insightful leader who could quickly spot opportunities for victory and determine when battles were not worth fighting. Although he expanded his influence throughout Europe, he also recognized he was not strong enough to cross the English Channel and successfully invade England. He did lead a force into the Mediterranean where he hoped to disrupt British trade and won several battles, but when the battle turned, he returned to France and joined an uprising against the ruling Directory. The success of the coup on November 9, 1799, made Napoleon France's de facto leader.

Napoleon has been described as "the greatest soldier of his age." Even today, his name is synonymous with military greatness. In spite of this, Napoleon was not very innovative. He did not develop any new weapons or military tactics. Rather, he became a master of adaptation. He maintained a high morale among his troops through his personal charisma and acts of bravery, but ensured their victory through careful planning.

Every military campaign was carefully planned. Before the battle, Napoleon personally briefed his subordinate commanders. Though willing to take risks, everything in a battle remained focused on the single objective of victory. He developed a staff system that defined accountability networks within the military while giving his officers liberty to lead as they saw fit. Although he never committed these principles to paper himself, others, including some who served with him, have attempted to define the principles of Napoleonic warfare and describe his system of organization and planning. Future generations of European and American leaders have all been students of his military organization, tactics, and strategy.

As he conquered much of Europe, he did implement the Napoleonic Code. The code abolished feudalism and serfdom, established freedom of religion, provided free education for all, and standardized law and administration throughout Europe. Much of the Western world continues to live under the influence of the "Little Corporal" today.

Leaders Who Plan to Lead

Lyle Schaller was describing the strategic leader when he wrote, "The person who has a systematic approach to the future and a frame of reference for evaluating alternatives has a tremendous advantage over the person who functions without either." Some leaders fail in times of prosperity because they lead without directions. Joseph modeled how to lead a country during an economic boom because he developed a strategic plan that prepared the country for the inevitable downturn in the economy.

Strategic leaders do not always have the highest profiles, but they are significant leaders throughout society. They include the generals who plan and execute battle plans that win wars. Their number includes businessmen and women who recognize a new challenge and prepare and implement a plan to rise above it while their competitors struggle to survive. They are the recruiters who find and enroll new students and the promoters who develop a plan to sell out the available seats for a concert. Strategic leaders also include pastors who develop church growth campaigns to reach new people for Christ and stewardship campaigns to help Christians grow into a deeper commitment to God.

The planning process itself, as important as it is to all leaders, can often be a source of frustration for strategic leaders. Sometimes they are called on to develop campaigns when the goals have not been clearly defined. On other occasions, they may have difficulty gathering all the information they need to develop the best strategy. In that kind of environment, there will always be difficulty gaining enthusiastic support for the plan.

Sometimes, the frustration faced by strategic leaders is not tied to the planning process but those involved in or affected most by that process. It is not uncommon for strategic planners to develop a plan more quickly than others are willing to accept. Group members may have difficulty believing a high goal is reachable, especially if the group has a history of failure in reaching previous goals. In some cases, these leaders may find themselves serving groups where many group members do not believe in planning. In some ministry settings, they may even be viewed as less spiritual than they should be, that is, trusting methodology rather than trusting God.

Strategic leaders are often gifted in administration. They depend greatly on the Law of Problem Solving in developing plans to deal with the challenges they face. They also use the Law of Accountability to ensure that work functions according to the plan. It is not uncommon for strategic leaders to be melancholy in temperament.

Because planning is so much of what strategic leaders do, they run the risk of trusting their own planning abilities more than trusting in God's ability. Sometimes they are guilty of overinvolving the group in organization, hindering the energizing zeal the group needs to accomplish the task. They may become inflexible in making changes to the plan once it has begun, even when those changes are advisable. This is especially a problem when the leader has personal blind spots that could have significant consequences for the group. Some strategic leaders tend to be reluctant to take advice from others with good insights, taking criticism of the plan personally. They are like the person who said, "Constructive criticism is when I criticize you. Destructive criticism is when you criticize me."

Horace Mann once suggested, "It is well to think well; it is divine to act well." Some strategic leaders struggle in this area. They tend to be more inclined to plan work than to work the plan. According to Mark

Twain, "The secret of getting ahead is getting started. The secret of getting started is breaking your complex, overwhelming tasks into small manageable tasks, and then starting on the first one."

Planning is a tool that all leaders need to incorporate into their personal leadership kaleidoscope. Planning saves time and money, identifies specific ways to accomplish goals, and avoids the problem of activity without accomplishment. George Small once reflected, "I read in a book that a man called Christ went about doing good. It is very disconcerting to me that I am so easily satisfied with just going about."

Planning is also an effective tool in communicating how a task should be accomplished. Looking back on a personal success in a particular project, Allen Berglund claimed, "Planning fosters success. We broke the project up into manageable chunks." In the planning process, leaders have the opportunity to recover from "failing on paper" and avoiding failure in the midst of a project. Someone put it this way: "He who fails to plan, plans to fail."

Ultimately, planning helps us recognize the significance of today in the context of the future. According to Rich Sorkin, "Most forward-looking people recognize that the future is on the line, and that the battle for market share is taking place now. If they marshal their resources, they can win. Some think they have plenty of time. I think they will be crushed by a company like Microsoft."

Joseph: Leading through Strategic Planning

Some Christians struggle with the concept of strategic planning, finding it hard to reconcile with the idea of trusting God. Yet many of these same Christians also believe in a planning God. They believe He does have a plan (will) for their life and that plan is good. Planning and faith are not mutually exclusive. According to Edward Dayton, "The entire concept of Christian planning is based on the premise that God would have us know Him more fully and that He desires to reveal to us His will for our lives and for His Church. . . . Inherent to planning is the end result. Effective planning is first the result of clear goals, the reason for planning. If we as Christians are to plan effectively, we must be convinced that setting goals is one way to respond to the will of God."

That was certainly Joseph's response to God's will. As a strategic leader, Joseph had foresight into the likely future of Egypt. That insight came from his God-given ability to interpret dreams. When brought before Egypt's ruler, "Joseph said to Pharaoh, 'The dreams of Pharaoh are one; God has shown Pharaoh what He is about to do'" (Gen. 41:25). Before he was finished, he added, "And the dream was repeated to Pharaoh twice because the thing is established by God, and God will shortly bring it to pass" (Gen. 41:32). Joseph understood strategic leadership begins with a clear vision of what God is doing. The leader with that vision sees first, sees farthest, and sees fullest.

But insight into the future alone is not enough to make a person a leader. Joseph had a plan to address the problem facing Egypt before that problem became too big to manage effectively. "Now therefore, let Pharaoh select a discerning and wise man, and set him over the land of Egypt. Let Pharaoh do this, and let him appoint officers over the land, to collect one-fifth of the produce of the land of Egypt in the seven plentiful years. And let them gather all the food of those good years that are coming, and store up grain under the authority of Pharaoh, and let them keep food in the cities. Then that food shall be as a reserve for the seven years of famine which shall be in the land of Egypt, that the land may not perish during the famine" (Gen. 41:33–36). His proposal may not have been widely popular initially, but in the longer term, he knew it was best for the country. In distinguishing politicians from statesmen, J. F. Clarke suggested, "A politician thinks of the next election; a statesman of the next generation."

The best plans are of little effect if those people with the authority to implement them are not convinced. Joseph was effective in "selling" his plan to Pharaoh, who was the only person who could really help him implement that plan. "So the advice was good in the eyes of Pharaoh and in the eyes of all his servants" (Gen. 41:37). As a result, Joseph was recognized and given the authority he needed to implement his plan. "And Pharaoh said to his servants, 'Can we find such a one as this, a man in whom is the Spirit of God?' Then Pharaoh said to Joseph, 'Inasmuch as God has shown you all this, there is no one as discerning and wise as you. You shall be over my house, and all my people shall be ruled according to your word; only in regard to the throne will I be greater than you.' And Pharaoh said to Joseph, 'See, I have set you over all the land of Egypt.' Then Pharaoh took his signet ring off his hand and put it on Joseph's hand; and he clothed him in garments of fine linen and put a gold chain around his neck. And he had him ride in the second chariot which he had, and they cried out before him, 'Bow the knee!' So he set him over all the land of Egypt" (Gen. 41:38–43).

As a strategic leader, Joseph prepared for the lean years during the years of plenty. "Now in the seven plentiful years the ground brought forth abundantly. So he gathered up all the food of the seven years which were in the land of Egypt, and laid up the food in the cities; he laid up in every city the food of the fields which surrounded them. Joseph gathered very much grain, as the sand of the sea, until he stopped counting, for it was immeasurable" (Gen. 41:47–49).

Next, Joseph managed resources wisely during the lean years. "Then the seven years of plenty which were in the land of Egypt ended, and the seven years of famine began to come, as Joseph had said. The famine was in all lands, but in all the land of Egypt there was bread. So when all the land of Egypt was famished, the people cried to Pharaoh for bread. Then Pharaoh said to all the Egyptians, 'Go to Joseph; whatever he says to you, do.' The famine was over all the face of the earth, and Joseph opened all the storehouses and sold to the Egyptians. And the famine became severe in the land of Egypt. So all countries came to Joseph in Egypt to buy grain, because the famine was severe in all lands" (Gen. 41:53–57).

Few political leaders have followed Joseph's example since. Rather, there is a tendency to raise the standard of living in the years of plenty, extend credit during the lean years, and slow the economic recovery of the nation in an attempt to balance the books later. In contrast, Joseph's actions during this fourteen-year period restructured the Egyptian economy and placed the nation in a position of strength coming out of the worldwide famine. This made Egypt the dominant world power of that day.

In his new position of power, Joseph finally had the opportunity to seek revenge on all those who had wronged him throughout his life. That list was long. It included his brothers who sold him into slavery out of jealousy, the Midianite traders who, for the sake of a business profit, conspired with his brothers and traded him in Egypt as a slave, Potiphar who enslaved him with no apparent plans to ever grant him his liberty, Potiphar's wife whose false accusation of sexual misconduct resulted in his imprisonment, and the butler who failed to mention his case for two years.

But Joseph refused to use his influence to settle old scores. He understood God had used their actions for His purposes. As he later explained to his brothers, "But as for you, you meant evil against me; but God meant it for good, in order to bring it about as it is this day, to save many people alive" (Gen. 50:20).

Developing a Strategic Plan

John Wesley advised his followers, "Do all the good you can, by all the means you can, all the ways you can, in all the places you can, at all the times you can, to all the people you can, for as long as you can." While his circuit riders traveled from village to village on preaching missions, Wesley understood they would be remembered for their actions more than their words. To accomplish Wesley's goal, the circuit riders needed to think through a careful plan of ministry to maximize their effectiveness. For some, that would be a challenge. According to Dryden, "They think too little who talk too much."

Solomon noted, "The plans of the diligent lead surely to plenty, but those of everyone who is hasty, surely to poverty" (Prov. 21:5). As you develop your personal leadership kaleidoscope, you will want to learn how to develop a strategic plan and then work that plan to accomplish your goal. According to Jim Brown, "Success is there for those that want it, plan for it, and take action to achieve it."

Dr. Philip Shelechty claims, "Leaders sometime do things that have never been done before." The first challenge in developing a strategic plan involves projecting the future. Projecting the future is sometimes described as "forecasting" in management literature. This is the work of estimating future trends and conditions. Leaders understand that conditions never remain the same. Even in a stable environment, when a leader implements his plans he changes the present equation.

Emphasizing the importance of the planning process, Carl F. George and Robert E. Logan suggest, "The plan means nothing, but planning means everything, because planning allows us to get vision from God concerning what He wants us to do. Time to think is one of the most important ingredients of leadership, so do not neglect planning time."

Based on your perception of the future and your understanding of God's vision for your life, the next step in the planning process involves establishing objectives. This is the work of setting goals that reflect the priorities expressed in the mission statement. If it is not clear where you are leading your group, no one will know when you get there.

Next, develop policies that will help you accomplish those objectives. Policies are standing decisions that apply to recurring questions and problems. Precedent sometimes establishes policies. The way you answer a question the first time may be the way that question is always answered. In other contexts, governing authorities may publish formal policy statements.

The next step in the process of developing a strategic plan involves developing programs to accomplish your objectives. Programming is the work of establishing the sequence and priority of steps involved in reaching the goal. Closely tied to this step is the need to develop procedures and schedules that will help you accomplish your objectives.

Developing procedures is the work of applying standardized procedures by which the work is done. When you schedule your plan, you establish a time sequence for each program step.

Finally, you need to budget adequate resources for the task. Leaders understand that no matter how great an idea is, it will not be pursued if there are not funds in the budget to pay for it. Budgeting is the work of allocating the necessary resources to accomplish the goal. Jesus warned His disciples to count the costs before undertaking a project (Luke 14:28–35). Your dreams will not be realized if you cannot afford to pay for them.

Taking the time to plan often saves time when it comes to implementing that plan to achieve the desired goal. The Chinese fortune cookie offered good advice when it contained the message, "Organize your work, and accomplishment will follow."

CHAPTER 6

Moses

The Charismatic Leader

A leader is a dealer in hope.

NAPOLEON BONAPARTE

According to John Gardner, "The prime function of a leader is to keep hope alive." United States President John Fitzgerald Kennedy so challenged his times that he became an icon for the Baby Boomer generation touched by his short-lived presidency. It is doubtful if anyone in that generation has forgotten where they were when they learned his life had been taken by an assassin's bullet. It seemed like his death marked the end of Camelot itself, a season of renewed hope in the future of America.

A native of Brookline, Massachusetts, Kennedy served his nation as a naval officer in World War II. In 1943, his PT boat was rammed and sunk by a Japanese destroyer. Despite grave injuries, Kennedy led the survivors to safety. Following the war, he became a Democratic congressman representing the Boston area. His political career advanced and in 1953 he moved on to the Senate.

But politics was not his only interest. While recovering from back surgery in 1955, he wrote the book, *Profiles in Courage*[1] which won the

Pulitzer Prize in history. His other interest was Jacqueline Bouvier, whom he married on September 12, 1953.

In 1956, Kennedy came close to securing the Democratic nomination for vice president. Four years later, he was their presidential candidate up against Vice President Richard Nixon. The 1960 campaign was the first political campaign in which television made a difference. During his campaign, Kennedy created the illusion of momentum by conducting press conferences in rooms able to handle about one-third of the press corps assigned to his campaign. He physically rested the day of the televised debates and used a make-up artist. Those who watched the debates on television saw a youthful, well-rested Kennedy; Nixon looked tired and old. Knowing his Catholic background was a barrier to being elected, he met with evangelical leaders in America's Bible Belt in an effort to win their support. Although he won by only a narrow margin in the popular vote, he was viewed as an extremely popular president.

Kennedy is often remembered for a memorable statement in his inaugural address. "Ask not what your country can do for you—ask what you can do for your country."[2] He had campaigned on a pledge to get America moving again. As he developed policies that would encourage continuous economic growth, he also called on Americans to do their part. As the civil rights movement became increasingly more popular, he adopted the cause as his own and called for new civil rights legislation. As the youngest president in American history, he captured the imagination of America's Baby Boomer generation just as it was coming of age.

When he assumed the oval office, the United States was clearly losing the space race. In response to news that the Soviet Union had succeeded in launching the first man into space, Kennedy raised the stakes by announcing America would land a man on the moon by the end of the decade. Having given the nation a new dream and hope of a better future marked by American superiority, he devoted large sums of money to space research and attracted many of the world's finest scientists to work for the National Aeronautics and Space Administration. Although he did not live to see it happen, in July 1969, it was an American who first stepped on to the lunar surface.

Though John F. Kennedy served as president little more than a thousand days, the Kennedy era seems shrouded in mystique to those who came of age in it. When he spoke, Kennedy touched the heart of his nation. When he died, it seemed like part of them died with him.

The Greeks Had a Word for It

There are some leaders who seem to have a mystical quality about them that draws others to them. That quality is often described by the Greek word *charisma,* which means "gifted." In his study of charismatic leadership, Douglas Porter described charisma as "the unusual quality of personal magnetism possessed by the gifted leader as it is used to arouse deep emotional and volitional responses in the lives of his followers toward the end of accomplishing the predetermined objectives of his movement."[3] In difficult times, people tend to be attracted to charismatic leadership that confidently communicates an appropriate vision with divine authority. Moses modeled charisma when he returned to Egypt to lead Israel to freedom. God's call upon his life illustrates several principles for developing personal charisma as part of a personal leadership kaleidoscope.

Charismatic leaders are the cultural innovators who dare to be different and successfully introduce a widely accepted new song, dramatic style, or approach to education. In the political arena, they rise as the people's candidate who will lead them into a brighter future. They have a way of capturing the imagination and hearts of the electorate. In ministry, charismatic leaders are often the church planters who dream of reaching a city for Christ and building a great church. But charismatic leaders also include the more mature pastors who dare a church in decline to dream again, recover its past glory, and build beyond its heritage.

Charismatic leaders are sometimes viewed as loose cannons within an organization. It is easy for them to dream beyond their potential followers to the extent that they are discouraged from following their leadership. In the early phase of their leadership, they lead in a culture that is initially nonresponsive to charismatic leadership. As they begin to succeed, they face critics who dismiss them as merely empire builders. They often have worthy dreams but lack the strategic plan to realize those dreams. That is because charismatic leaders usually lack the administrative skills to lead the movement they spawn. When their dreams do become reality, they are often frustrated in the management of their movement. Throughout their leadership, they always run the risk of encountering other charismatic leaders with a different vision who may attract followers from their group.

Those who lead with charisma often have a unique gift mix that includes evangelism, prophecy, and exhortation. When they lead through their gift of evangelism, they are effective in winning others to their cause. They use their gift of prophecy when addressing the crisis of the moment. Their gift of exhortation helps them guide followers in the steps required of them. Perhaps more than other leaders, charismatic leaders lead through the Law of Dreams as they share their vision of the future. They also use the Law of Motivation to gain a commitment to their cause on the part of their followers. They are often sanguine in temperament.

According to Peter Drucker, "Charisma becomes the undoing of leaders. It makes them inflexible, convinced of their own infallibility, unable to change." Sometimes charismatic leaders dream beyond reality, creating situations in which their dreams can never be implemented. When their personal worldview is defective, they tend to implement dreams that self-destruct. If they overestimate the significance of the crisis, they also fail to gain a following. When they do attract followers, they sometimes attract followers to themselves but not their cause. Sometimes even they have difficulty in defining a personality apart from the cause or movement they lead.

It is not uncommon for charismatic leaders to overlook the myriad of details necessary to successfully implement their vision. If that happens, the movement may grow beyond their ability to lead. Unable to make the kind of changes necessary to ensure the movement's continued success, the leader who begins the movement is often the one who destroys it.

Notwithstanding the above, there are good reasons for leaders to incorporate charisma into their personal leadership kaleidoscope. Charisma attracts followers. There is no leadership without followers. It is especially effective in the early days of a new movement, when promoting new ideas or a new vision for the future, and in times of social crises or confusion. Charisma allows followers to personify great ideas and pursue them by following a great leader.

Responding to the Call of God

In what Moses initially thought was a curious anomaly in the desert, he met God and understood God's call upon his life. The time spent at that burning bush forever changed his life. When God spoke, Moses was responsive to the prompting of God in his life. "So when the LORD saw that he turned aside to look, God called to him from the midst of the bush and said, 'Moses, Moses!' And he said, 'Here I am' " (Exod. 3:4). Before the conversation ended, God was inviting Moses to return to Egypt as the instrument of God's deliverance (Exod. 3:10).

Businesswoman Nora Watson mused, "I think most of us are looking for a calling, not a job. Most of us, like the assembly line worker, have jobs that are too small for our spirit. Jobs are not big enough for people." In contrast, when God calls individuals to a specific task, that task tends to be God-sized.

Moses became assured of God's presence and gained direction for his leadership through time spent alone with God. "So He said, 'I will certainly be with you. And this shall be a sign to you that I have sent you: When you have brought the people out of Egypt, you shall serve

God on this mountain'" (Exod. 3:12). Someone has suggested, "The direction of a man's life follows the unseen influence of what he admires, what he lives, and what he believes in." According to Wendell Phillips, "One on God's side is a majority."

That time spent alone with God also gave Moses significant insight into the character of God. "And God said to Moses, 'I AM WHO I AM.' And He said, 'Thus you shall say to the children of Israel, "I AM has sent me to you"'" (Exod. 3:14).

According to Humphrey Mynors, "Leadership is the power to evoke the right response in other people." God directed Moses to those who would be most responsive to his people. "Go and gather the elders of Israel together. . . . Then they will heed your voice" (Exod. 3:16, 18). German Field Marshall Erwin Rommel advised, "The commander must try, above all, to establish personal and comradely contact with his men, but without giving away an inch of his authority."

Moses understood there would be significant opposition to his plan to liberate Israel. God warned him, "But I am sure that the king of Egypt will not let you go, no, not even by a mighty hand" (Exod. 3:19). But he also became convinced of God's ability to overcome the obstacles he would face in pursuing God's call upon his life. "So the LORD said to him, 'What is that in your hand?' He said, 'A rod.' . . . And Moses took the rod of God in his hand" (Exod. 4:2, 20). According to James M. Kouzes and Barry Z. Posner, "Leaders act in ways that are consistent with their beliefs, they are persistent in pursuit of their visions, and they are always vigilant about the little things that make a big difference."

Writers M. Z. Hackman and C. E. Johnson claim, "To be effective, leaders must know how to communicate their visions effectively and how to enlist the cooperation of others." Moses felt this would be a problem because of his inability to speak without stammering. He sought and got the assistance of others. "Is not Aaron the Levite your brother? I know that he can speak well. And look, he is also coming out to meet you. When he sees you, he will be glad in his heart. Now you shall speak to him and put the words in his mouth. And I will be with your mouth and with his mouth, and I will teach you what you shall do. So he shall be your spokesman to the people. And he himself shall be as a mouth for you, and you shall be to him as God" (Exod. 4:14–16).

Joe J. Sparagna claims, "Leadership requires changing the 'business-as-usual' environment." Military analyst Karl Von Clausewitz adds, "Never forget that no military leader has ever become great without audacity." Moses boldly challenged the status quo and called for a significant change in keeping with the nature of his call. "Afterward Moses and Aaron went in and told Pharaoh, 'Thus says the LORD God of Israel: "Let My people go, that they may hold a feast to Me in the wilderness"'" (Exod. 5:1). "Great leaders are never satisfied with current levels of performance" according to Donna Harrison. "They are restlessly driven by possibilities and potential achievements." In a previous generation, President Kennedy challenged his fellow Americans, "Let us go forth to lead the land we love, asking His blessing and His help, but knowing here on earth God's work must be truly our own."

Moses remained true to his calling despite opposition from the very people he had come to liberate. "So Moses spoke thus to the children of Israel; but they did not heed Moses, because of anguish of spirit and cruel bondage" (Exod. 6:9). Sometimes, as Havelock Ellis noted, "To be a leader of men one must turn one's back on men." But Moses endured until his enemy weakened and his goal could be accomplished. The night eventually came when Pharaoh conceded and told Moses, "Rise, go out from among my people, both you and the children of Israel. And go, serve the LORD as you have said" (Exod. 12:31).

When leaders go places, they take others with them. One test of leadership is to turn around and see if anyone is following you. Followers will never go any farther than their leaders. As Moses led Israel out of Egypt, he reinforced the vision that birthed the movement by establishing the Passover as a memorial that would commemorate a significant milestone in the movement's history. He described it as "a night of solemn observance to the LORD for bringing them out of the land of Egypt. This is that night of the LORD, a solemn observance for all the children of Israel throughout their generations" (Exod. 12:42). He continued to lead his people to celebrate various victories God gave them as they continued pursuing God's call in their lives. When the nation crossed the Red Sea, "Then Moses and the children of Israel sang this song to the LORD, and spoke, saying: 'I will sing to the LORD, for He has triumphed gloriously!'" (Exod. 15:1).

Uncovering Your Personal Charisma

While it is true some leaders have an unusual quality of charisma that characterizes their personality, every leader has a degree of charisma that touches those within his personal sphere of influence. There are things leaders can do to enhance their charisma, extend their sphere of influence, and influence more people. As you seek to incorporate charisma into your personal leadership kaleidoscope, consider the following actions.

First, those who would desire greater charisma should spend time with charismatic leaders and let their charisma rub off on you. In an earlier book, author Elmer Towns coined the phrase "hot poker" to describe this strategy of leadership development he witnessed in revivalistic churches and Bible colleges. This principle states, "Just as heat transfers from the coals to the poker, so the qualities and attitudes of effective leadership are assimilated."[4]

Second, get some practical ministry experience that will equip you to implement your vision. Everyone wants to follow a successful leader. Developing the skills you need for success will enable you to begin building a ministry that will attract people. Your initial success in ministry will extend your ministry, enabling you to take the next step in pursuing your vision.

The strength of charismatic leaders is the ability to communicate their vision to their followers in a way that results in their followers buying into their dreams and making it their own. Dave Patterson described the leader as "the evangelist for the dream." Therefore, study communication theory and methodology to become a more effective communicator. Joseph Conrad claimed, "Give me the right word and the right accent and I will move the world."

Third, take time to learn and apply the spiritual disciplines that will result in personal growth in your relationship with God. Leaders must learn to seek ideas, and those ideas come from God. If charisma is "gifted leadership," then those who would desire greater charisma in their personal leadership kaleidoscope must spend time with "the Father of lights" who gives "every good gift and every perfect gift" (James 1:17). Jesus reminded His disciples of the need to remain connected to Him, explaining, "Without Me you can do nothing" (John 15:5).

Fourth, take inventory to determine your personal strengths and weaknesses as a leader. Dr. Joseph P. Cangemi described leadership as "a quality that inspires trust, confidence and faith." Great leaders know their strengths and work to increase their effectiveness. Likewise, they also know their limits and work to minimize the impact of their weaknesses. When you know your strengths, you can build on them and be a more effective leader.

CHAPTER 7

Moses

The Administrative Leader

*Many churches have been seriously damaged and the work of a
number of Christian institutions has been handicapped by
well-meaning spiritually minded men who have never learned
the principles of effective management.*

ROBERT G. RAYBURN

She was born into one of England's wealthiest families but is best
remembered today for her work among the poor and outcasts of
British society.

Elizabeth Gurney's father was a highly successful banker who was
able to provide far beyond the necessities for her family. His wealth
became so legendary that the expression "as rich as the Gurneys"
became a popular British idiom to describe those who were very rich.
Although her family's wealth insulated her from the darker side of
British society, her Quaker faith taught her to be sensitive to the needs
of others and to treat all people as equals. She married Joseph Fry, who
was also a Quaker, and began a family that eventually included eleven
children and twenty-five grandchildren.

Elizabeth Fry first heard about conditions in London's Newgate Prison in 1813 and found it difficult to believe such a place could exist. The prison itself was located in one of the oldest and worst parts of the city. As she began looking into the situation, she learned four hundred women were incarcerated there, crowded into four small rooms. As some of the women were also mothers, the prison also housed fifty children. A visit to the prison confirmed there were no beds or bedding, toilets, heat, ventilation, or light in the prison, and those living there were dressed in rags. Something had to be done about the appalling conditions, but what could one woman do in nineteenth-century Britain?

Fry had watched her father succeed by managing his business well. Borrowing a page from his book, she began talking to people about the needs in the prison and networking with others to begin making reforms. She understood the reform of Newgate Prison could not be accomplished alone, so she organized others to help. Together with other Quakers, she provided warm clothes for the prisoners and began a school to educate the children incarcerated with their mothers. She urged the women to take steps to reform themselves and urged jailers to treat inmates more humanely. As many of the women were imprisoned for minor debts, she helped them organize cottage industries that enabled them to earn enough money to pay their debts and earn their freedom.

The kindness shown the prisoners by Fry and those she enlisted to help her in her endeavor began softening the hardened hearts of the female prisoners in the Newgate Prison. As they began working on various projects organized by Fry, their new attitude was reflected in the way they treated themselves, others, and the facility in which they were incarcerated. What had been a filthy and dangerous place to live became a clean and edifying environment. Prison and government officials quickly recognized Fry's reforms were having a positive effect. Her ideas on prison reform spread quickly beyond the Newgate Prison and were implemented in prisons throughout Britain.

The mother who had organized a few friends to try to make a difference in one prison eventually became a widely admired spokesperson for prison reform throughout Europe. She was the first woman who was not a monarch ever invited to address the British Parliament. The governments of France, Holland, Denmark, and Prussia all invited her to advise them on making prison reforms. When Fry's ideas were applied in a new prison in St. Petersburg, Russia, the effect was so positive the emperor of Russia called her "one of the wonders of the world." Her attitude toward the treatment of prisoners was perhaps best expressed in the final statement of a report she prepared for the king of France. "When thee builds a prison, thee had better build with the thought ever in thy mind that thee and thy children may occupy the cells."[1]

Management and Leadership

Lawrence A. Appley described management as "getting things done through other people." Many leaders limit their leadership potential or quickly burn out in leadership because of their failure to delegate. Moses faced this risk in his own life as he led Israel through the wilderness, but on the advice of his father-in-law, he appointed judges to do work he was doing that could be done as well or better by others. His actions in that context describe him as an administrative leader.

Administrative leadership is the traditional approach to management widely used in both large and small companies throughout America. Cultural institutions such as schools, theaters, and orchestras use administrative leaders in planning, organizing, leading, and controlling various efforts to better educate their students or entertain their patrons. Church leaders who have been trained in management principles use this approach to organize, implement, and evaluate stewardship campaigns, church growth campaigns, and mission conferences. They also use this approach to administer various aspects of their ministry such as Sunday school or small group ministry.

Because of their organizational skills, administrative leaders are often called in to salvage poorly organized projects as things begin falling apart. This can lead to their being subjects of resentment by those who are talented but lack administrative gifts and abilities. They may also find it difficult to work in some environments where traditional policies tend to hinder progress. Working with creative people who resent the systems they establish can also be challenging. Administrative leaders tend to think long-term. This can create problems when they attempt to communicate how their plans will address a problem, especially when those they are leading are in a panic mode. Because administrative leaders tend to be project-oriented, coming to the end of a project without a new project on the horizon can result in frustration.

Perhaps the greatest danger facing administrative leaders is the possibility—some would say the probability—that they will some day take on a project beyond their ability and not realize it until they are well into the project itself.

Administrative leaders tend to be well equipped to face these challenges. They lead best when they lead through their gift of administration. They often use the Law of Rewards to recognize the work of their staff. They also rely on the Law of Accountability to ensure that the work done is accomplished according to mutually agreed-upon standards. Administrative leaders are often choleric in temperament.

Skilled administrative leaders may at times appear to be well organized even when they really are not. Sometimes, in addressing the broad picture, they may overlook important details. In their commitment to develop a plan, they sometimes appear to be insensitive to people. This sometimes results in their being accused of being cold, pushy, or using people to build their empire. Sometimes, their success in "getting the job done" may be used to justify rather than deal with character deficiencies. In desperate situations, they may resort to manipulating others to ensure the project is completed on time. They may even use delegation as an excuse for their own laziness.

Notwithstanding the above, delegation is an important tool that needs to be part of every leader's personal leadership kaleidoscope. It is impossible for leaders to do everything themselves without burning out. Often, there are people within the organization who can do a job better than their leaders. Others can be stretched by new challenges and rise to new levels of personal growth when given the opportunity. Many people doing smaller tasks well usually results in greater effectiveness and efficiency in a project and greater commitment within the organization. Learning to delegate allows leaders to focus on what only they can do and do well.

Moses: Leading through Delegation

Moses used various approaches to leadership throughout his forty years of leading Israel through the wilderness. In the initial phase of his leadership, Moses relied heavily on charisma to gather a following and lead them to take on a great vision. But Moses learned quickly the ongoing responsibilities of leadership demanded a different approach. In a meeting with his father-in-law, Moses learned and applied the principle of delegation to his personal leadership kaleidoscope.

Moses established his leadership reputation through accomplishing significant tasks. The story of Israel's success over the Egyptians spread far beyond the nation itself. "And Jethro, the priest of Midian, Moses' father-in-law, heard of all that God had done for Moses and for Israel His people; that the LORD had brought Israel out of Egypt" (Exod. 18:1).

Moses understood the importance of memorials to remind his followers of past successes. Following a battle that saw Israel victorious over the Amalekites, "Moses built an altar and called its name, The-LORD-Is-My-Banner" (Exod. 17:15). In doing so, Moses enhanced his leadership credibility.

Another way Moses expanded his leadership influence was through storytelling, recounting past victories. When he met with Jethro, "Moses told his father-in-law all that the LORD had done to Pharaoh and to the Egyptians for Israel's sake, all the hardship that had come upon them on the way, and how the LORD had delivered them" (Exod. 18:8).

One reason Moses was a successful long-term leader was that he was willing to listen to others who saw problems that limited his leadership. He had fallen into a common problem faced by successful leaders—that of confusing activity with productivity. But Moses was unaware of his problem until Jethro asked, "What is this thing that you are doing for the people? Why do you alone sit, and all the people stand before you from morning until evening?" (Exod. 18:14).

Moses faced the same problem many pastors face today. In a study examining growth potential in congregations, Carl F. George and Robert E. Logan reported, "We discover that when a pastor primarily does the ministry in the congregation, rather than leading others to do the ministry, growth potential remains small. That type of ministry management will not allow the congregation to grow beyond a hundred or so. By increasingly focusing on leading others into ministry, a pastor increases church-growth potential, because the entire congregation becomes capable of working in ministry. As the pastor leads others to do ministry, those people share in the leadership creating a 'snowball effect.'"

Leaders who do the work rather than enlist others to work with them as part of the team are leaders at high risk for burnout. In optimum conditions, a leader's span of control should be about one to six, that is, the leader has six people directly accountable to him with direct access to him. According to George and Logan, "Moses' . . . span of control was 1 to about 2 million." Under those circumstances, leaders no longer have time to give priority to leading. According to Robert J. McKain, "The reason most major goals are not achieved is that we spend our time doing second things first."

Jethro helped Moses in this situation refocus on his mission in life. When Jethro asked him the purpose behind this activity, he answered, "Because the people come to me to inquire of God . . . and I make known the statutes of God and His laws" (Exod. 18:15–16). Moses clarified his role as God's representative to the people and the primary teacher of the law.

Once the purpose of the activity had been clarified, Jethro was able to suggest a more effective strategy by which Moses could accomplish that purpose with greater efficiency and endurance. "Listen now to my voice; I will give you counsel, and God will be with you. . . . If you do this thing, and God so commands you, then you will be able to endure, and all this people will also go to their place" (Exod. 18:19, 23). Jethro then outlined a five-step plan by which Moses could establish a judicial system that would free up his time to be the leader God called him to be.

First, Moses was urged to keep his personal mission and vision in life constantly before the Lord. "Stand before God for the people, so that you may bring the difficulties to God" (Exod. 18:19). According to George and Logan, "Those who have no clear goals tend to work much harder, to get nowhere in particular."

Second, Moses was urged to invest significant energy in communicating the governing vision for the nation. "And you shall teach them the statutes and the laws, and show them the way in which they must walk and the work they must do" (Exod. 18:20). By way of application to pastors today, George and Logan argue, "Too many pastors underestimate the power of the pulpit. Preaching is one of the primary tools of vision casting in the church. You teach incidentally through your outlines. You teach irresistibly through your stories."

The next step in delegation involved enlisting capable men to assist him in the work of realizing his vision. According to John C. Maxwell, "Acquiring and keeping good people is a leader's most important task."[2] Jethro advised Moses, "Moreover you shall select from all the people able men, such as fear God, men of truth, hating covetousness; and place such over them to be rulers of thousands, rulers of hundreds, rulers of fifties, and rulers of tens" (Exod. 18:21). According to Andrew Carnegie, "It marks a big step in your development when you come to realize that other people can help you do a better job than you could do alone."[3] David Jackson claims, "The real turning point in a company is when you go from one to two people. Then, at least, there is someone to answer the phone while you eat your lunch."[4]

Once capable men had been enlisted, Moses then needed to delegate to others who could do the job as well. "And let them judge the people at all times. Then it will be that every great matter they shall bring to you, but every small matter they themselves shall judge. So it will be easier for you, for they will bear the burden with you" (Exod. 18:22). According to Henry Brandt, "Your leadership position requires meeting the demands of growth. Growth requires change and sharing the work through delegation. Neglecting or ignoring this principle jeopardizes both your personal ability and your church's ability to minister effectively."

George and Logan have written extensively about delegation. They define delegation as "the process of identifying your work responsibilities and assigning portions of your work to others, so that the workers become fulfilled and the work is accomplished." They suggest pastors "recruit people to help organize and systematize ministry by assessing needs and recommending solutions," arguing "an hour each week spent with such an assistant can free you from at least five to six hours of work per week." They also identify five levels of delegation: "(1) Do it and don't report back; (2) Do it and report back immediately; (3) Do it and report back routinely; (4) Investigate and make recommendations to me, and we will decide together; and (5) Gather data for me, and I will decide."

Finally, Jethro urged Moses to make himself available to assist the judges when they really needed his help. "Then it will be that every great matter they shall bring to you, but every small matter they themselves shall judge" (Exod. 18:22). As John F. Kennedy was preparing to assume the office of president of the United States, outgoing President Dwight D. Eisenhower warned him, "You'll find no easy problems ever come to the President of the United States. If they were easy to solve, somebody else has solved them."

Tom Peters urges leaders, "Find the specialness in people, set them free to reach their potential, believe in them, affirm them, rebuke them when necessary, and care for them." When Moses appointed judges, he looked for four things to identify their leadership potential: (1) ability, (2) wisdom, (3) integrity, and (4) character.

According to Konrad Adenauer, "We all live under the same sky, but we don't all have the same horizon."[5] Understanding that various people had different limits to their ability, Moses appointed some leaders to have authority over as few as ten people whereas others were given authority over thousands. He assigned responsibilities for each, according to the abilities they demonstrated.

Moses also looked for men of wisdom, men who feared God, which is the beginning of wisdom. In discussing the differences between two Russian leaders, Henry Kissinger described the one he admired most as "a second-class man who has surrounded himself with first-class men." The other was described as "a first-class man who has surrounded himself with second-class men." In making that evaluation, Kissinger was applying a principle suggested centuries earlier by Niccolo Machiavelli. "The first method for estimating the intelligence of a ruler is to look at the men he has around him."[6]

A third essential for leadership was integrity. According to V. Gilbert Beers, "A person of integrity is one who has established a system of values against which all of life is judged."[7] It is the kind of person about whom Socrates was thinking when he said, "The first key to greatness is to be in reality what we appear to be."[8] According to Ann Landers, "People of integrity expect to be believed. They also know time will prove them right and are willing to wait."[9] Billy Graham argues, "Integrity is the glue that holds our way of life together. We must constantly strive to keep our integrity intact."[10]

Former president and distinguished military leader Dwight Eisenhower claimed, "In order to be a leader a man must have followers. And to have followers, a man must have their confidence. Hence, the supreme quality for a leader is unquestionably integrity. Without it, no real success is possible, no matter whether it is on a section gang, a football field, in an army, or in an office. If a man's associates find him guilty of being phony, if they find that he lacks forthright integrity, he will fail. His teachings and actions must square with each other. The first great need, therefore, is integrity and high purpose."[11]

The importance of integrity is also a common theme in business leadership literature. Peter Drucker writes, "The final requirement of effective leadership is to earn trust. Otherwise there won't be any followers. And the only definition of a leader is someone who has followers. To trust a leader, it is not necessary to agree with him. Trust is the conviction that the leader means what he says. It is a belief in something very old-fashioned called 'integrity.' A leader's actions and a leader's professed beliefs must be congruent or at least compatible. Effective leadership—and again this is very old wisdom—is not based on being clear; it is based primarily on being consistent."[12]

John Maxwell distinguishes between image and integrity. "Image is what people think we are. Integrity is what we really are." He adds, "A person with integrity does not have divided loyalties (that's duplicity), nor is he or she merely pretending (that's hypocrisy). People with integrity are 'whole' people; they can be identified by their single-mindedness. People with integrity have nothing to hide and nothing to fear. Their lives are open books."[13]

Moses strove to find men of character to assume leadership, men who hated covetousness and therefore would be hard to bribe. Someone said, "When wealth is lost, nothing is lost; when health is lost, something is lost; when character is lost; all is lost."[14] According to John Foster, "A man without decision of character can never be said to belong to himself. He belongs to whatever can make captive of him." Emerson claimed, "Every great institution is the lengthened shadow of a single man. His character determines the character of the organization."

Stephen Covey, whose study of the habits of highly successful people has become a classic, claims character is essential to success. He writes, "If I try to use human influences, strategies and tactics of how to get other people to do what I want, to work better, to be more motivated, to like me and each other—while my character is fundamentally flawed, marked by duplicity or insincerity—then, in the long run, I cannot be successful. My duplicity will breed distrust, and everything I do—even using so-called good human relations techniques—will be perceived as manipulative. It simply makes no difference how good the rhetoric is or even how good the intentions are; if there is little or no trust, there is no foundation for permanent success. Only basic goodness gives life to technique."[15]

With delegated leaders in place, Moses was able to share his insights as a leader to train other leaders. Within the Pentateuch he recorded various laws governing the behavior of kings and judges. He was also able to invest significant time training his successor. Moses became an equipper of other leaders.

According to C. Peter Wagner, "Studies of growing churches show that the leadership role of the pastor is the key to church vitality. The ideal role for a church growth pastor is now being described as an 'equipper,' rather than an 'enabler.' This implies pastoral initiative in setting goals, obtaining goal ownership from the people, and mobilizing the laity for effective ministry aimed at accomplishing the goals."

Mastering the Art of Delegation

One of the most important skills of the administrative leader is delegation. Knowing when to delegate, how to delegate, and who can be entrusted with delegated responsibility and authority are all part of the challenge. Leaders who delegate well free their time and energy to focus on their priorities. In the process, they usually extend and strengthen their influence, becoming better leaders. Mastering the art of delegation is a worthy goal for leaders to develop their personal leadership kaleidoscope.

Delegating well usually begins with recognizing the need to delegate. There are several conditions that arise in a leader's life that may be viewed as warning signs that it is time to reevaluate what you are doing and consider delegating responsibilities and authority to others. Many of these conditions relate to job performance. When you are not doing the big jobs that need to be done, missing deadlines, and spending time on trivial tasks that others could do, it is time to delegate. But the job performance of the leader is not the only factor to consider. When you have people who with training could accomplish a task as well as or better than you, or your staff needs new challenges to keep them motivated, it may be time to delegate.

Once the need to delegate has been determined, the next step involves identifying what could be delegated. Business guru Peter Drucker developed three diagnostic questions to help leaders identify work that could be delegated. First, "What am I doing that really does not need to be done at all by me or anyone else?" If a task is redundant, it can be eliminated. Second, "Which of the activities on my time log could be handled by someone else as well, if not better?" The answer to this question will identify areas that can and should be downloaded to others. Third, "What do I do that wastes the time of other people?" This question will help you identify areas of your work that should be reevaluated to make the whole organization more effective.

As you prepare to delegate work to others, write a clear job description that clarifies both the responsibility and authority of the worker. A good job description usually includes seven elements. First, begin with a job title that reflects the nature of the job. Many churches have changed the title of their "Bible Teachers" to "Bible Study Group Leaders" to reflect the more relational emphasis in their educational ministries. Next, include a job summary that gives a general overview of the job. This is usually followed by a list of specific duties and responsibilities involved in the job. Fourth, there should be some mention of organizational relationships in a job description. This explains the relationship of this job position to both supervisors and subordinates. Also, the job description should identify the qualifications required. These are the gifts and skills necessary to do the job right.

Often, job descriptions also include a section on training and development, identifying the training that is provided or encouraged to help a person develop skills that result in greater productivity in the job. Every job description should also include a notice of scheduled reviews. It is only fair that a worker knows when and how the work done in this job will be evaluated.

When this has been done, delegate appropriate work to qualified staff. Be sure to communicate to them and others that they also have the authority to accomplish the tasks assigned. As they begin their work, provide resources as necessary to enable them to accomplish their newly assigned tasks. Then check back periodically to ensure the delegated work is being accomplished by others. Although one purpose in delegating work to others is to release you from that work, you will want to be available to assist as necessary, especially in the transition stage, without becoming directly involved in the delegated work.

CHAPTER 8

Moses

The People Management Leader

Leadership has a harder job than just choosing sides.
It must bring sides together.

JESSE JACKSON

Vincent Thomas Lombardi was born into a Catholic home in Brooklyn, New York, and studied the priesthood for two years before transferring to St. Francis Preparatory High School. While there, he was the star fullback on the football team. In college, he played guard in Fordham's defensive line despite weighing only 170 pounds. When he graduated, he stepped up to playing semi-pro football with Delaware's Wilmington Clippers while working at a finance company and taking night school classes at Fordham's law school. But as much as he loved the game, it was not as a player that Lombardi would make his mark.

As early as 1939, Lombardi began coaching football at a New Jersey high school as part of his teaching contract. A decade later, Earl Blaik, West Point's football coach, hired him to manage their varsity defensive line. Blaik was considered the best coach in the country at the time, and the two men spent as much as seventeen hours a day together. During the five years they worked together, Blaik taught Lombardi to stick to basic plays, strive for perfect execution, and conduct himself appropriately on the field.

Lombardi believed in winning. "Winning is not a sometime thing; it's an all the time thing. You don't win once in a while; you don't do things right once in a while; you do them right all the time."[1] That was the philosophy by which Vince Lombardi lived and the discipline he brought out in the players he coached.

Lombardi left West Point to begin his career coaching in the National Football League as an assistant coach with the New York Giants. He was placed in charge of the offensive strategy of the team that had scored the least number of points in the league the previous year. Within three years, the Giants were a championship team. As offensive coach, he was responsible for moving a defensive player named Frank Gifford to offense as a halfback. During his five years with the team, Gifford was nominated as halfback on the all-pro team and the Giants did not have a losing season.

Tired of being an assistant, Lombardi signed a five-year contract as head coach of the Green Bay Packers. The Packers had a well-established reputation as perpetual losers, winning only one game the previous season. The new coach told the players he expected obedience, dedication, and 110 percent effort from each player. But he also promised them they would become a championship team if they obeyed his rules and used his methods. When he left the Packers nine years later for retirement, the Packers dominated football, having won six division titles, five NFL championships, and two Super Bowls.

Less than a year into his retirement, Lombardi realized he was not ready to quit coaching. He became the head coach of the Washington Redskins in 1969 and led the team to its first winning record in fourteen years. In fact, throughout his coaching career, Lombardi never had a losing season even though the teams he coached had experienced

THREE APPROACHES TO CONFLICT RESOLUTION

There is always more than one way to solve a problem, but not all approaches to conflict resolution produce the same results. The following chart compares three different approaches to resolving conflict with three different outcomes.

Features	Confrontation	Collaboration	Joint Problem-Solving
The parties are	Adversaries	Friends	Joint Problem-Solvers
The target is	Victory	Agreement	A wise outcome
Attitudes toward relationship	Demands concessions as a precondition	Encourages concessions as an entry fee	Separates relationships from the problem
The values are to be	Hard on people and hard on the problem	Soft on people and soft on the problem	Soft on people, but hard on the problem
The positions are	To dig in	To change readily	Not important; the future is the focus
Offers	Threats	Compromises	A creative solution
Outcomes	I win, you lose	You win, I lose	You win, I win
Priorities	Insist on my position	Insist on agreement	Insist on objective criteria

several prior to his arrival. His death in the fall of 1970 prevented him from coaching the Redskins to yet another Super Bowl.

As a coach, Lombardi helped the men on his teams play up to their potential. He gave his players pride and victory. His perseverance, hard work, and discipline as a coach made him one of the most admired and respected coaches of all time. At his funeral, tough football players cried openly. In 1971, he was inducted into the Professional Football Hall of Fame and the Super Bowl trophy was renamed in his honor. Thirty years after his death, ESPN named him "Coach of the Century."

Managing People

According to James M. Kouzes and Barry Z. Posner, "Teamwork is essential for a productive organization. Collaboration is needed to develop the commitment and skills of employees, solve problems, and respond to environmental pressures. Fostering collaboration is not just a nice idea. It is the key that leaders use to unlock the energies and talents available in their organizations."

From time to time, all leaders encounter pockets of resistance among their followers. Moses faced this problem with a strong representative team that he had developed to assist him in people management. This gave him both liberty and authority to address conflict situations as they arose and to resolve them.

People managers are an important part of every organization. In business, they are the human resources directors responsible for the work force. They also include mediators in legal, industrial, and business settings who seek to resolve conflict with as little fallout as possible. Their number includes the artistic directors of theater groups and deans of colleges who manage to get people who would otherwise not associate with one another to work together in a significant undertaking. They also include the pastors who reconcile warring factions in the church and help individuals resolve their conflicts with one another.

Leaders of people know the task of managing people never ends. People managers cannot always tell what, if any, progress is being made in their work. They constantly deal with people's expectations. Much of their work tends to be repetitive as they work with the same problem people year after year. Working with people problems tends to produce a significant energy drain in one's life. It is not uncommon for people managers to get exhausted by failure.

People managers often lead others effectively through their shepherding gift. Some may lead through a unique blend of the gifts of prophecy and empathy, confronting people with a genuine concern for helping them in their need. They tend to use the Law of Communication to ensure that people understand what is expected of them and the Law of Accountability to ensure that people do what is expected. People managers are often sanguine in temperament.

Managing people can be exhausting. People managers run the risk of becoming weary in their work. When they are tired, they may grow callous in their attitude toward other people. They serve in a context in which they are rarely rewarded or recognized for success in their work and are highly accountable for failure. When the team does not play well, the coach is the first one fired. It is no wonder that people managers tend to be among those most prone to burnout.

WHY DO THE NATIONS RAGE?

A comparison of the causes of international and interpersonal conflicts reveals a remarkable similarity. Territorial conflicts in groups happen when there is competition for roles and responsibilities. Border conflicts arise when the roles and responsibilities of team members are not clear. Resource conflicts usually relate to time and money, the fundamental resources of small groups, but could also include such things as room space and equipment use. Ethnic conflicts are the result of being threatened by differences in others. Influence conflicts arise as spheres of influence begin developing around strong personalities. Ideological conflicts are the result of placing value judgments on people based on our understanding of perceived fundamentals of the faith. Personality conflicts are the result of people who feel threatened, lashing out at other personality types that intimidate them.

Effective leaders need to incorporate conflict resolution skills into their personal leadership kaleidoscope. Conflict within human relationships is inevitable. This includes the relationship between leaders and their followers. Healthy groups will experience conflict as part of the give-and-take of group experience. Unhealthy groups will experience significant conflict and probably lack the resources to deal with it. In both situations, no leader is good enough to lead without the consent of the group he or she leads.

Preserving unity within the church is a key spiritual factor in evangelistic success. In His high priestly prayer, Jesus said, "I do not pray for these alone, but also for those who will believe in Me through their word; that they all may be one, as You, Father, are in Me, and I in You; that they also may be one in Us, that the world may believe that You sent Me" (John 17:20–21). Promoting unity within the church may also be a key to bringing spiritual revival to that church (Ps. 133).

According to Grace Murray Hopper, "You manage things. You lead people." Former U.S. President Theodore Roosevelt claimed, "Whatever power I at any time had, I obtained from the people. I could exercise it only as long as the people heartily backed me up." Effective leaders in every generation have managed people well.

Moses: Leading through Conflict Resolution

Throughout his tenure as leader, Moses faced both internal and external conflict. In the process, he learned how to work through conflict. He also knew that conflict would be an ongoing reality in the experience of Israel. As he instructed the nation as they prepared to enter the land, he outlined the principles by which he had resolved conflict and applied them to the kind of situations they were about to face.

One of the toughest lessons for leaders to remember is not to take conflict personally. Moses reminded the people that the battles they would encounter are really God's battles. "When you go out to battle

A LEADER'S VOCABULARY

Words are the chief means by which leaders communicate ideas and values. Someone has collected a series of key words and phrases that need to be part of every leader's vocabulary.

The Six Most Important Words: "I admit I made a mistake."
The Five Most Important Words: "You did a good job."
The Four Most Important Words: "What is your opinion?"
The Three Most Important Words: "If you please."
The Two Most Important Words: "Thank you."
The Single Most Important Word: "We"
The Least Important Word: "I"

against your enemies, and see horses and chariots and people more numerous than you, do not be afraid of them; for the LORD your God is with you, who brought you up from the land of Egypt" (Deut. 20:1). Lest they failed to understand this principle, he added, "For the LORD your God is He who goes with you, to fight for you against your enemies, to save you" (Deut. 20:4).

Moses urged individual Israelites to disqualify themselves before the conflict began if they were prone to distraction. He identified several specific concerns people might have that could distract them in battle. Some might be concerned about their personal assets. "Then the officers shall speak to the people saying: 'What man is there who has built a new house and has not dedicated it? Let him go and return to his house, lest he die in the battle and another man dedicate it'" (Deut. 20:5). Others might be concerned about their work responsibilities. "Also what man is there who has planted a vineyard and has not eaten of it? Let him go and return to his house, lest he die in the battle and another man eat of it" (Deut. 20:6).

Relationships were another concern that could disqualify someone from battle. "And what man is there who is betrothed to a woman and has not married her? Let him go and return to his house, lest he die in the battle and another man marry her" (Deut. 20:7). Still others might have concerns about the future. "The officers shall speak further to the people and say, 'What man is there who is fearful and fainthearted? Let him go and return to his house, lest the heart of his brethren faint like his heart'" (Deut. 20:8).

The next step in this process involved organizing all their resources for maximum efficiency. "And so it shall be, when the officers have finished speaking to the people, that they shall make captains of the armies to lead the people" (Deut. 20:9). But even though the army was now ready for battle, Moses advised Israel to seek a peaceful resolution to the conflict before escalating the battle. "When you go near a city to fight against it, then proclaim an offer of peace to it" (Deut. 20:10). Part of effective leadership involves giving people more than they deserve. Johann Wolfgang von Goethe urged, "Treat people as if they were what they ought to be and you may help them to become what they are capable of being."

If the city rejected the offer of peace, Israel's next step involved using a siege to give the other side time to change and become more responsive to a peaceful solution. "Now if the city will not make peace with you, but makes war against you, then you shall besiege it" (Deut. 20:12). Dwight Eisenhower claimed, "You do not lead by hitting people over the head—that's assault, not leadership." When Moses described this siege, he emphasized several key elements. First, the siege represented a long-term commitment ("when you besiege a city for a long time"—Deut. 20:19). Second, the siege provides an opportunity to demonstrate your strength and ability to win without maximum effort ("while making war against it to take it"—Deut. 20:19). It is also an attempt to conserve ("you shall not destroy its trees"—Deut. 20:19). The consistent focus of the siege is conflict resolution ("until it is subdued"—Deut. 20:20).

Moses advised Israel if the need to fight finally arises, they should be thorough in battle. "And when the LORD your God delivers it into your hands, you shall strike every male in it with the edge of the sword" (Deut. 20:13). In giving this instruction, Moses recognized the harmony of the Law of Timing ("when"), the Law of Sovereignty ("the LORD your God delivers it"), and the Law of Responsibility ("you shall strike every male").

Moses encouraged the people to take time to enjoy and celebrate the victory when God gave them a resolution to their conflict. "But the women, the little ones, the livestock, and all that is in the city, all its spoil, you shall plunder for yourself; and you shall eat the enemies' plunder which the LORD your God gives you" (Deut. 20:14). This involved both embracing former enemies as family and enjoying the new resources God provides. But this was not a license for the victors to abuse the victims. According to Dr. Joseph P. Cangemi, "Unhealthy people will behave well under good leadership. Healthy people will behave poorly under poor leadership." When leaders heed the advice of Edward Hale, "You can never lead unless you lift," they create a healthy environment even in the midst of a battle.

While this strategy was designed to be the norm in Israel's experience, Moses warned them never to use this strategy as an excuse for making an alliance with the enemies of God. He reminded them God had commanded the destruction of His enemies. "But you shall utterly destroy them . . . just as the LORD your God has commanded you" (Deut. 20:17). He warned his people that a long-term close association with God's enemies would distract them in their own relationship with God. "Lest they teach you to do according to all their abominations which they have done for their gods, and you sin against the LORD your God" (Deut. 20:18).

A Strategy for Resolving Conflict

Jesus said, "It is impossible that no offenses should come, but woe to him through whom they do come!" (Luke 17:1). While not justifying those who create conflict, He warned His disciples that conflict was

THE TEN COMMANDMENTS OF LEADERSHIP

Some creative writer has developed an ethical code known as "The Ten Commandments of Leadership." Although these commandments do not come down with the same authority as the laws engraved in stone on Mount Sinai, they are certainly worth considering.

1. Thou shalt love people, not just use them. The greatest thing in the world is a person. The greatest thing about a person is his motive, and the greatest motive is love.

2. Thou shalt develop understanding. If every person's cares were written on his brow, how many would our pity share who bear our envy now?

3. Thou shalt not criticize more than compliment. You had better cover your neighbors' faults with a cloak of charity. You may need a circus tent to cover your own!

4. Thou shalt not get angry. If you are right, you don't need to. If you are wrong, you cannot afford to.

5. Thou shalt not argue. It is no use to win the argument and lose the people. Beware of the attitude which says: In matters controversial, my attitude is fine. I always see two points of view: the one that's wrong and mine.

6. Thou shalt be kind. You had better be kind to the people you meet on the way up. They are the same ones you will meet on the way down.

7. Though shalt have a sense of humor. A sense of humor is to a person what springs are to a wagon. It saves him many jolts.

8. Thou shalt smile. No person is ever fully dressed until he has a smile on his face. Remember, "Laugh, and the world laughs with you. Weep, and you weep alone."

9. Thou shalt practice what thou preachest. One example is worth one thousand arguments.

10. Thou shalt go to the school of the Headmaster of the universe, the Master of men, the Secretary of human relations, namely Jesus Christ. He is the greatest leader of people the world has ever known.

an inevitable part of group life. Anyone who has led a group for long can verify the accuracy of Jesus' conclusion. That is why growing leaders incorporate conflict-resolution skills into their personal leadership kaleidoscope.

Recognizing the inevitability of conflict and being prepared for it when it arises is an important first step in the process of conflict resolution. As each group is unique, the longer a leader leads, the easier it will be for him to identify the usual sources of conflict within the group and see the problem as it emerges. In some groups, certain issues tend to be the focal points of conflict. One long-term pastor claimed every dispute he experienced in his ministry was over youth or music. In other groups, certain people tend to be the focal points of conflict. In a church business meeting, a man voted against the motion he had proposed. When asked why he answered, "It looks like everyone supports the idea, and I don't think it is healthy for a church to make a unanimous decision." Others in the church thought otherwise.

In other groups, conflict tends to arise on a seasonal basis. Some people are affected by the lack of sunlight in winter and become irritable in the first quarter of the year. In contrast, others are affected by the heat of summer and likewise become irritable. In some churches, as the anniversary of a former church problem comes up, people become tense as old wounds are remembered.

As you begin dealing with conflict, recognize your options in pursuing peace. There are essentially three kinds of peace that can be achieved in any conflict situation. First, there is the peace of mutual destruction: "I lose, you lose." This was the underlying philosophy of the Cold War era of the last half of the twentieth century. It tends to have the same chilling effect on groups today. Second, there is the peace of victory and loss: "I win, you lose." Many groups that value the democratic process tend to use this approach to end conflict quickly. The down side of this approach is that no one really likes to lose. Third, there is the peace of compromise: "I win, you win." In this approach, all parties involved attempt to find common ground and resolve the problem in a way that pleases everyone.

Establishing a peace of compromise is not easy. It involves a willingness of all parties to work toward reconciliation. As you begin working with the parties involved in the conflict, it is important to establish some basic ground rules.

First, each member must have equal rights of expression, consideration, support, and love. Second, there must be mutual respect for everyone. While one may not agree with another's view, he can assume that person holds this view with sincerity and honesty. Also, each member can assume others share a genuine desire to reach an agreement and resolve the problem in a way that respects each position and the personal feelings involved.

Third, there needs to be a commitment to factual accuracy. Agreement and reconciliation cannot be based on sentimentality or subjective emotion. Also, all parties need to agree on a commitment to build consensus. Group members need to be committed to finding common ground and unwilling to live with the consequences of an ongoing rift within their group.

In dealing with others, apply common sense principles of communication that help strengthen human relations. Sometimes, it is not the things you say but the way you say them or your timing in saying them that has the greatest impact. Catherine the Great explained her general policy in dealing with people when she said, "I praise loudly; I blame softly." Many leaders use the "sandwich" approach to address difficult situations. They plan their conversation to ensure any criticism that needs to be communicated is sandwiched between praise or commendation for work the person being addressed has accomplished. Because people tend to remember criticism and forget commendation, effective leaders need to praise often and criticize only when necessary to build healthy and lasting relationships with group members.

CHAPTER 9

Joshua

The Equipped Leader

*He who walks with wise men will be wise, but the companion of
fools will be destroyed.*

PROVERBS 13:20

One would think there would be little opportunity for advancement for a military leader during peacetime, especially for a young officer who graduated sixty-first in a class of only 164. But West Point's class of 1915 produced more than fifty future generals, including Dwight David Eisenhower.

In his initial assignments, Eisenhower earned his reputation by developing training for the infantry and the tank corps. Although he never saw combat during World War I, he did benefit from the rapid promotions of the times and was Major Eisenhower by 1920. During the two decades following, he served in various positions and used the time to continue preparing himself for the future.

At Fort Leavenworth, Kansas, Eisenhower finished first in his Command and General Staff College class. This brought him to the attention of several American generals under whom he served and continued to learn. In 1929, he worked for General Pershing and produced a guidebook to the battles of World War I. In 1935, he joined General MacArthur at the Office of the Army Chief of Staff and accompanied MacArthur to the Philippines. He quickly became known as the consummate staff officer and rose to the rank of lieutenant colonel before America entered World War II.

The impression he had made on generals Pershing and MacArthur, along with his personal performance, resulted in his being appointed to head the army's Operations Division by Army Chief of Staff George Marshall shortly after the bombing of Pearl Harbor. He was a major influence in developing the Allies' strategic plan of containing the war in the Pacific while focusing first on victory in Europe. He became Marshall's choice to assume control of American troops assembling in Great Britain. The new assignment came with a promotion to major general. In July 1942, he was promoted to lieutenant general and placed in command of U.S. forces involved in the invasion of North Africa. After an initial setback, Eisenhower reorganized his staff and launched an offensive that led to the mass surrender of Nazi and Italian soldiers. In the process of achieving victory, he also demonstrated his ability to control headstrong and flamboyant subordinate leaders, including Montgomery and Patton.

His accomplishments in North Africa resulted in a promotion to full general and increased responsibilities. In December 1943, he became commander of the Supreme Headquarters, Allied Expeditionary Force, charged with the responsibility of planning and executing the invasion of France. His years of study and preparation bore fruit as the Allies gathered the largest invasion force in history while keeping both the time and place of their invasion secret. Following the successful landing at Normandy, Eisenhower commanded the multi-million-man force as it moved toward the German capital. Only a last-minute decision based on faulty intelligence prevented Eisenhower from capturing Berlin, and perhaps Hitler himself.

Following the war, Eisenhower returned to replace Marshall as Chief of Staff. In 1948, he retired from military service to become president of

Columbia University. Three years later, he returned to Europe to lead NATO, but that involvement was short-lived. In 1952, he campaigned as the Republican candidate for the presidency and won the largest popular vote margin to date. In the oval office, as in other assignments he had assumed previously, this equipped leader proved to be the right person for the right job at the right time.

Equipped for Effectiveness

Equipped leaders are the students of leadership principles who have learned how to lead people and are competent in the application of those principles. According to Henry Ford, "The question, 'Who ought to be boss?' is like asking, 'Who ought to be tenor in the quartet?' Obviously, the man who can sing tenor." In contemporary business culture, an executive MBA opens doors for leaders that are closed to others who lack formal education. Part of Joshua's initial success as a leader was tied to his mentoring by Moses. The principles of mentoring leaders and being mentored by a leader are illustrated in the unique relationship between these two great leaders.

Every organization is looking for equipped leaders. Their number includes college graduates who are already able to perform well in a responsible position when they join the company. They are also the product of company training programs for people in management who continue growing, learning the principles taught in leadership seminars, and thus becoming a more valuable resource to the company. They include college presidents with a successful track record of leadership experience in other similar settings. Equipped leaders are also found among pastors, especially pastors of their second and subsequent churches who have learned how to apply the lessons learned in seminary and have discovered the things they were not taught in seminary.

Equipped leaders sometimes struggle, especially when those they lead commit to strategies they know will not work. Often their expertise may not be recognized until they have struggled to achieve credibility and the project is nearing completion. People seldom have experience until after they need it. After they do achieve success, some equipped leaders stop growing and burn out. Their reputation, based on past success, enables them to function at an inferior level.

Others struggle with a sense they are being underutilized and could assume more responsibility than has been offered. This may result in their feeling unchallenged as they become even more proficient and the risk element in various projects becomes minimal. They may come to think of themselves as having arrived and stop learning and growing as leaders. Equipped leaders may also fail to train others to do the work because they feel they can do the job so much better.

Equipped leaders are those who have discovered their spiritual gifts and know how best to use them to accomplish tasks for the glory of God. They tend to use the Law of Credibility to convince others to follow their advice. This credibility is sometimes tied to specialized training or previous experience. They also use the Law of Problem Solving because they understand the problem best and are aware of ways others have successfully addressed that kind of problem in similar situations. While any temperament may be equipped for leadership, equipped leaders often manifest a type of melancholy perfectionism.

Sometimes, equipped leaders may appear more competent than they really are. This could make them reluctant to take on new challenges in areas in which they feel inadequately trained. On other occasions, their training can be detrimental. They may rely on their training and begin to operate independently of what God wants to do in their ministry. Their success and background sometimes result in their struggling with humility. They may become so confident in their own abilities that they fail to recognize and utilize other equipped leaders. They may even begin minimizing the value of others within the organization. They may become selective in the projects they address and neglect others that require their attention.

Despite the potential danger, every leader needs to be equipped for the tasks he or she will face. When leaders fail, they cause others to fail with them. Equipped leaders are less likely to fail than those who have been inadequately trained for the task at hand. When leaders are successful, others enjoy their success with them. Equipped leaders are more likely to be successful than those who have been inadequately trained.

Leaders guide others to take on and accomplish significant tasks. The importance of these tasks calls for equipped leaders. Leaders who fail to lead hinder the progress of churches and other ministries. Equipped leaders are more confident in their leadership abilities. If something is worth doing, it is worth doing well. Therefore, leaders ought to be the very best they can be in preparation for their very best work.

Joshua: The Equipped Leader

Abraham Lincoln once said, "I will get ready and then perhaps my chance will come."[1] That thought may well have occurred to Joshua during the forty years he served Moses in the wilderness. Before he ever led Israel, he was led by Moses and trained for the unique role to which God had called him. The lessons he learned in that school in the wilderness equipped him for the challenges he would face later as a leader. His leadership curriculum was developed through significant experiences with his mentor, Moses.

Great leaders often begin as followers of great leaders. In that context, someone once said, "Be humble enough to obey. You will be giving orders yourself someday." Effective leaders are those who use their time as followers to learn the lessons they need to learn to accomplish the tasks they will face later.

The first lesson Joshua learned in the wilderness was that God is committed to the defense of his people. According to Samuel Butler, "You can do very little with faith, but you can do nothing without it." Following a battle with Amalek, "the Lord said to Moses, 'Write this for a memorial in the book and recount it in the hearing of Joshua, that I will utterly blot out the remembrance of Amalek from under heaven.'

THINGS A LEADER NEEDS TO KNOW

The United States Army Manual suggests a dozen things leaders need to know. Though originally prepared as a list for military leaders, it identifies things every effective leader would want to incorporate into his or her personal leadership kaleidoscope.

1. How to motivate people in general and your subordinates in particular.
2. Your own strengths and weaknesses.
3. The strengths and weaknesses of your subordinates.
4. How beliefs and values become instilled in people and how they can be changed.
5. How character is developed.
6. How to communicate in a way that builds bonds of mutual trust, confidence, respect, and understanding among soldiers and between leaders and troops.
7. How people learn.
8. How to develop morale, cohesion, and discipline.
9. How soldiers can deal effectively with stress.
10. How to teach the individual and team skills necessary for unity and effectiveness.
11. How informal group norms and rules become instilled as beliefs and values in group members.
12. How to teach and train others to become good leaders. You must have the knowledge required to create favorable situations. This knowledge includes:
    a. How to identify, analyze, and influence the important forces in a situation.
    b. How to plan.
    c. The technical and tactical knowledge necessary to do your job.
    d. The important lessons of military history.

And Moses built an altar and called its name, The-LORD-Is-My-Banner; for he said, 'Because the LORD has sworn: the LORD will have war with Amalek from generation to generation'" (Exod. 17:14–16). Later, Moses explained this lesson further. "You must not fear them, for the LORD your God Himself fights for you" (Deut. 3:22). In the battle against Amalek, Joshua learned God will not abandon His people when they need Him.

That battle also taught Joshua that prayer is mightier than the sword. According to Ralph Waldo Emerson, "Great men are they who see that the spiritual is stronger than any material force." As they prepared for that battle, "Moses said to Joshua, 'Choose us some men and go out, fight with Amalek. Tomorrow I will stand on the top of the hill with the rod of God in my hand.' So Joshua did as Moses said to him, and fought with Amalek. And Moses, Aaron, and Hur went up to the top of the hill. And so it was, when Moses held up his hand, that Israel prevailed; and when he let down his hand, Amalek prevailed. But Moses' hands became heavy; so they took a stone and put it under him, and he sat on it. And Aaron and Hur supported his hands, one on one side, and the other on the other side; and his hands were steady until the going down of the sun. So Joshua defeated Amalek and his people with the edge of the sword" (Exod. 17:9–13).

It was in the wilderness that Joshua also learned leaders need time alone with God to evaluate themselves and determine their personal core values in life. When Moses climbed Mount Sinai to receive the Ten Commandments carved in stone by the finger of God, Joshua accompanied him up the mountain (Exod. 24:13). Moses alone went into the dense cloud at the top of the mountain, leaving Joshua for his own forty days of fasting and reflection. According to Walter Gropius, "Leadership does not depend on innate talent only, but very much also on intensity of conviction and willingness to serve."

Former President John F. Kennedy used his time recovering from back surgery to prepare for future leadership challenges by studying the accomplishments of great leaders of the past. He wrote a book about these leaders, calling it *Profiles in Courage.* According to Kennedy, "Courage—not complacency—is our need today, leadership not salesmanship." In a culture where image is everything, there is always a risk of a leadership vacuum as salesmen become increasingly more influential.

Time alone with God is the best investment leaders can make with their time. Joshua learned that lesson from the example of Moses and began practicing that discipline in his own life. "So the LORD spoke to Moses face to face, as a man speaks to his friend. And he would return to the camp, but his servant Joshua the son of Nun, a young man, did not depart from the tabernacle" (Exod. 33:11). Some Bible teachers believe Moses wrote Psalm 91 and was thinking about Joshua's time in the tabernacle as he wrote it. The psalm begins, "He who dwells in the secret place of the Most High shall abide under the shadow of the Almighty" (Ps. 91:1).

One of the most difficult lessons Joshua struggled to learn was never to resist the moving of the Spirit of God simply because God chooses to act in a way different from his expectations. On one occasion, two of Israel's elders prophesied in the camp despite the clear instructions of Moses to first leave the camp prior to prophesying. "So Joshua the son of Nun, Moses' assistant, one of his choice men, answered and said, 'Moses my lord, forbid them!' Then Moses said to him, 'Are you zealous for my sake? Oh, that all the Lord's people were prophets and that the LORD would put His Spirit upon them!'" (Num. 11:28–29).

Someone said, "The man who leads the orchestra must turn his back on the crowd." Part of a leader's responsibility is to lead even when the road ahead is unpopular. Truth never changes. Joshua understood this and refused to compromise what he believed was right, even when it seemed the whole world was against him. When he returned from an investigative trip into the Promised Land with eleven other spies, it quickly became apparent the people were reluctant to go in and claim what God had promised them. Joshua urged the nation, "The land we passed through to spy out is an exceedingly good land. If the LORD delights in us, then He will bring us into this land and give it to us, 'a land that flows with milk and honey.' Only do not rebel against the LORD, nor fear the people of the land, for they are our bread; their protection has departed from them, and the LORD is with us. Do not fear them" (Num. 14:7–9). The people responded to Joshua's appeal by attempting to stone him.

Some have suggested one synonym for leadership may be loneliness. There are moments in the life of all leaders when they, like Joshua, need to stand alone. The message in a Chinese fortune cookie warned, "The man who follows the crowd will never be followed by a crowd."

Effective leaders understand "the gifts and the calling of God are irrevocable" (Rom. 11:29). God's call on the life of a leader is His guarantee of assistance. "He who calls you is faithful, who also will do it" (1 Thess. 5:24). Leaders who understand this promise are more comfortable in their leadership and, according to Robert Rochefoucauld, "the confidence one has in oneself chiefly creates the confidence one inspires in others." Describing her own leadership success, Maria Straatmann claimed, "I really believed we could do it. I was personally enthusiastic and helped others in any way that I could. The Key: show them the way."

Knowing Joshua's own confidence as a leader would have a significant impact on the nation, "Moses called Joshua and said to him in the sight of all Israel, 'Be strong and of good courage, for you must go with this people to the land which the LORD has sworn to their fathers to give them, and you shall cause them to inherit it. And the LORD, He is the one who goes before you. He will be with you, He will not leave you nor forsake you; do not fear nor be dismayed' " (Deut. 31:7–8).

The best leaders are led leaders. The key to Joshua's success would be his willingness to submit to the control of the Holy Spirit. "Now Joshua the son of Nun was full of the spirit of wisdom, for Moses had laid his hands on him; so the children of Israel heeded him, and did as the LORD had commanded Moses" (Deut. 34:9). We cannot lead someone else to the light while we are standing in the dark.

Learning to Lead

Just as Joshua was equipped to lead before assuming responsibility for the nation, so effective leaders today need to learn how to lead before they realize their potential. According to Max De Pree, "We are sentenced to live with who we become." As we develop our personal leadership kaleidoscope, there are several things we can do in an attempt to learn and prepare for future leadership challenges.

First, study the principles of leadership as you train to be a better leader. B. C. Forbes observed, "Few people are born leaders. Leadership is achieved by ability, alertness, experience and by keeping poised; by willingness to accept responsibility; a knack for getting along with other people; an open mind, and a head that stays clear under stress." While it may be true that education cannot make us all leaders, it can teach us which leader to follow. Charles Barkley advises, "Educate yourself. Have pride and self-respect. Do the best you can." Shakespeare's observation, "There is no darkness but ignorance," is a good motto for the student of leadership principles.

Next, be a loyal follower of good leaders and learn their leadership style by watching their example. According to Sam Rayburn, "You cannot be a leader, and ask other people to follow you, unless you know how to follow too." There are aspects of leadership that are better caught than taught, and these lessons can only be learned through establishing a relationship with another leader.

Be discerning as you watch how others lead and learn from their mistakes. Many leaders claim to be graduates of the "School of Hard Knocks." A wise student will learn from the mistakes of others, learning lessons from that school's alumni and not having to enroll himself.

Part of learning leadership involves learning how God has equipped you to accomplish the specific tasks to which He has called you as leader. When you know your personal temperament, you will understand why you act as you do and why others relate to you the way they do. Understanding your spiritual gift will help you identify a ministry focus that enables you to lead from your strengths. It is good to take inventory periodically to determine how various experiences and learned abilities help shape you for specific leadership challenges.

As you prepare for leadership, take time to identify the nonnegotiables in your life. There will be many opportunities to compromise these core values and little time to develop an ethical standard in the midst of a project. Knowing what you believe and value will enable you to make ethical decisions as you lead your group to accomplish God's vision for your life.

Ultimately, growing leaders need to nurture their relationship with God. As they learn to become good followers of Christ, they become better leaders. This is the essence of discipleship. No one can lead others where he himself has never been.

CHAPTER 10

Joshua

The Confrontational Leader

I would rather fail in a cause that will ultimately succeed, than succeed in a cause that will ultimately fail.

WOODROW WILSON

Born in a dirt-floored log cabin in the frontier wilderness of Kentucky, Abraham Lincoln was raised in difficult times and learned early the value of honesty and protecting one's reputation. The family moved several times in search of a better life and ended up in Illinois. As a nine-year-old boy, he endured the sorrow of his mother's death. His father later remarried, and Lincoln's new stepmother taught him to read and instilled a love of learning in the young man.

Ten years later, Lincoln was six feet four inches tall and known as a strong young man of integrity. That reputation resulted in an invitation to take cargo a thousand miles downriver to New Orleans on a flatboat. When the cargo was safely delivered, he toured the city before returning home. It was there he saw his first slave market. Though he was aware slavery was practiced in some states, seeing slaves auctioned in New Orleans only confirmed his belief that the practice was inherently evil.

At the time, fighting slavery was not a popular cause. But his commitment to do what he could to abolish slavery was not based on a desire to be popular. Lincoln affirmed, "I am not bound to win, but I am bound to be true. I am not bound to succeed, but I am bound to live up to what light I have. I must stand with anybody that stands right: stand with him while he is right and part with him when he goes wrong."

In 1855, slavery became a national political issue. Lincoln spoke out against slavery in a failed campaign for a U.S. Senate seat. In 1858, he ran against incumbent Steven A. Douglas in a campaign that once again raised the issue of slavery. In a series of seven public debates with Douglas, Lincoln condemned slavery "as a moral, social and political evil." Although Douglas won the election, Lincoln gained a national reputation for his position. That resulted in his being nominated by the antislavery Whig Party as their presidential candidate in the 1860 election. On November 6 of that year, he was elected president.

Within two years, Lincoln addressed the issue of slavery directly by issuing his Emancipation Proclamation freeing all slaves in the Confederate states. Though Lincoln's life was cut short by an assassin's bullet, the process he began eventually led to the Thirteenth Amendment to the Constitution, which abolished slavery throughout the United States.

Taking on the World and Winning

Nobody really enjoys conflict, but sometimes conflict is necessary. Confrontational leaders understand there are times when they must stand up and be counted. They see problems as opportunities. Strong opposition is an opportunity for ultimate victory. Obstacles encountered along the way are a challenge to be overcome. They tend to rise to the challenge when faced with a significant task, take it on directly, and accomplish it. They view their primary tasks as leading forward to victory. They do not get sidetracked trying to "win friends and influence people."

There are many biblical examples of the confrontational leader. They include every judge, king, and general who led Israel into battle. They include the prophets who challenged the culture values of their day as they announced their message from God. They include the apostles who challenged the heretical movements that threatened the survival of the early church. But none of these leaders models this leadership style better than Joshua. He led Israel from victory to victory in both the military and governing phases of his leadership over Israel.

Even though the idea of confrontation may not be popular, the need for confrontational leaders is immense. Confrontational leaders are needed in business to meet various challenges that must be overcome to ensure continued success. The business community is depending on them to develop strategies to address increased competition in the marketplace and to resolve significant issues in labor relations. Schools need confrontational leaders to meet the challenges of recruiting students, raising funds, and ensuring high standards of academic excellence. When confrontational leaders lead churches, they win souls, raise money, build buildings, start new ministries, and lead moral crusades in their community.

Life for confrontational leaders is not without problems. We live in a culture that tends to pride itself on being nonconfrontational. Tolerance is the great value of our day, and it applies to everyone and everything except those who dare to challenge that value itself. Confrontational leaders stand alone against the culture.

Some people will resist confrontational leaders simply because of their leadership style. It is not uncommon to see confrontational leaders blamed for the problems they address. Also, if confrontational leaders challenge one of their core values, people tend to resist the leaders to protect their values. When Vice President Dan Quayle attacked the values taught by the popular sitcom character

Murphy Brown, he was personally ridiculed and the media largely ignored the issue raised. A decade later, the actress who played Murphy Brown claimed Quayle was right and lamented the fact there were not more people like him to stand for traditional family values. With confrontational leaders, the distinction between issues and personalities is not always clear.

Confrontational leaders are prone to take on problems that are too big to handle. This is a major risk because failure can be fatal for confrontational leaders. In contrast, these kinds of leaders may not be able to rally the troops without a problem. They may be guilty of creating problems to maintain their leadership. Also, when they are victorious, they may have difficulty adjusting to that victory. Confrontational leaders sometimes begin attacking their friends when they have no more enemies to fight. Some church leaders believe this tendency among some early fundamentalist leaders led to the failure of Fundamentalism to become the powerful influence for God it could have been. According to Plato, "When the tyrant has disposed of foreign enemies by conquest or treaty and there is nothing to fear from them, then he is always stirring up some war or other, in order that the people may require a leader."

The greatest challenges for confrontational leaders may be to move beyond problem solving and begin casting a vision for the future. A pastor may do well in a troubled church because of his trouble-shooting abilities, but when the church becomes healthy under his leadership, it may need a new pastor to lead them into the future. A hardnosed businessman may be successful in leading a company out of the red, but he may not be the same leader needed to take that company into the *Fortune 500* list.

Confrontational leaders lead best when they lead from their strengths. The confrontational pastor tends to be gifted in prophecy. He finds it easy to discern problems and address them directly. The confrontational manager uses the Law of Problem Solving to build his leadership credibility. Confrontational leaders are often choleric in temperament.

It can be dangerous being confrontational leaders. They often appear more insightful than they really are. They may not have all the answers, but because they have stumbled across a few right answers in specific situations, expectations are elevated. Because they are affirmed in their ability to resolve problems, they may neglect other areas of leadership they need to develop for continued success. It is easy for confrontational leaders to use their success in resolving problems to cover areas of personal deficiency.

Over the long term, confrontational leaders face other unique challenges. They are likely to become exclusively task-oriented in their approach to problem solving. In resolving organizational problems, they may unwittingly be the cause of people problems within that organization. Long-term involvement in problem solving may result in a mind-set that is only problem-focused. Their continued success may make them reluctant to involve others in the problem-solving process, hindering the growth of others in the organization. Then there is the confrontational leaders' worst nightmare. Sooner or later, they are likely to face a problem they cannot resolve.

The greatest ability of confrontational leaders is their ability to resolve problems. Sooner or later, every leader has a problem. Leaders need to know how to solve problems because the inability to solve problems has serious consequences for their leadership. Many problems do not just go away on their own. Sooner or later, they must be addressed. Problems tend to grow when they are not addressed quickly. Knowing how to address problems quickly often results in better solutions at less expense with minimal disruption to the organization.

The ongoing presence of problems not being addressed tends to erode the credibility of leaders. Just as the Law of Problem Solving builds leaders' credibility, so failure to solve problems erodes their credibility. Also, unresolved problems are like rabbits; they tend to multiply. The presence of unsolved problems tends to breed new problems that also remain unresolved. In contrast, effective problem solving recognizes the potential for problems, preventing them before they happen.

Joshua: The Confrontational Leader

Someone may have been thinking of the confrontational leader when he said, "They conquer who believe they can." That principle certainly applied in the life of Joshua. The account of his conquest of Canaan describes him as one of the most successful military leaders of all time. Yet even before he crossed the Jordan River, God Himself assured Joshua of victory. "No man shall be able to stand before you all the days of your life; as I was with Moses, so I will be with you. I will not leave you nor forsake you" (Josh. 1:5). Resting on that promise, Joshua confronted his enemies and led Israel from victory to victory. The record of his life suggests eight steps in the process that led to ultimate victory.

First, Joshua recognized the key to his success in this venture would be tied to the discipline of meditating on the Word of God. The promise God gave him was tied to that responsibility. "This Book of the Law shall not depart from your mouth, but you shall meditate in it day and night, that you may observe to do according to all that is written in it. For then you will make your way prosperous, and then you will have good success" (Josh. 1:8).

Shortly after assuming the leadership of Israel, Joshua met with Israel's other leaders to dedicate both himself and the people to the will of God. Having witnessed the constant murmuring of the previous generation in the wilderness, Joshua understood it was imperative to have everyone's support as they began this new venture. When faced with the situation, Israel's other leaders formed a "death covenant" with Joshua. "All that you command us we will do, and wherever you send us we will go. Just as we heeded Moses in all things, so we will heed you. Only the LORD your God be with you, as He was with Moses. Whoever rebels against your command and does not heed your words, in all that you command him, shall be put to death. Only be strong and of good courage" (Josh. 1:16–18).

Winning popular commitment to the cause before conflict erupts is imperative for any leader confronting a widely held cultural value. Everybody likes to win. In the midst of a struggle, those who are not deeply committed to the cause will become discouraged, especially if it looks like they might lose. They may quit just when you need them most, or worse, transfer their allegiance to the enemy just when you are depending upon their support.

Although Joshua was confident of ultimate victory, he also recognized the need to gather intelligence. Before engaging the enemy directly, Joshua took time to investigate the way of God by sending two men into the land on a covert mission with specific instructions. "Go, view the land, especially Jericho" (Josh. 2:1). The men scouted the area and entered Jericho itself to gather intelligence. They understood they could see a lot just by watching. Beyond that, they also talked with people who confirmed what God had promised was in fact happening (Josh. 2:9–11). When they had finished the assigned task and confirmed it was safe to return to Joshua, they reported, "Truly the LORD has delivered all the land into our hands, for indeed all the inhabitants of the country are fainthearted because of us" (Josh. 2:24).

Because this conflict had to be won at the spiritual level first, Joshua called on his people to initiate a walk with God. "Sanctify yourselves, for tomorrow the LORD will do wonders among you" (Josh. 3:5). As he led the people to cross the Jordan River, he was also leading them to trust God. He began the march toward the flooded river and did not stop even though the river only began to recede when "the feet of the priests who bore the ark dipped in the edge of the water" (Josh. 3:15). Because Joshua was able to lead Israel to trust and obey God, the Canaanite kings heard what God did for Israel, "and there was no spirit in them any longer because of the children of Israel" (Josh. 5:1).

Joshua understood he needed to be completely separated to God if he expected the blessing of God. Before taking on the enemy, Joshua called on the men of Israel to be circumcised at Gilgal (Josh. 5:2). Circumcision was a rite practiced in Israel as a symbol of Israel's covenant relationship with God. It demonstrated their separation from other cultures. Even when Israel was in bondage in Egypt, they continued to circumcise male children when they were eight days old. But during their forty years in the wilderness, the practice had been abandoned. By requiring the men to be circumcised, Joshua was leading them to reaffirm their relationship to God and eliminating the potential cause of the wrath of God on them. Gilgal, which means "rolling" in Hebrew, was so named because it was there God "rolled away the reproach of Egypt" from Israel (Josh. 5:9).

The toughest enemy most people face lives within. That's why self-control is the greatest of all victories. Solomon claimed, "Whoever has no rule over his own spirit is like a city broken down, without walls" (Prov. 25:28). Only those who can command themselves can command others. "He who is slow to anger is better than the mighty, and he who rules his spirit than he who takes a city" (Prov. 16:32).

Above all, Joshua knew the battle in which he was engaged was the Lord's battle. Therefore, he chose a battle strategy at his first conflict that would clearly demonstrate the wonder of God. He was willing to wait on God to show him the best way to destroy Jericho, knowing he who endures with patience is the conqueror (Josh. 6:2–5). But as soon as he knew the Lord's battle plan for Jericho, he began mobilizing the nation for war.

The Book of Joshua records a remarkable succession of victories throughout the conquest of Canaan. If there is a point in which Joshua failed, it was in the battle of Ai. Admittedly, that defeat was key to ensuring the success of the subsequent victorious battle plan. Still, Joshua failed to anticipate the wisdom of God in judging Israel for hidden sin in the camp. When he complained to God over the initial defeat, the Lord responded, "Get up! Why do you lie thus on your face?

Israel has sinned, and they have also transgressed My covenant which I commanded them. For they have even taken some of the accursed things, and have both stolen and deceived; and they have also put it among their own stuff" (Josh. 7:10–11). When Joshua learned of the problem, he took the steps necessary to resolve it so the nation could once more experience the blessing of God.

According to Marshall Foch, "Greatness does not depend on the size of your command, but on the way you exercise it." Throughout the remaining battles in Canaan, Joshua was careful to identify what God was doing on Israel's behalf and to participate in the work of God. Before he faced Ai a second time, he had a face-to-face meeting with the Lord (Josh. 8:1). Because he had met with God before meeting the enemy in the battle to protect Gibeon (Josh. 10:8), Joshua had boldness to command even the sun and the moon to cooperate to ensure a decisive military victory (Josh. 10:12–14). Joshua's victories in the north were also preceded by an encounter with God (Josh. 11:6).

Joshua may well be the most successful military leader ever to lead a nation into war. His was not an easy road, but his success on the battlefield gave him the credibility he needed later as he divided the land among the twelve tribes and ruled them in an age of relative peace. As Epicurius noted, "Skilful pilots gain their reputation from storms and tempests."

Learning to Solve Problems

The primary skill needed by confrontational leaders to ensure success is problem solving. Some will never become the competent leader God wants them to be because they are intimidated by problems. Unfortunately, problems are an integral part of life. According to Jerry Falwell, "One of three things is always true. Either you find yourself in the midst of a problem, or you have just come out of a problem, or any day now, you are in for the surprise of your life."[1] If problems are inevitable, it is imperative to learn a better way to deal with problems as they arise.

First, learn to recognize the source of your problems. Generally, problems tend to arise from one of three sources. Some problems come from changes we experience. Others reflect differences between ourselves and other people. Still others arise from our circumstances.

Because problems are so prevalent in life, it is important to learn to choose your own battles rather than wasting energy fighting everyone else's battles. There is always a problem to solve, but problem solvers are most effective when they choose the problems they can solve.

Leaders need to develop "problem-solving" eyes to gain balance and discernment into problems. They need eyes to see the positive, eyes to see the people involved, and eyes to see the facts of every situation. Good leaders see everything;, overlook a great deal, and correct a little. Charles Haddon Spurgeon taught his students to have "one blind eye and one deaf ear." He claimed successful pastors must learn to look at some things with their "blind eye" and hear some things with their "deaf ear."[2]

Problem solving begins by asking the right questions to gain insight into the problem itself. How big is the problem? Who is involved in the problem? What do others think about this problem? Asking these kinds of questions helps the leader understand the issues he is dealing with.

Great leaders learn to discern the best course of action in addressing a specific problem. Usually, there are many options available. The leaders may be tempted to launch an all-out war over the problem. In other situations, it may be wiser to attack the problem with a little less passion. They may fuss over the problem and treat it like a minor irritation. Some leaders may feel threatened by the problem and surrender. Others may retreat and try to suppress the problem. But good problem-solving leaders will develop a unique strategy to solve the problems they face.

One way to become more effective in problem solving is to study the Scriptures to gain insight into how to resolve problems. Many leaders find reading a chapter of Proverbs each day gives insight into human nature and life's problems. The "testimonies" (biographies) of Scripture reveal how other people solved similar problems. In the New Testament, Paul addresses how to resolve various specific church problems in his epistles.

The ultimate challenge in problem solving is remaining consistent. Be consistent in implementing decisions when you resolve problems. As you solve problems, you establish policy by precedent. A policy is a standing answer to a recurring question. Consistent leaders will eventually resolve problems they never faced by the policies established by their previous actions. They can train others to solve problems on their behalf by modeling consistency in their own problem-solving strategy.

CHAPTER 11

Samson

The Flawed Leader

He who walks with integrity walks securely, but he who perverts his ways will become known.

PROVERBS 10:9

H e may have been the most intelligent twentieth-century president of the United States. He was certainly better versed than most on international affairs. Understanding the times, he led the nation to establish diplomatic relations with China when others tended to ignore the largest nation on the face of the earth. He managed one of the world's two superpowers during an era of Cold War diplomacy. Though he had previously served as vice president under Dwight D. Eisenhower, a great American general, he inherited the poorly managed war in Vietnam which he sought to bring to an end. But when people think back on the presidency of Richard Nixon, one word quickly comes to mind: *Watergate.*

Despite all he accomplished during his years of public service, Nixon's legacy includes one of the darkest hours in American political history. When the office of a psychiatrist in the Watergate Plaza was broken into, most people assumed it was just another random act of

THE GOOD BOOK ON LEADERSHIP

violence in a city that had grown accustomed to it. A junior reporter for the *Washington Post* assigned to cover the story discovered one of those arrested for the crime had links to an agency of the American government. It seemed the deeper he looked into the story, the more sordid it became. While others reported the break-in and subsequent arrest of suspects, the *Post* assigned two reporters to continue looking into the possibility of a conspiracy. Eventually, that effort led to a congressional committee looking into allegations of White House involvement, the attempted suicide of a presidential aide and arrest of others, and the resignation of the president himself.

Some defenders of the president argued he had not done anything more than his predecessors. Indeed, there is evidence of wrongdoing by others who held that office. But when Nixon's sins were widely published, his consistent denials of involvement served only to erode his credibility as the mounting evidence continued to suggest otherwise. Gerald Ford, a man whose integrity and character was highly regarded by both Democrats and Republicans, replaced him. While that began a healing process in the nation, it was not enough to undo the damage that had been done when the nation went to the polls two years later. President Ford was defeated as voters vented their anger against his predecessor.

Someone has said, "The only lesson men can learn from history is that men do not learn from history." Sadly, that often proves true. While the trauma of Watergate raised the character issue, temporarily torpedoing the careers of a few politicians on the fast track to power, less than a generation later the absence of moral character among leading American corporate executives created widespread suspicion among financial investors, resulting in a significant economic slowdown in the nation.

Character Counts!

The failure of leaders to rise to their potential is often linked to character. The flawed leader is one with potential and opportunity to lead a group to accomplish a significant task, but fails to do so because he lacks the character to rise to the challenge of being the leader. The story of his life is often not defined in his accomplishments but by his failure to accomplish more. At the end of his life, the flawed leader is haunted by the question, "What might have been?"

In the Scriptures, Samson was that kind of leader. Before he was born, God called Samson to lead Israel from Philistine oppression (Judg. 13:3–5). Early in his life, "the Spirit of the LORD began to move upon him" (Judg. 13:25). Yet despite these advantages, Samson's flawed character limited his leadership potential and accomplishments.

Flawed leaders are present in every area of society. They lead businesses without the ethical values needed to ensure long-term success. When their flaws become public, they may be charged with fraud or other crimes associated with financial mismanagement. Flawed leaders are also involved in various cultural institutions, including schools and choirs. Their distorted moral values and lack of discipline often lead to inappropriate behavior, resulting in charges of abuse. When pastors seek to lead churches without character, they may engage in activities that disqualify them from ministry or limit the growth of the ministries they lead. Character is defined as habitually doing the right thing in the right way. Character is fundamental to effective long-term leadership in any organization or institution.

Unlike other leaders, the problems faced by flawed leaders are often problems of their own making. They tend to relate directly to that part of their life that is flawed. Leaders who are flawed intellectually may have difficulty gaining the insight they need to make good decisions and cast vision for those they lead. These leaders who are flawed emotionally may lack the stability to lead under pressure. Leaders who are flawed socially may experience difficulty in relating well to their followers. Those who are flawed morally may lack the character to avoid undermining their moral authority as leaders.

Flawed leaders tend to lead from some area of weakness in their life. They may have difficulty in discerning the use of their spiritual gift in ministry. Often, they have difficulty in consistently applying the laws of leadership in all situations. They may also lack insight into their unique temperament or personality and how that effects their leadership style.

The problem with flawed leaders is that their flaw may not be readily apparent to others. They may look like they have it all together, when they really do not. As a result, they may tend to overcompensate in other areas of their life to mask the flaw in their leadership. They are likely to have a significant blind spot in their own perception of things caused by their flaw. As they recognize their own inability to lead others adequately, they often become deeply insecure. It is not uncommon for these kinds of leaders to use their limited success in some areas to justify their deficiencies in other areas. They may begin building walls between themselves and those around them to hide their flaws, creating distance in the leader-follower relationship. Eventually, they face the challenge of a constant decline in the confidence and numbers of followers as their flaws are recognized.

Character development is essential in every leadership style, but especially in the case of the flawed leader. By definition, biblical faith shows up in the way we live our life. The Scriptures were written in part as a behavioral manual (2 Tim. 3:16–17). Our Christian faith is dead when it is not evident in the way we live and lead (James 2:26).

The absence of godly character in Christians has a tendency to weaken the impact of Christianity on society. A Christian leader from India visiting the West wondered why Christianity in Europe and North America was not impacting society like the dominant religion of his homeland was impacting Indian society. He came to the conclusion the answer was in part due to perceptions of leadership. In the West, the successful pastor was an effective manager of resources, skillful in the use of the latest techniques used in business. In the East, the religious leader was viewed as "a holy man."

While leadership principles are important, character is essential. There is a clear correlation between what we believe (the content of our faith), the process by which we believe (the foundation of our faith), how we live (our lifestyle), and who we are (our character). Our character is the very foundation of our credibility as leaders. Without it, the days of even the most popular leader of our times are numbered.

Samson: The Flawed Leader

If there were ever a leader who failed to realize his potential, it was Samson. Even before he was conceived, his destiny was described to his mother by an angel. Samson was one of only two men described as "a Nazarite from birth." Normally, the Nazarite vow was taken by a man to express his commitment to God. God had a special purpose in that man's life. But in Samson's case, it was not until moments before his death that he really got serious about his commitment to God. Several actions throughout his years of service to Israel reveal character deficiencies and a lack of personal discipline and commitment to God that apparently limited his leadership.

Samson's flawed character is most evident in his failure to live up to his calling as a Nazarite. He was destined to be "a Nazarite to God from the womb to the day of his death" (Judg. 13:7), but ultimately, he failed to live up to each requirement of the vow. Under Jewish law, when a man took the vow of the Nazarite, he was required to abstain from all alcoholic beverages and any product of the vineyard (Num. 6:1–4). Also, he was required to let his hair grow uncut throughout the duration of his vow as an expression of his personal holiness (Num. 6:5). Further, the Nazarite was required to stay away from all dead bodies so as to avoid making himself unclean (Num. 6:6–8).

Although theoretically separated to the Lord by his Nazarite vow from birth, Samson's choice of a Philistine wife suggests otherwise. When he came of age, he told his father, "I have seen a woman in Timnah of the daughters of the Philistines; now therefore, get her for me as a wife" (Judg. 14:2). In the culture of that day, the choice of a wife for his son was usually the responsibility of the father. When Samson's parents objected about his choice of a wife, he insisted, "Get her for me, for she pleases me well" (Judg. 14:3).

Samson's lack of clear communication with his parents suggests he had difficulties establishing the most basic of relationships. This became evident when Samson violated his Nazarite vow by eating honey out of the hive in the carcass of a lion he had killed earlier. He shared the honey he had found with his parents, "but he did not tell them that he had taken the honey out of the carcass of the lion" (Judg. 14:9). Had he done so, he would have revealed his violation of the Nazarite vow. Samson chose to hide his failure rather than repent of his sin and renew his vow as prescribed in Jewish law.

Taking the honey from the carcass of the lion was a violation of his most basic commitment in life, his Nazarite vow (Judg. 13:7). Some Bible teachers believe the initial attack of the lion was a message from God to encourage Samson to change his ways (Judg. 14:5–6). A Nazarite in a vineyard exposed himself to unnecessary temptation. This suggests Samson lacked commitment to basic core values in life that could help him in making moral decisions.

Samson's relationship with both his wife and Delilah suggests he lacked discernment into the character of women. His wife was willing to sacrifice him to maintain her relationship with others in her community (Judg. 14:17). Later, Delilah chose the wealth and respect of the lords of the Philistines over her relationship with Samson (Judg. 16:18). In a very real sense, this lack of discernment cost Samson his liberty and strength.

The biblical record suggests Samson also had an anger control problem. His lack of self-control is evident in several accounts of violent outbursts throughout his life. When the guests at his wedding guessed his riddle, he had to pay off his "wager" to them. "He went down to Ashkelon and killed thirty of their men, took their apparel, and gave the changes of clothing to those who had explained the riddle. So his anger was aroused, and he went back up to his father's house" (Judg. 14:19). When he later returned to claim his wife and found she had been married to his best man, "Samson went and caught three hundred foxes; and he took torches, turned the foxes tail to tail, and put a torch between each pair of tails" (Judg. 15:4). This way Samson burned up the enemy's crops. When the Philistines sought revenge for the damage done to their crops, Samson "attacked them hip and thigh with a great slaughter" (Judg. 15:8). Later, he killed a thousand men with the jawbone of a donkey (Judg. 15:15–16).

While it might be argued this was part of Samson's mandate from God, the manner and motive of his actions suggest his anger resulted in a lot of energy expended that could have been harnessed for greater accomplishment.

Samson also lacked insight into real danger, resulting in no sense of caution in the presence of recognized danger. This is particularly evident in his relationship with Delilah. Despite her repeated attempts to learn his secret and betray him to the lords of the Philistines, he continued to maintain his relationship with her. Eventually, he told her what she wanted to know (Judg. 16:15–17). Had he recognized the danger and exercised appropriate caution, it is doubtful he would have remained in a relationship with her long enough to reveal his secret.

Perhaps Samson's real problem was that his personal relationship had become so distant he could not discern the difference between the presence and absence of the Spirit of God in his life. In the Old Testament, the presence of the Holy Spirit in one's life was usually temporary and an indication that God intended to use that person in a special way. This had often been Samson's experience throughout his life (Judg. 13:25; 14:6, 19; 15:14), but when he awoke after revealing the secret of his strength to Delilah, "he did not know that the LORD had departed from him" (Judg. 16:20).

While he had some success against the Philistines throughout his life, Samson clearly fell short of his goal to deliver Israel from their enemy. It was not until moments before his death that he came to the place of total commitment to God. When he prayed, "just this once" (Judg. 16:28), he was for the first time in his life asking God to assist him in his work. His previous efforts were based on his personal strength rather than the power of God. This act of faith earned Samson mention in Paul's "Hall of Faith" (Heb. 11:32). Even though it cost him his life, this single act of faith by Samsom accomplished more than the sum total of everything else he had done (Judg. 16:30). It leaves one wondering what might have been.

Building Character

Within the leadership kaleidoscope, character is essential to maintaining the balance of leadership styles and ensuring effectiveness in various situations faced by the leader. When the child's toy was dropped and the mirrors of the kaleidoscope were cracked or misaligned, there was no longer a beautiful design to see regardless of other adjustments that might be made. Likewise, without character, the most skilled leader in management theory is eventually exposed by his character deficiency, and it is not a pretty picture to behold. Moses warned Israel, "Be sure your sin will find you out" (Num. 32:23).

Because character is foundational to leadership, every leader needs to engage in the process of character development. Peter describes that process in his second epistle. "God has given us powerful yet precious promises in Scripture that will break our old lusts and change us to become followers of Christ. To change your life, add faith to your knowledge of Scripture, then add virtue (estimation or expectation), next add the attitude of self-control (temperance), also add patient actions, and finally, the results will make you live like God, kind and loving others. If these qualities increase in you, they will keep you from being ineffective and unproductive" (2 Pet. 1:4–8, authors' translation). This passage suggests four steps in the process of character development.

Step one involves changing the way you think. When you change your thinking, you change your beliefs. It does make a difference what you believe. The Scriptures use various words to describe belief. When examined together, these words outline the normal steps to developing biblical belief. The word *hope* describes the desires we may have. On the basis of this hope, we make plans reflecting that which we anticipate. As we are persuaded in our faith, we express our confidence. The fullest expression of that confidence is in the statement, "I know." When we come to that point in the growth of our faith, we have moved into the realm of conviction. Ultimately, belief is the conviction that something is true. This process is rooted in the Scriptures, which are called "the word of faith" (Rom. 10:8). "So then faith comes by hearing, and hearing by the word of God" (Rom. 10:17).

The second step in the process of character formation involves developing vision. Your expectations or vision must come from God's Word. "Where there is no revelation [i.e., vision or expectation], the people cast off restraint; but happy is he who keeps the law" (Prov. 29:18). Some people never have a vision because their faith in God does not create new expectations from God.

There are at least six different responses people may have with regard to a God-given vision. Some never see a God-given vision. They have a mechanical problem. Others see a God-given vision, but do not understand it. They have a mental problem. Others see the God-given vision, but never pursue it. Their problem is with the will. Others see the God-given vision, but never feel it. They have an emotional problem. Others see the God-given vision and through obedience achieve it. But there are a few who see and share a God-given vision with others, demonstrating their capacity for leadership.

Leaders pursuing God's vision for their life may find four steps helpful in grasping it. First, look within yourself to determine how God has enabled and gifted you. Then, look behind yourself to see how God has used past events to shape you and prepare you for something greater. Third, look around yourself to others whom you admire. Your choice of heroes reveals what you will be like in ten years. Finally, look ahead to determine where the Lord is leading in your life.

The third step in this process involves changing your attitude. Your attitude is the predisposition of your life's focus. As you consistently apply attitudes, you develop habits that form your character. As John Maxwell notes, "Your attitude determines your altitude."[1]

There are usually four steps in developing new attitudes. First, identify the problem you wish to address. For illustration's sake, let's assume the problem is chronic lateness. The next step involves identifying the right thinking that will lead to changing an emotional habit. At this point, a person needs to decide he wants to be on time. Third, begin relating to positive people. We become like those with whom we associate. If you want to become punctual, begin associating with people who tend to be punctual. Finally, develop a plan that will encourage positive attitudes and develop a new habit. Begin by being on time for your next meeting, then the next one, and so on. By being on time for one meeting at a time, you will develop the habit of being on time and earn the reputation of being a punctual person.

When you change your attitude, you change your actions. Your actions earn your reputation and communicate to others the kind of person you are. Solomon got it right when he wrote, "Even a child is known by his deeds, whether what he does is pure and right" (Prov. 20:11). In the New Testament, Jesus taught, "For every tree is known by its own fruit. For men do not gather figs from thorns, nor do they gather grapes from a bramble bush. A good man out of the good treasure of his heart brings forth good; and an evil man out of the evil treasure of his heart brings forth evil. For out of the abundance of the heart his mouth speaks" (Luke 6:44–45). Our actions are the fruit by which others determine the kind of people we are.

The fourth step is to change your habits. Since an accomplishment is the outcome of an action, so a habit is the outcome of character. The process by which we develop character in our life may be described in seven steps: (1) we think it; (2) we know it; (3) we dream it; (4) we begin to focus on it; (5) we act on it; (6) we accomplish it; and finally (7) we become it.

CHAPTER 12

Saul

The Failed Leader

*The fear of the wicked will come upon him, and the desire of
the righteous will be granted.*

PROVERBS 10:24

Some people think he came very close to ruling the world, but ultimately his name is linked with horrific crimes against humanity and a national embarrassment with which one of the world's strongest nations continues to lives. As the absolute dictator over Germany, Adolph Hitler conquered the largest parts of Europe, Asia, and Africa ever subdued by a single military force. But in the process, his actions led to an international conflict that resulted in the death of more than thirty-five million people. He was one of history's most influential yet diabolical leaders.

Adolph Hitler failed high school and began his adult life as a common laborer and street artist. His continuous failures left him sleeping in parks and eating in soup kitchens. He began blaming his problems on the state of Austria and multicultural populations. He later confessed, "I hated the motley collection of Czechs, Ruthenians, Poles, Hungarians, Serbs, Croates, and above all that ever-present fungoid growth—Jews."[1] Growing increasingly bitter over his lot in life, he moved to Germany, his father's homeland, looking for conditions more favorable to a "really great German" like himself.

In 1914, he volunteered for the Sixteenth Bavarian Infantry Regiment and served throughout World War I on the western front. Despite being decorated for bravery four times, he never advanced beyond the rank of corporal. At the end of the war, he returned to Munich and joined the socialist German Worker's Party. By April, he had assumed leadership of the group, enlarged its organization and changed its name to the National Socialist German Worker's Party (Nazis). Using his public speaking abilities and organizational skills, the Nazis grew in influence and conspired with local military units to seize control of Bavaria. When local officials put down the "putsch" of November 8–9, 1923, Hitler and others were arrested and charged with treason.

Hitler spent nine months in the Landsberg Prison before being released as part of a general amnesty. While in jail, Hitler wrote *Mein Kampf*[2] outlining his views and goals. By 1927, he had restored the Nazi Party to prominence and continued expanding it largely through his personal public speaking. By the time the Great Depression hit Germany in 1929, his promises of jobs, economic reform, and the restoration of Germany's former glory and power gained widespread support among the German population. What he had previously failed to do by force, he accomplished through the ballot box. The election of 1932 gave the Nazi Party control of the Reichstag. The following year, the former army corporal became Germany's chancellor.

Now with the power to pursue his ambitions, Hitler secured his position as Germany's absolute dictator by murdering or jailing his opponents. Through a combination of his personal charm and tendency to blame others for Germany's economic woes, he continued to be widely popular among the German people. He began restructuring the nation's military in violation of international treaties, replacing those he viewed as responsible for losing World War I with friends who would remain loyal to him. By 1936, he began an offensive by occupying the Rhineland. In the years following, he annexed Austria, the Sudetenland, and Czechoslovakia. It was not until he invaded Poland that France and England declared war on Germany. Even then, there were many in England and America who secretly stood in awe of his incredible leadership.

Germany controlled much of Europe within a few years, but Hitler had even larger ambitions. In June 1941, he broke a nonaggression treaty and invaded Russia. In his desire to create a "Jew-free Europe," he established centers throughout his territory where he killed and cremated Jews and other "undesirables." His barbaric murder of six million Jews during this Holocaust became his legacy.

Following his failure to conquer Britain, Hitler increasingly acted as his own military commander in chief. He assumed the title "Grofaz," a German acronym for "the greatest commander of all time." Believing he was indeed history's greatest commander, he accepted no responsibility for military defeat. When his generals failed to accomplish his goals, they were executed or sent to the Russian front as punishment. Those closest to Hitler lived in fear as reports of defeat arrived at headquarters with greater frequency. He survived two assassination attempts organized by loyal Germans who came to believe Germany would be better off with any leader but Hitler. In the end, he took his own life just days before his inevitable capture and defeat. Many of his closest advisors fled the country looking for safe havens around the world.

Ironically, his actions to create a Jew-free Europe did much to win international support for an independent Jewish state. Within three years of the war's conclusion, the state of Israel was established, a state that, despite ongoing opposition from its Arab neighbors, has already survived six times as long as Hitler's "thousand-year Reich."

When Everything Goes Wrong

People will follow leaders who look and act like leaders. But sometimes even the most promising leaders fail to lead their followers to accomplish their goal. Despite that promise at the beginning of their tenure, the anticipated results are not realized and organizational objectives fail to be realized. Saul, Israel's first king, began his career as Israel's new leader with strong popular support, but failed in the long term because of his wavering and failure to meet the expectations of his followers.

Failed leaders are present in every area of silence. In the business community, they lead businesses that fail to make a profit and become subjects of hostile takeovers, mergers, or bankruptcies. When they lead cultural institutions like schools, theaters, and orchestras, those institutions are usually in decline. As coaches they fail to bring out the best in their talented players and turn a winning team into a losing season. When they pastor churches, those churches tend to be plateaued, declining, and then closing.

The problem with failed leaders is that their minor successes tend to be hindered by a record of major failure. They are unable to live up to the expectations of others and struggle to maintain esprit de corps among their followers. Often, they have difficulty maintaining the momentum needed to accomplish major projects. Because people prefer to follow successful leaders, leaders with a track record of failure have difficulty maintaining a solid team of followers. That poor track record eventually closes doors for failed leaders. They tend to dig themselves into a hole from which they cannot escape.

Failed leaders tend to lead from their weaknesses rather than from their strengths. They either fail to recognize or choose not to minister out of the strength of their spiritual gift. Their leadership tends to be haphazard as they fail to apply consistently the eight laws of leadership. It is likely they do not understand their unique personality or know how to lead out of the strength of their temperament.

Failure is the ultimate mark of the failed leader. Failed leaders fail to lead. In doing so, they cause their followers to flounder and may create significant problems for those who remain loyal. Their pattern of failure may influence their followers to fail in other areas of their life. The longer they remain with an organization, the more likely they will sap the strength out of that organization. In an effort to defend themselves, they may convince others the office served by the leader is flawed and begin dismantling a solid organizational infrastructure. When that fails to solve the problem, their followers may conclude that the whole concept of leadership is flawed, resulting in a tendency toward anarchy.

While effective leaders tend to learn best from other effective leaders, there are important lessons that should be learned from failed leaders and incorporated into your personal leadership kaleidoscope. First, the potential for failure is found in every successful leader, organization, and institution. Insightful leaders may be able to recognize the path taken by self-destructive leaders early enough to prevent the impending disaster. Leaders with this insight will recognize these symptoms in leaders they might otherwise follow and followers who might otherwise be elevated to a leadership position within the organization. Leaders who recognize the symptoms of failing leadership have a standard by which their own leadership may be periodically evaluated to ensure their continued leadership success.

Saul: The Failed Leader

Saul's reign as Israel's first king began with great promise but ended in disaster. He failed to rise to the expectations of his followers. He even failed to rise to his own personal expectations. The story of his reign is that of a king who began well but continued on a downward spiral until he undid much of the good he had done in his early life.

When he first met Samuel, who would anoint him king, Saul was looking for his father's donkeys. His failure to find them may have been a warning sign of what was to come. In an act of desperation, Saul's servant suggested they consult with Samuel, who was by then a widely reputed prophet in Israel. "Then Saul said to his servant, 'But look, if we go, what shall we bring the man? For the bread in our vessels is all gone, and there is no present to bring to the man of God. What do we have?' And the servant answered Saul again and said, 'Look, I have here at hand one fourth of a shekel of silver. I will give that to the man of God, to tell us our way'" (1 Sam. 9:7–8). Saul's willingness to offer a fourth of a shekel to Samuel as an offering suggests a lack of spiritual values in his life. "For where your treasure is, there will your heart be also" (Matt. 6:21).

Saul's first meeting with Samuel further suggests a lack of spiritual interest in Saul's life. "Then Saul drew near to Samuel in the gate, and said, 'Please tell me, where is the seer's house?'" (1 Sam. 9:18). Although Samuel had faithfully served the Lord for generations and was well known and loved by the people of Israel, Saul was unable to identify Samuel even when they talked face to face.

When the time came to publicly anoint Saul, he was nowhere to be found even though he had been told previously he would be Israel's new king. "But when they sought him, he could not be found. Therefore they inquired of the LORD further, 'Has the man come here yet?' And the LORD answered, 'There he is, hidden among the equipment'" (1 Sam. 10:21–22). Some Bible teachers see Saul's hiding at his installation service as a false humility, masking his hurt pride and embarrassment over the proverb, "Is Saul also among the prophets?" (1 Sam. 10:11).

Although Saul began well as king, his eventual intrusion into the priest's office by offering a sacrifice demonstrated his lack of understanding into the way God wanted the kingdom governed. "And Samuel said to Saul, 'You have done foolishly. You have not kept the commandment of the LORD your God, which He commanded you. For now the LORD would have established your kingdom over Israel forever. But now your kingdom shall not continue. The LORD has sought for Himself a man after His own heart, and the LORD has commanded him to be commander over His people, because you have not kept what the LORD commanded you' " (1 Sam. 13:13–14).

One factor that undermined Saul's authority as king was his tendency to make rash decisions that made life more difficult for his most loyal followers. His hasty decision in the midst of a battle tended to weaken his own people when they needed to be strongest. "And the men of Israel were distressed that day, for Saul had placed the people under oath, saying, 'Cursed is the man who eats any food until evening, before I have taken vengeance on my enemies.' So none of the people tasted food" (1 Sam. 14:24).

When his own son, who had not heard that command, violated it and encouraged others to taste honey to regain their strength, Saul was willing to execute Jonathan. "But the people said to Saul, 'Shall Jonathan die, who has accomplished this great deliverance in Israel? Certainly not! As the Lord lives, not one hair of his head shall fall to the ground, for he has worked with God this day.' So the people rescued Jonathan, and he did not die" (1 Sam. 14:45). Although Saul ultimately bowed to the will of the people, his intent revealed his controlling personality. He had difficulty with others acting on his behalf with his best interest at heart and if he were not personally directing their activities.

Saul's incomplete obedience in his battle with Amalek revealed his rebellious heart. He had been commanded to utterly destroy the nation and all that belonged to it, but he chose to save the best herds "for sacrifices." When he tried to excuse his actions, Samuel responded, "Has the LORD as great delight in burnt offerings and sacrifices, as in obeying the voice of the LORD? Behold, to obey is better than sacrifice, and to heed than the fat of rams. For rebellion is as the sin of witchcraft, and stubbornness is as iniquity and idolatry. Because you have rejected the word of the LORD, He also has rejected you from being king" (1 Sam. 15:22–23). Saul's continued unwillingness to yield completely to the Spirit of God had its tragic consequence. "But the Spirit of the LORD departed from Saul, and a distressing spirit from the LORD troubled him" (1 Sam. 16:14).

As David became more prominent in the life of Israel, deficiency in Saul's character became increasingly more apparent. First, he began actively opposing David because his pride was wounded over his loyal soldier's success. "Then Saul was very angry, and the saying displeased him; and he said, 'They have ascribed to David ten thousands, and to me they have ascribed only thousands. Now what more can he have but the kingdom?' So Saul eyed David from that day forward" (1 Sam. 18:8–9).

Next, his uncontrolled anger and jealousy toward David began eroding some of his most basic relationships in life. When Jonathan granted David permission to be absent from a feast where he felt his life might be threatened, "Saul's anger was aroused against Jonathan, and he said to him, 'You son of a perverse, rebellious woman! Do I not know that you have chosen the son of Jesse to your own shame and to the shame of your mother's nakedness?' " (1 Sam. 20:30)

As Saul's jealousy continued to grow and control him, he ended up destroying loyal subjects in his own kingdom because he suspected them of being involved in a nonexistent conspiracy. When the priests aided David by giving him the sword of Goliath and bread, Saul sentenced them to death, even though they had acted on an assumption that David was on a secret mission for their king. When Saul's loyal Israelite soldiers refused to carry out the order, "the king said to Doeg, 'You turn and kill the priests!' So Doeg the Edomite turned and struck the priests, and killed on that day eighty-five men who wore a linen ephod" (1 Sam. 22:18).

Lacking direction in his life, Saul began using illegitimate means of getting counsel. "Then Saul said to his servants, 'Find me a woman who is a medium, that I may go to her and inquire of her'" (1 Sam. 28:7). The king who began his service to the nation by disposing of mediums ended his career by consulting one. In his years as king, he managed to alienate or destroy his most loyal subjects and found himself surrounded by those who had no difficulty finding the kind of people who had been banned from the kingdom in better days.

Why Leaders Fail

As most leaders seek to improve their leadership skills, it is only natural to focus on new ideas and strategies that promise to expand their influence. Biographies of great leaders and books, videos and audiotapes of recognized authorities in the field are the natural resources to access to achieve that goal. But there is good reason also to take time to understand why some leaders never realize their dreams. The best leadership principles and strategies will not produce the desired results if they are unable to withstand the pressure that produces leaders.

There are several reasons why leaders fail. Some leaders fail when they fail to develop personal core values that place a high value on character and one's relationship with God. Leadership is more than a mystical mix of charisma and strategies. Character counts. And leaders who lack allegiance to something bigger than themselves rarely experience long-term allegiance from their followers.

Leaders also fail when they fail to humble themselves. Solomon warned, "Pride goes before destruction, and a haughty spirit before a fall" (Prov. 16:18). The failure to develop personal humility often leads to personal humiliation. Perhaps that is why he added that it is "better to be of a humble spirit with the lowly, than to divide the spoil with the proud" (Prov. 16:19).

When leaders fail to understand and restrict themselves to the limits of their authority, they move on to the expressway of failure. By its very nature, power has a corrupting influence. When a leader does not have accountability to another person or group, he is left with no means to counter that corrupting influence. Successful leaders have a small circle of people to whom they have given permission to ask questions and hold them accountable. Also, as their organization grows, they place various checks and balances in place to ensure there are limits to the power they may exert within the organization.

Leadership also fails when leaders fail to make good decisions that make life easier on their followers. People will endure hardship for a cause for a time, but they must realize personal benefit eventually. The people of Britain rallied around their prime minister during World War II when he had nothing to offer them but "blood, toil, tears, and sweat," but when the war ended they elected a new leader who promised a peace dividend.

Leaders who fail to share parts of their leadership with others ultimately fail to achieve their dream. When a leader insists on maintaining absolute and personal control of every detail, he limits his leadership potential. There are natural limits to what one person can do even if he is extremely gifted. Leaders who build a team to work with them toward achieving a common goal usually get there faster and stay there longer.

When leaders fail to accomplish their goals by making unacceptable compromises, they create a leadership crisis they will not survive. A similar situation develops when leaders surround themselves with poor advisors. A leader's personal credibility diminishes when he establishes a pattern of neglecting good advice and being controlled by bad advice and influences.

Ultimately, successful leadership is dependent on followers trusting their leaders and committing themselves to their cause. When leaders fail to recognize the value of their followers, they risk a similar response on the part of their followers toward their leader. The leaders who begin lashing out at others for personal reasons are the leaders whose days are numbered.

CHAPTER 13

David

The Growing Leader

He also chose David His servant, and took him from the sheepfolds; from following the ewes that had young He brought him, to shepherd Jacob His people, and Israel His inheritance. So he shepherded them according to the integrity of his heart, and guided them by the skillfulness of his hands.

PSALM 78:70–72

As a child, the boy who would become Frederick the Great offered no clue of his future military success. His father, King Frederick William I, considered his son a weakling and was disappointed with his natural interest in philosophy and art. As a result, young Frederick grew up the victim of both physical and mental abuse. It was only under duress that he finally accepted a commission in his father's personal bodyguard unit of grenadiers. By the time he was twenty, he unsuccessfully attempted to desert to France with a fellow officer. He was forced to watch the execution of his friend and spent eighteen months in jail.

During his prison term, Frederick resigned himself to his destiny and reconciled with his father. In 1732, he accepted a commission as colonel in the Ruppin Infantry Regiment and two years later fought in the War of the Polish Succession under the command of Prince Eugene of Savoy. The future king of Prussia learned from Prince Eugene the principles of war—principles on which he would build his future.

On May 28, 1740, Frederick assumed the throne of Prussia and leadership of the army three days after the death of his father. He began making both civil and military reforms immediately. Among his reforms, he guaranteed individual rights by abolishing censorship and establishing freedom of the press. He also banned the torture of civilian prisoners. He quickly established that he, and he alone, would be the leader of the military. Addressing a group of senior generals appointed by his father, he announced, "In this kingdom, I am the only person to exercise authority."

Frederick realized his military responsibilities did not have to prevent him from pursuing his interests in the arts. Indeed, his commitment to continue learning in various disciplines contributed to his success as both a military and civil leader. He studied the art of war while learning more about music and the arts. He also established a long-term correspondence with the French philosopher Voltaire.

Within months of assuming leadership, Frederick developed a strategy by which he would lead during the remainder of his career. He determined the best way to defend his nation was to go on the offensive. He mastered the use of terrain, maneuverability, and surprise to his advantage in battles with more powerful armies. In *The Instruction of Frederick the Great for His Generals*[1] (1741), Frederick detailed his ideas on the role of tactics and maneuvers in battle. In the process, the one-time deserter rewrote the book on modern warfare.

Many of the king's ideas grew out of his initial attempt at leading his nation into battle. He attacked Austria during a transition of power following the death of Austrian emperor Charles VI. After initial success, the Austrians rallied at the battle of Mollwitz on April 10, 1741. Suffering heavy losses in their cavalry, the Prussian cavalry commander convinced Frederick to withdraw. In his absence, the Prussian infantry stayed on and ultimately won the battle. The embarrassed leader returned to the front, vowing to never again retreat from an undecided battle and to improve his cavalry. In the next two decades, he built a strong military, invested heavily in infrastructure projects with both civilian and military benefits, and established a fund to finance future military conflicts.

At the conclusion of the Seven Years' War (January 16, 1763), Frederick changed his focus and began rebuilding his nation with the same zeal he had demonstrated in military conflict. He improved the quality of life for his citizens without compromising the strength of his military. Even without his direct involvement, the Prussian army remained a dominant force in Europe. Indeed, they did not experience defeat in battle until the rise of Napoleon, long after the death of Frederick.

Avoiding the Peter Principle Curse

In his book *The Peter Principle*,[2] Dr. Laurence Peter argues organizations tend to promote people to their level of incompetence. The principle itself has been well documented in a variety of contexts and is generally accepted as an axiom of contemporary management thought. It is a product of the natural tendency to reward success with increased responsibilities. Peter argues this tendency to promote people beyond their ability to perform turns productive employees into unproductive employees.

Many leaders also fall victim to the "Peter Principle Curse." They tend to rise to a level of competence and then stagnate. The only way to break the curse is to continue growing. Growing leaders continue to achieve personal growth throughout their tenure as leaders. As they grow with each new task they undertake, they continue to stretch the natural limits of the Peter Principle and not fall victim to it.

David demonstrated personal growth as a leader throughout his life. He rose to prominence and a position of influence in Israel as a result of a victorious one-on-one conflict with a Philistine champion. Later, he became a leader of other soldiers in Saul's army. Circumstances over which he had no control resulted in his becoming a leader of a standing private militia. Ultimately, his influence grew as he took his place on the throne of Israel as king.

Growing leaders are in high demand throughout society. They are the long-term leaders of growing businesses that establish the economic climate of the community. They include political leaders who begin serving their community as school board trustees but grow to represent their community on the national stage. They also include the pastors of small churches who continue to lead as their church grows into a multicongregational church. They make the successful transitions necessary to move from being the sole pastor of a congregation to leading a larger pastoral staff.

Finding time to grow leadership skills can be a challenge. Growing leaders usually develop their skills as they lead people. Their activities as leaders usually limit the time available to devote to their personal growth. Also, although there is much literature being produced on leadership, some of it is not very helpful. Growing leaders need to discern between good and bad advice being offered those who would lead.

Leadership is more than principles and practices. The intangible aspects of leadership are often gleaned through close association with great leaders. Growing leaders are not always able to work closely with other leaders. Other alternatives may be expensive or inappropriate. Leadership training seminars and adventure-based conferences can cost thousands of dollars. Much of the training available in these venues is designed as executive training for corporate leaders. While the principles of leadership never change, the strategic application of those principles will differ greatly in nonprofit organizations such as churches and schools.

Growing leaders must also be training other leaders. They cannot afford to outgrow their followers. Nor can they afford to stop growing personally. When they do so, their organization will stop growing or outgrow them.

Growing leadership is not dependent on any particular spiritual gift. Rather, growing leaders have identified their dominant gifts and learned to use them to their maximum potential. Likewise, they have also learned to use all the laws of leadership. Their desire to grow causes them to study leadership principles and incorporate them into their personal leadership style. Leaders with any type of temperament can become growing leaders if they learn to build on the strengths of their personality and compensate for their natural weaknesses.

While the personal growth of leaders is important, it is also fraught with danger. Growing leaders may devote so much energy to training that they neglect present leadership responsibilities. It is not uncommon for them to make mistakes that could undermine their credibility. Making mistakes is part of the learning process, but it bears a high price in leadership. Also, they may adopt the practices of other successful leaders that do not contribute to their personal success. The young pastor may adopt the accent or dress of a famous preacher, yet fail to have that preacher's spiritual power in the pulpit.

Growing leaders have increased pressures on their time as their leadership influence grows. Many struggle in the area of time management. They may also struggle to give up aspects of their leadership that hold them back from continued growth. Delegation is a difficult practice to begin, especially for entrepreneurs faced with the need to transition their leadership style to continue to grow their business or church that is now more than a one-man operation.

Growing leaders sometimes come to a place of maturity in which they are tempted to believe they have arrived. That temptation to stop growing becomes stronger as leaders grow. Also, they may struggle to consistently apply the lessons of leadership they are learning, especially if they adopt a learning strategy that involves prolonged periods of intensive leadership training.

Despite its challenges, leaders need to be committed to a personal and ongoing growth plan. Without it, the Peter Principle kicks in. They will rise to their level of incompetence and stagnate unless they begin to grow again. Also, failure to grow as a leader limits the influence of the leader. Growing leaders understand leadership is an emerging science. New literature being published in this field continues to suggest new principles and practices that may work in various settings. Because different kinds of people respond to different kinds of leaders, growing leaders need to continually expand their personal leadership kaleidoscope and learn how to lead the people who are not currently responding to their leadership. The alternative is unacceptable. People and institutions that stop growing usually begin to decline. Growing personal leadership skills not only helps prevent personal leadership decline; it potentially helps expand our influence.

David: The Growing Leader

David was one of Israel's most significant leaders and one of the greatest leaders in world history. His life is described in over eighty chapters, not including the Psalms. While many kings of Israel are listed in the royal genealogy of Christ in Matthew 1, David alone is described as "the king." It is hard to imagine any Jew not identifying David on a top-ten list of great Jewish leaders. Most would include him in the top three along with Abraham and Moses. Yet the recorded details of his life reveal David's growth in leadership over many decades.

David qualified as a candidate for leadership by developing a heart for God. When Samuel was prepared to anoint one of David's brothers as Israel's next king, God stopped him, advising the prophet, "Do not look at his appearance or at the height of his stature, because I have refused him. For the LORD does not see as man sees; for man looks at the outward appearance, but the LORD looks at the heart" (1 Sam. 16:7).

David's training as a growing leader began with an opportunity to serve King Saul in the palace. In that context, he witnessed what happened to a leader who did not grow. "And so it was, whenever the spirit from God was upon Saul, that David would take a harp and play it with his hand. Then Saul would become refreshed and well, and the distressing spirit would depart from him" (1 Sam. 16:23). Although David was only one of many palace servants in that setting, it was his first up-close exposure to how kings lead.

When David defeated Goliath, he opened the door to further growth as a leader. "Saul took him that day, and would not let him go home to his father's house anymore" (1 Sam. 18:2). This enabled David to develop relationships with other leaders, including both Saul and Jonathan. As he accomplished various assignments well, Saul eventually "set him over the men of war, and he was accepted in the sight of all the people and also in the sight of Saul's servants" (1 Sam. 18:5).

David earned a greater reputation and expanded his influence by achieving military victories as a leader in Saul's army. His victories were popularized in the music of the people. "Now it happened as they were coming home, when David was returning from the slaughter of the Philistine, that the women had come out of all the cities of Israel, singing and dancing, to meet King Saul, with tambourines, with joy, and with musical instruments. So the women sang as they danced, and said: 'Saul has slain his thousands, and David his ten thousands'" (1 Sam. 18:6–7).

David continued to grow and increase his influence and popularity by strengthening his relationships with his followers even as he came into disfavor with King Saul. "Therefore Saul removed him from his presence, and made him his captain over a thousand; and he went out and came in before the people" (1 Sam. 18:13). David's wise behavior in a difficult circumstance further alienated the king, "but all Israel and Judah loved David, because he went out and came in before them" (1 Sam. 18:16).

Even Saul's growing and intense opposition to David helped him grow as a leader. This forced David to learn how to relate to a different kind of follower in the wilderness. "And everyone who was in distress, everyone who was in debt, and everyone who was discontented gathered to him. So he became captain over them. And there were about four hundred men with him" (1 Sam. 22:2).

As David rose to that challenge and proved victorious under difficult situations, his leadership influence continued to grow. That growing influence was reflected in the growth of his army. It was not long before the four hundred men became six hundred men (1 Sam. 23:13). By the time Saul died in battle, the tribe of Judah was ready to declare David as their king. "Then the men of Judah came, and there they anointed David king over the house of Judah" (2 Sam. 2:4). David proved himself capable as king of Judah for seven and one-half years before his kingdom was expanded to include all Israel (2 Sam. 2:11).

David had learned to grow in adversity in the wilderness. The civil war between Israel and Judah resulted in his continued growth in strength as Israel's king weakened. "Now there was a long war between the house of Saul and the house of David. But David grew stronger and stronger, and the house of Saul grew weaker and weaker" (2 Sam. 3:1).

Despite his growing position of strength, David was willing to reach out to others outside his sphere of influence to welcome them. His response to the death of Abner (2 Sam. 3:37) and Ishbosheth (2 Sam. 4:12) communicated to others that he was willing to embrace former enemies as friends. His overtures to his enemies resulted in an invitation to expand his kingdom to include Israel. "Therefore all the elders of Israel came to the king at Hebron, and King David made a covenant with them at Hebron before the LORD. And they anointed David king over Israel" (2 Sam. 5:3).

Developing a Personal Growth Strategy

Personal growth is not an option for leaders; it is essential to guarantee ongoing success in long-term leadership settings. Leaders who would be most effective and would influence the most people to accomplish the greatest projects, are the leaders who are continually expanding their personal leadership kaleidoscope. While time and financial restraints may place some leadership training options out of reach, there are several things leaders can do to develop a personal growth strategy.

First, set a personal goal to become all the leader you can be for God. The desire to excel is the starting point for a growing leader. If a leader is content with who he is, he is usually not motivated to become more. In contrast, leaders who want to become better at what they do will find the time and resources they need to grow.

Next, identify your personal strengths as a leader. Growing leaders know what they do best and build on those strengths to become more effective. Growing leaders also need to know their limits and take steps to compensate for personal weaknesses.

One inexpensive way to grow in your leadership is to take advantage of your public library. Study the lives of great leaders in various disciplines for both inspiration and insight into the task of leading people. The pastor of a growing church may not expect to find much help in the biography of a basketball coach or a World War II general, but the principles by which these leaders lead people in different circumstances can be adapted by the pastor and applied in his church.

Most libraries also have a selection of books on leadership theory. Study the theory and principles of leadership to learn better ways to lead people. Once again, many of these books are written for the business market, but principles that work in business often work well in other settings when adapted to the unique culture of a school or church.

As you study leadership, do not neglect your study of the Scriptures. The Scriptures reveal God's insights on leadership.

Sometimes these principles are illustrated in the biographies of Scripture. You can learn important leadership principles from both effective and poor leaders described in Scripture. Also, portions of the Scripture were written initially to train leaders. This includes Jesus' training of the Twelve in the Sermon on the Mount and the Upper Room Discourse and also the Book of Proverbs, which may have been used in the training of Israel's kings. Some leaders find it helpful to read a chapter from Proverbs daily, studying the entire book every month.

As you grow, *take periodic personal inventories to identify progress and plot personal growth strategies for continued growth.* Give other people permission to evaluate your leadership and identify ways you can become all the leader God wants you to be. These times of evaluation will encourage you with the progress you have made and help you identify priorities in the next phase of your personal growth plan.

CHAPTER 14

Solomon

The Transitional Leader

*Be diligent to know the state of your flocks, and attend to
your herds; for riches are not forever, nor does a crown
endure to all generations.*

PROVERBS 27:23–24

Anglican church leaders in South Africa quickly noticed the leadership potential of a young priest, Desmund Tutu. Recognizing that white academics would not always be involved in the training of black clergymen, they saw in Tutu a candidate who could help them make this transition. He had already earned two under-graduate degrees and was an experienced teacher. In order to prepare further for a new ministry, the thirty-two-year-old left South Africa in 1962 to pursue his master's degree at King's College at London University.

While living in Britain, Tutu and his family enjoyed a life free from apartheid. He grew to believe interracial harmony might be possible in his own country where apartheid was so ingrained in the culture. Tutu later claimed his stay in Britain also gave him the confidence to dis-agree with whites.

Tutu returned to South Africa in 1967 and continued teaching black African clergy. In 1976, Tutu's profile was raised when he was consecrated as the bishop of Lesotho, an independent conclave within South Africa. When asked to speak at the funeral of a black activist who died in police custody in 1977, Tutu became convinced the church needed to become involved in the political process if apartheid was to be dismantled without bloodshed. In 1978, he became the general secretary of the South African Council of Churches, an organization with a distinct political agenda.

His new position gave Tutu increased media exposure, resulting in opportunities to speak on talk shows around the world. Tutu became one of many who called for economic sanctions against South Africa. The South African government responded by revoking his passport. Although isolated from the rest of the world, he was not forgotten. In 1982, the president of Columbia University traveled to South Africa to present Tutu with an honorary degree. Two years later, he became South Africa's second black Nobel Peace Prize laureate. A month later, he became the first black Anglican bishop of Johannesburg. In 1986, Tutu assumed the highest position in South Africa's Anglican Church—Archbishop of Capetown.

Tutu used his personal success to denounce his government's failure to end apartheid. While many in the anti-apartheid movement had resorted to violence, Tutu followed the example of Gandhi and Martin Luther King Jr. in leading nonviolent protests. His actions may have been a factor in the election of F. W. de Klerk as president of South Africa. The new president had pledged to speed up reforms and abolish apartheid. At the end of 1993, de Klerk's promise was kept with the promise of South Africa's first all-race elections. On April 17, 1994, South Africans elected Nelson Mandela as their first black president, a symbol that assured apartheid was finally over.

The young man who was enlisted to help the Anglican Church make an important transition within his denomination became a chief spokesman during his country's most significant cultural transition.

That experience uniquely equipped him to provide transitional leadership in the next major challenge faced by his nation.

The struggle had been long and hard, and many wrongs had been committed during the apartheid years. While some in the new government wanted to seek revenge, Tutu disagreed. "If we are going to move on and build a new kind of world community there must be a way in which we can deal with a sordid past," he claimed. There was a way. In 1995, Tutu assumed the chair of South Africa's Truth and Reconciliation Commission. While the mandate of the committee is to investigate apartheid-era crimes, its goal is to find ways to reconcile whites and blacks into an interracial harmony Tutu has dreamed of for his nation throughout much of his adult life.

Transitional Leadership

One of the most difficult periods in a leader's life is a season of transition. Transitional leaders serve in two similar contexts. First, some are those who assume control during the difficult period following the end of a successful leader's tenure. Others lead through the uncertainty associated with significant change in the culture and/or the particular organization they lead.

When leadership changes within an organization, that time of transition presents unique challenges for the leader assuming control. Solomon modeled the principles of transitional leadership during such a time when he assumed the throne of Israel from his father, David.

Transitional leaders include those who lead their business through a period of downsizing to make their company more competitive in the changing marketplace. They include those who lead schools in the implementation of new curriculum guidelines for new study programs. Some lead cultural institutions to adapt to the changing values of the community they serve. They also include the pastors who transform declining churches into growing churches by guiding the church to identify more closely with the community they are seeking to reach.

Transitional leadership can be challenging at times. These leaders are called on to lead without the benefit of precedent to guide them in their decision making. Often, they are leading a discouraged people who may not be certain the proposed changes will prove beneficial. They may lack the funds and other resources they would prefer to have to accomplish all they would like to accomplish. Even the secure infrastructure of their organization may need to change to become more adaptable to changing conditions.

Those called on to lead an organization through transition always do so in the context of a history. Some face the challenge of leading in the shadow of a great leader. Others face an equally difficult challenge of leading in the shadow of a poor leader. In either case, it is not uncommon for a transitional leader to be called on to lead people who are reluctant to change. People who resist change will also resist leaders who call them to change.

Like all other leaders, transitional leaders need to learn to lead from their strength rather than their weakness. Effective transitional leaders often use their gift of prophecy to identify what needs to be done and call people to do it. They also use their gift of exhortation to motivate and guide followers in the steps required to pursue the new vision. Their gift of empathy (showing mercy) is also important in their dealings with those who are deeply committed to the former leader. Often phlegmatic in temperament, effective transitional leaders often use the Law of Decision Making to quickly build credibility as new leaders of an organization.

The challenge of transitional leadership involves overcoming problems that threaten the leader's effectiveness. Some leaders try to carry on in the leadership style and vision of the former leader, even though that may not be their style. They struggle with the expectations of followers who become frustrated with their new leader's lack of experience and expertise. As a result, they may come to resent the work of the former leader and abandon the heritage of the group they are leading. They may also become frustrated with those reluctant to change even though they may be responsible for that reluctance by having failed to clearly communicate the need to change.

As the relationship between leader and follower disintegrates, they may question the loyalty of followers who were also loyal to their former leader. This is especially true when they attempt to assume authority faster than their followers are ready to yield. It is not uncommon for a transitional leader to become frustrated living with the consequences of the former leader's decisions, especially in the early years of his tenure, until his own decisions begin to bear fruit.

Learning how to assume leadership from others is an important part of any leader's personal leadership kaleidoscope. Few leaders are the first leaders in an organization; therefore, they need to learn to build on the successes of others. Also, few leaders are the last leaders in an organization; therefore, they need to learn to establish conditions for a smooth transition to the next leader. Further, in larger organizations, leadership is shared among many; therefore, they need to learn how to work with one another in a nonthreatening environment.

We learn leadership from the great leaders of previous generations. Transitional leaders need to learn how to discern the personal expectations of their followers based on their previous experiences with other leaders. We also need to know how to rise to become the great leaders of this generation whom others will follow.

Solomon: Assuming His Father's Throne

When he assumed the throne of his father David, Solomon modeled several principles and steps involved in effective transitional leadership. David had been a highly successful king, one by whom future kings would be measured. Also, there was another person contending for the throne during this transitional period. Yet despite the difficulties he faced, Solomon successfully assumed the throne and quickly earned his own reputation distinct from that of his father.

Solomon had those in positions of influence who supported his leadership as the next king. Their support for Solomon was so obvious they were not even invited to the attempted coronation of Adonijah. These men included both Nathan the prophet and Benaiah, one of David's mighty men (1 Kings 1:10).

Solomon also won the approval of the former king, his father David, before being installed into the regal office. "And the king took an oath and said, 'As the LORD lives, who has redeemed my life from every distress, just as I swore to you by the LORD God of Israel, saying, "Assuredly Solomon your son shall be king after me, and he shall sit on the throne in my place," so I certainly will do this day'" (1 Kings 1:29–30).

Following that personal commitment to Solomon, David was true to his word and formally installed his son into the office of king in a public ceremony celebrating that appointment. "And King David said, 'Call to me Zadok the priest, Nathan the prophet, and Benaiah the son of Jehoiada.' So they came before the king. The king also said to them, 'Take with you the servants of your lord, and have Solomon my son ride on my own mule, and take him down to Gihon. There let Zadok the priest and Nathan the prophet anoint him king over Israel; and blow the horn, and say, "Long live King Solomon!"'" (1 Kings 1:32–34).

During that induction service, Solomon was given the symbols of power as he assumed his new office. "So Zadok the priest, Nathan the prophet, Benaiah the son of Jehoiada, the Cherethites, and the Pelethites went down and had Solomon ride on King David's mule, and took him to Gihon. Then Zadok the priest took a horn of oil from the tabernacle and anointed Solomon. And they blew the horn, and all the people said, 'Long live King Solomon!'" (1 Kings 1:38–39). When Solomon rode his father's mule, that act communicated to others he had the right to be king because only the king rode that mule. Also, the act of anointing with oil was a symbol to the people that God had anointed Solomon to be king of Israel.

In an effort to win the support of a former enemy, Solomon gave Adonijah the opportunity to work within certain guidelines so he could find his rightful place within the kingdom. In the process, he also warned him of the consequences of continuing to resist his authority, noting, "If he proves himself a worthy man, not one hair of him shall fall to the earth; but if wickedness is found in him, he shall die" (1 Kings 1:52).

Although he had authority to rule any way he wished, Solomon sought the counsel of his father to learn how to faithfully fulfill the duties of his new office (1 Kings 2:1). David reminded Solomon to honor the commitments and promises that he as king had made to others, including "the sons of Barzillai the Gileadite," who supported him during the rebellion of Absalom (1 Kings 2:7). He also warned Solomon to be alert to potential problems and deal with them in wisdom as king. "Moreover you know also what Joab the son of Zeruiah did to me, and what he did to the two commanders of the armies of Israel . . . And see, you have with you Shimei the son of Gera, a Benjamite from Bahurim, who cursed me with a malicious curse in the day when I went to Mahanaim" (1 Kings 2:5, 8).

Solomon firmly established his new authority by dealing quickly with those who were insubordinate to him or challenged his right to rule. When the first act of rebellion was confirmed, Solomon responded, "Now therefore, as the LORD lives, who has confirmed me and set me on the throne of David my father, and who has established a house for me, as He promised, Adonijah shall be put to death today!" (1 Kings 2:24). When Joab ran to the altar in the temple and refused to leave after being exposed as a rebel, Solomon ordered his men, "Strike him down and bury him, that you may take away from me and from the house of my father the innocent blood which Joab shed" (1 Kings 2:31).

When Shimei rebelled against the conditions that had been established for him, Solomon told him, "You know, as your heart acknowledges, all the wickedness that you did to my father David; therefore the LORD will return your wickedness on your own head" (1 Kings 2:44).

These three decisive acts did much to ensure "the kingdom was established in the hand of Solomon" (1 Kings 2:46).

Solomon also renewed his dedication to the Lord as he began to reign as king. "Now the king went to Gibeon to sacrifice there, for that was the great high place: Solomon offered a thousand burnt offerings on that altar" (1 Kings 3:4). As a burnt offering in the Old Testament was an expression of complete consecration to God, Solomon's sacrifice was an extreme statement of commitment.

Understanding the great challenge that lay before him, Solomon turned to God for wisdom from on high. He prayed, "Now, O LORD my God, You have made Your servant king instead of my father David, but I am a little child; I do not know how to go out or come in. And Your servant is in the midst of Your people whom You have chosen, a great people, too numerous to be numbered or counted. Therefore give to Your servant an understanding heart to judge Your people, that I may discern between good and evil. For who is able to judge this great people of Yours?" (1 Kings 3:7–9).

Guidelines for Making Smooth Transitions

China made history in the fall of 2002 when power was peacefully transferred from one generation to the next in that country's Central Committee. It was the first transfer of power since the death of Mao that did not involve a blood bath, purging the system of those loyal to the former administration. Although most churches and businesses do not experience conflict to the same degree as China in transitions, many transitions of power do not go as well as they could. There are several principles the transitional leader will want to embrace as part of his leadership kaleidoscope to ensure greater success in this area.

First, gather a strong transitional team around you as you prepare for transition. This team should be composed of people of influence who support your leadership within the organization. Not only should they be people with great confidence in you as a leader; you also need to have great confidence in them. Having to wonder if your closest advisors are loyal will hinder you as you work through a transition.

When possible, secure the public support of former leaders who may still have significant influence within the organization. When Woodrow Kroll assumed the leadership of Back to the Bible, he and Warren Wiersbe, Back to the Bible's former radio teacher, shared a broadcast together. The broadcast departed from the usual Bible teaching format, but it served to convince a loyal radio audience that Kroll would be building upon Wiersbe's ministry and that he had the full support of their former Bible teacher in this endeavor.

Next, arrange a formal installation service in which you are publicly installed into your new office. During the service, there should be a presentation made to you of something that adequately symbolizes your new authority and right to lead within the organization. When a pastor begins his ministry in a new church, it is customary during the pastor's installation service for the chairman of the pulpit committee to present the pastor with a Bible on which both his name and that of the church have been printed on the cover.

Once you have been installed into your new office, identify the problem people within the organization and clearly communicate the terms by which they can remain involved should they decide to do so. If they are unwilling to remain under those terms, let them go. If they agree but later prove not to be abiding by those terms, remove them.

As you expect others within the organization to be loyal and committed to your leadership, be loyal and reaffirm your commitment to the vision and commitments of the organization you lead. While changes will no doubt take place during your tenure as leader, your new followers need to know they can trust you to continue pursuing God's vision for their church. When the time comes to make changes, take time to explain how these changes will serve to advance your mutual goals.

The early days of your leadership in a new organization are among the most crucial. People will make decisions about you as a leader that they will assume to be true for years to come. Unfortunately, as a new leader you will be required to make decisions before you have time to get to know your new organization well. That is why it is urgent that you seek wise counsel from others with experience and insight as you begin to lead. A call to a former pastor seeking advice on how to deal with a situation that arises early in one's ministry in a new church has saved many pastors from years of heartache and helped build their credibility quickly among their new followers.

CHAPTER 15

Hezekiah
The Crisis Leader

So shall they fear the name of the LORD from the west, and His glory from the rising of the sun; when the enemy comes in like a flood, the Spirit of the LORD will lift up a standard against him.

ISAIAH 59:19

For years he had tried to warn his government of an impending danger in Europe. He understood the peace achieved at the end of World War I was only temporary, and he was among the first to see the evidence of a gathering storm over the continent once again. But by the time his views were accepted, Hitler was well on his way to controlling much of Europe. When Winston Churchill was finally given the opportunity to lead his nation, he assumed control of a country ill equipped for an inevitable war with a much stronger enemy.

Churchill was not unfamiliar with the problems of war. As a student of history, he had written an authoritative history of the English-speaking people. His interest in his own family heritage had resulted in a rather thorough study of John Churchill, the Duke of Marlborough, and one of Britain's greatest military leaders. During the previous international conflict, he knew personally most of the leaders of that era and had even been involved in solving a minor crisis for the British.

During World War I, Britain's enemies had frustrated their ability to move artillery by placing various kinds of barriers on major transportation routes that could not be overcome by trucks and automobiles. As Churchill had thought about the problem and doodled, he came up with the idea of a vehicle that relied on a moving track rather than tires to move from place to place. His "tank" gave Britain the break they needed to break the stalemate and give them the upper hand in battle.

But this time, everything would be different. Churchill had been collecting intelligence for years, and he knew Germany was a far superior military force. The air force was much larger than the combined Commonwealth force and boasted much more efficient planes. Their scientists had developed rockets that could be launched safely from the continent and cause havoc in major cities throughout the nation. Their submarines were scattered throughout the North Atlantic, meaning Britain could no longer boast of ruling the seas.

As Poland and then France fell, Churchill knew it was only a matter of time before Hitler would vent his anger on the island nation. Before long, German authorities developed Operation Sea Lion and set phase one into motion. The plan called for the German air force to bomb Britain and destroy its air and other defenses prior to a planned invasion by sea.

Knowing he had limited resources, Churchill came up with a plan to convince Germany the British air force was much larger than they had anticipated. He ordered that all planes would fly in battle fifteen minutes before returning to base for refueling. Further, he wanted a third of his planes on the ground as reserves at any point in the battle. When the large German air force crossed the English Channel, only a portion of the British force met them. The initial encounter confirmed German intelligence reports of superior German numbers, but as fresh planes continually joined the battle to meet them, German authorities began wondering about the validity of their own information.

The Battle of Britain continued throughout much of the summer of 1939, and England suffered heavy losses. Churchill spoke to his nation often, confirming reports his people had already heard and preparing them for continued losses. He vowed to fight on to victory when no victory was in sight and convinced his nation to hang in just a little longer. The valiant pilots of the British force continued their ruse until German authorities concluded the battle would not be won, scaled back, and then eventually ended the attack.

While no one really won the battle, the really important issue for England was that Churchill had not lost. There would be more battles during the next five years of war, and more crises to be faced, but Churchill knew if he held on long enough, help would come and victory would eventually belong to him and his allies. Throughout the dark and desperate early years of World War II, Churchill managed the resources at his disposal through the crisis, waiting for the inevitable opportunities to take advantage of enemy errors.

Shortly after the war ended, his views once again fell out of vogue. Still, he felt it was necessary to warn a world that was not listening to a problem they could not see. He was the first to recognize the growing dominance of Russia over the nations of Eastern Europe and coined the phrase "the iron curtain" to describe conditions that would thrust the world into the Cold War. That is what crisis leaders do best—identify a crisis. Then, when given an opportunity to do something about it, they manage as best they can through the crisis to an acceptable solution.

Facing a Leadership Crisis

Crisis leadership rises to the challenge of the darkest hour and brings hope and enthusiasm to followers to pay the price, endure the pain, and pass through the crisis to the victory side. Different leaders work through a crisis in different ways. Elsewhere in this book, the authors use the expression "interventional leader" to describe leaders who tend to be more proactive in facing a crisis. The term "crisis leader" in this book is used to describe those who manage themselves and their organization through a crisis, taking advantage of various opportunities as they arise.

Just as success gives leaders great credibility in the eyes of their followers, so failure tends to create a leadership crisis. But crisis leaders can continue building their personal credibility by managing through a crisis to a better day. Hezekiah modeled the principles of crisis management that leaders need to use to face a crisis and continue leading even in moments of weakness.

Crisis leaders are essential throughout society, especially in contexts where groups are struggling. They include the businessman called to turn a failing business around and restore it so that it becomes a contender in a competitive market. Coaches who assume control of a losing team and lead it to a winning season are also in this group. Pastors of churches with a significant debt who help that church restructure and adopt a workable strategy to become debt-free and those who pastor divided churches but work with various factions within the church to achieve reconciliation and establish spiritual unity within the body also demonstrate this leadership style. Their success in resolving a major ministry crisis often results in establishing a foundation for effective ministry in the community they serve.

The task of crisis leaders is not an easy one. They tend to lead people who feel threatened and organizations at risk in an uncertain context with significant time and resource pressures. They are called on to provide leadership without the benefit of a strong support network to provide them and their followers with the emotional support needed in a crisis. If they fail in this task, they are often blamed for the demise of the organization. In contrast, if they are successful, they are seldom valued once the crisis is past.

Those who lead groups through a significant crisis must do so from their strength. These leaders tend to use their giftedness in prophecy to discern the cause of the crisis and attack that directly. They rely heavily on the Law of Problem Solving to resolve the crisis they face. It is not uncommon for them to be choleric in temperament.

Crisis leaders practice the fine art of brinkmanship. They run the risk of suffering the losses feared most when they encounter the crisis. In the midst of the pressure cooker, it is easy for them to become irritated with people who resist the changes they perceive to be necessary for survival. The lack of resources needed to achieve what needs to be done serves as a constant source of frustration. If the crisis lasts too long or the solution appears too distant, they may become discouraged in their work. That discouragement can quickly become depression, especially if the group rejects them when the crisis is past. The very nature of this leadership style and context suggests a high potential for personal burnout. Leaders who use this leadership style with success may even be tempted to create new crises so they can continue leading the group.

While most leaders work hard to avoid problems, it is inevitable that problems will come. That is why effective leaders incorporate crisis management skills into their personal leadership kaleidoscope. These skills help leaders distinguish between a real and an apparent crisis. When they do encounter a real crisis, there is usually little time available to begin developing crisis management skills prior to addressing the problem. When leaders already have these skills and begin dealing with the problem quickly and effectively, they become a source of comfort and encouragement to followers who would otherwise be overcome with fear.

Just as a crisis may threaten the continued existence of a group, if managed well it can also be the means of bonding leaders and followers into a cohesive team. The leaders who manage a crisis successfully tend to expand their influence significantly among their followers.

Hezekiah: The Crisis Leader

Crisis leadership rises in response to conditions over which the leader has no control. But when crisis leaders face the crisis, they use the skills they have acquired to manage through the crisis to a positive future. Hezekiah's crisis was precipitated by the invasion of Judah by Sennacherib's army. "Now it came to pass in the fourteenth year of King Hezekiah that Sennacherib king of Assyria came up against all the fortified cities of Judah and took them" (Isa. 36:1).

When faced with the crisis, Hezekiah refused to become involved in any rhetoric that might further inflame the situation. Despite the challenge of Sennacherib, the king's officials "held their peace and answered him not a word; for the king's commandment was, 'Do not answer him'" (Isa. 36:21).

Hezekiah investigated conditions and came to a personal realization of the seriousness of the situation he faced. "And so it was, when King Hezekiah heard it, that he tore his clothes, covered himself with sackcloth, and went into the house of the LORD" (Isa. 37:1). There, he turned to God in prayer to seek His assistance in the midst of this crisis. He prayed believing "it may be that the LORD your God will hear the words of the Rabshakeh, whom his master the king of Assyria has sent to reproach the living God, and will rebuke the words which the LORD your God has heard. Therefore lift up your prayer for the remnant that is left" (Isa. 37:4).

The king turned to others, including Isaiah, for insight on how to proceed. "So the servants of King Hezekiah came to Isaiah. And Isaiah said to them, 'Thus you shall say to your master, "Thus says the LORD: 'Do not be afraid of the words which you have heard, with which the servants of the king of Assyria have blasphemed Me. Surely I will send a spirit upon him, and he shall hear a rumor and return to his own land; and I will cause him to fall by the sword in his own land'"'" (Isa. 37:5–7).

Hezekiah implemented a workable plan to address the crisis. In this case, because the battle was to be fought by God, Hezekiah's part was to pray and wait on God. "Then Hezekiah prayed to the LORD" (Isa. 37:15). Then the plan was allowed to take its effect to resolve the crisis. "Then the angel of the LORD went out, and killed in the camp of the Assyrians one hundred and eighty-five thousand; and when people arose early in the morning, there were the corpses—all dead" (Isa. 37:36).

Hezekiah's experience with Sennacherib helped prepare him for a greater crisis he was about to face. "In those days Hezekiah was sick and near death. And Isaiah the prophet, the son of Amoz, went to him and said to him, 'Thus says the Lord: "Set your house in order, for you shall die and not live" ' " (Isa. 38:1). Unfortunately, when that crisis was averted through the healing touch of the Lord, Hezekiah's enthusiasm clouded his judgment, resulting in his making unwise decisions that created an even greater crisis for Israel generations later.

When Babylonian officials visited the king to congratulate him on his recovery, "Hezekiah was pleased with them, and showed them the house of his treasures—the silver and gold, the spices and precious ointment, and all his armory—all that was found among his treasures. There was nothing in his house or in all his dominion that Hezekiah did not show them" (Isa. 39:2). Because of that action, God through Isaiah warned the king, "Behold, the days are coming when all that is in your house, and what your fathers have accumulated until this day, shall be carried to Babylon; nothing shall be left" (Isa. 39:6).

Leading through a Crisis

The leader who gets all the credit when problems are resolved is also blamed when they are not. Even when the leader has done all he could to avoid a problem, disgruntled followers will often make him their easy target. The longer the problem continues, the larger it begins looking to others, and before long, even those loyal to their leader will struggle not to join in the chorus of criticism. Long-term leaders need to incorporate basic crisis management skills into their leadership kaleidoscope to survive the crises that will inevitably come their way.

One of the first challenges facing a leader in a crisis is to identify the source of the crisis and those factors that contribute to it. While there is often an obvious source to the present manifestation of a crisis, a wise leader will look beyond the rebel leader or problematic situation to identify ongoing concerns that contribute to the crisis environment. Just as there are many potential answers for a problem, so there are often many contributing factors that give birth to problems.

Christian leaders need to seek wisdom from God to gain needed insight into the appropriate course of action. This involves praying for wisdom in those areas where you lack understanding. James wrote, "If any of you lacks wisdom, let him ask of God, who gives to all liberally and without reproach, and it will be given to him" (James 1:5). While prayer is important, there are other things we can and should do to acquire wisdom. "The testimony of the LORD is sure, making wise the simple" (Ps. 19:7). Therefore, we should study the Scriptures regularly and receive wisdom as a by-product of that spiritual discipline.

Also, we can consult others to gain their insight into the nature of the problem and the best means to resolve it. "Listen to counsel and receive instruction, that you may be wise in your latter days. There are many plans in a man's heart, nevertheless the LORD's counsel—that will stand" (Prov. 19:20–21).

After a thorough investigation of the situation, it is the responsibility of the leader to choose the most appropriate course of action to resolve the crisis. When that decision has been made, implement the chosen strategy and allow it to take effect. Sometimes the most difficult part of the process is just letting the solution take effect in an appropriate time when others are looking for immediate gratification.

Be careful in this process not to make unwise decisions or to take careless actions when the crisis is past that might lead to a greater crisis in the future. Crisis management involves leading groups through and out of difficult situations, not into them.

CHAPTER 16

Ezra

The Spiritual Leader

When the righteous are in authority, the people rejoice; but
when a wicked man rules, the people groan.

PROVERBS 29:2

W hen the young evangelist arrived at the Christian conference
ground, he had already established a reputation among evangelical churches where he had preached as an effective evangelist, especially good at communicating with youth. But within himself, young
Billy Graham knew he was struggling in his relationship with God, a
struggle that was bound to impact the direction of his future ministry.

Forest Home was a Christian retreat in the San Bernardino
Mountains just outside Los Angeles. Graham knew he was scheduled
to return to the area for a citywide crusade, but accepted the invitation
to speak at the annual briefing for Christian colleges held at the camp-
ground. Because he had high regard for Henrietta Mears, the director
of Christian Education at First Presbyterian Church in Hollywood,
California, and founder of the camp, he discussed his struggle several
times with the godly lady. Mears talked with him about his commitment to Christ. At the same time, J. Edwin Orr, another speaker at the

171

camp, challenged Graham to consider the possibility that America was on the verge of a national revival.

While these two were giving him good advice, Graham's personal faith crisis was largely due to conversations he was having with yet another speaker at the conference. Long-time friend and fellow evangelist Charles Templeton had changed his theology during his Ph.D. studies at Princeton University. He had adopted the "new" theology of German theologian Karl Barth and questioned the inspiration and authority of the Scriptures. Although his new views were not yet publicly known in the Christian community, out of his personal friendship with Graham, Templeton was urging his friend to abandon his fundamentalist attitude toward the Scriptures.

Graham was not a trained theologian like his friends Orr and Templeton. Nor had he the benefit of long ministry experience like the three people trying to influence him in his decision. Ultimately he understood the decision had to be his to make. And it was a decision he did make before leaving the camp.

One night, Graham walked under the full moon and dropped to his knees. He opened his Bible and looked up to God. "Lord, there are many things in this Book I don't understand," he confessed. "I can't answer the philosophical and psychological questions people are raising." Then after a pause, he continued. "Father, I'm going to accept this as Your Word by faith. If You said it, that's good enough for me."

When Graham rose from his knees, he was a changed man. His renewed confidence in the Scriptures was reflected in a new phrase added to his vocabulary that soon peppered his sermons, "The Bible says." As far as he was concerned, he did not have to understand it or respond to those who would deny it. He would simply preach the Bible as it was to people as they were and see what God would do.

As the upcoming "Christ for Greater Los Angeles" crusade approached, Graham believed God would honor his renewed commitment and bless the meetings. He increased the crusade budget significantly and insisted crusade organizers double the size of the tent they had planned to use. Despite some criticism and opposition, organizers went ahead with the changes. As the crusade began, it quickly became apparent God was at work. By the time it finally ended seventy-two nights later, thousands professed faith in Christ, including several individuals with celebrity status. Newspapers across America reported revival had come to Los Angeles. And the young evangelist from North Carolina had become the world's most respected spiritual leader, a distinction he would continue to hold for more than half a century.

Graham's personal celebrity growing out of the Los Angeles crusade, and subsequent highly successful crusades throughout America and Europe, opened doors the young evangelist would never have thought possible. At the invitation of heads of state around the world, he has served monarchs, presidents, and prime ministers as their spiritual counselor. The young evangelist who decided to simply preach the gospel and assume the Word of God would produce results, has personally communicated the gospel in his crusades and through various media to more people than anyone else in history.

Spiritual Leadership

In his book *Spiritual Leadership,* J. Oswald Sanders states, "A God-appointed spiritual leader is perfectly safe when, and only when, he walks humbly with his God, for God is very jealous of the authority of those who He has endorsed." Leading people into a deeper relationship with and commitment to God requires a special kind of leader. Ezra is described in Scripture as just such a leader. He modeled the principles of spiritual leadership in his significant ministry among the remnant in Jerusalem.

Spiritual leaders have been largely neglected in American business in recent decades. That practice is beginning to change with the rise of corporate chaplains serving as spiritual counselors and evangelists within the workplace. In education, the chancellors and deans of students in Bible colleges and Christian universities are charged with encouraging spiritual growth among the faculty and student body. Spiritual leaders are most apparent within the Christian community. They include the revivalists raised up by God to draw Christians into a deeper relationship with God, often in an itinerant revival or Bible conference ministry. They also include pastors who faithfully care for the spiritual needs of the flocks over which the Holy Spirit has given them oversight. They lead their people to develop new spiritual disciplines that result in long-term spiritual growth.

Spiritual leaders face unique problems as they attempt to exert their influence. The spirit of this age tends to cause many people, even many Christians, to minimize the importance of the inner life. Much deeper-life literature is theoretical and difficult to apply by the average Christian. The task of spiritual leaders is to show Christians how to apply these principles where they live. When they are applied, they will eventually produce spiritual growth. Unfortunately, we live in a generation conditioned to expect instant gratification that is often unwilling to wait, even for good things. Also, there is some confusion among evangelical Christians about the nature of spirituality. This variance of opinion may hinder growth in the lives of those exposed to various views.

The pressures and responsibilities of ministry make it easy for spiritual leaders to be sidetracked and fail to nurture their own walk with God. This danger grows as they become more successful in ministry. Prosperity tends to discourage interest in spiritual things. The cares of this world tend to choke out spiritual truth before it takes root in lives. Also, there are forces at work in our world committed to discouraging spiritual growth. Spiritual leaders are constantly engaged in spiritual warfare.

Spiritual leaders often use their gift of teaching to communicate biblical truth to their followers. Their goal is to lead them into a deeper understanding of who God is. They also use their gift of exhortation to guide followers into a closer walk with God. They use the Law of Dreams when they describe their vision of a deeper spiritual life to their followers. They also use the Law of Accountability as they organize their followers into accountability relationships that promote ongoing spiritual growth. Ironically, spiritual leaders are often melancholy in temperament. Many great men and women of God have not only experienced times of deeper communion with God, but also prolonged periods of depression.

Spiritual leadership has several unique dangers inherent to this leadership paradigm. People often fall at their strongest point. Therefore, those with a great passion for God may be tempted to wander after other passions that will hinder their relationship with God. Also, those who experience times of intense communion with God often have desert experiences in which they distance themselves from Him. Further, those who live by faith may struggle in making long-term plans and commitments because they are unsure of their future.

Leaders who manifest the fruits of spirituality in their lives are often neglected in the prayers of others. This problem is compounded because those who would follow Christ as spiritual leaders should expect to encounter the same kind of resistance Christ experienced from the enemies of the gospel. They are subject to spiritual attack from the enemy of our souls and often find themselves in the heat of spiritual warfare. They are a particular challenge to carnal Christians. If carnal Christians choose not to repent and follow their leadership, they will often become their enemy.

One of the most important lessons all leaders need to incorporate into their personal leadership kaleidoscope is how to walk with God. The responsibilities of leadership are greater than any person can bear without the assistance of God. Because followers rarely hold their leaders accountable to the degree they ought, leaders need to be aware of their own accountability to God. Walking humbly with God is a prerequisite for being elevated to a higher level of leadership. It also gives leaders a sense of direction. Spiritual leaders need to walk with God before they can lead others into a deeper experience with God.

Ezra: The Spiritual Leader

In a culture in which many Jews found comfort in the Babylonian lifestyle they had adopted, Ezra believed there were greater values by which life should be governed. He prepared himself for ministry before ministry opportunities became apparent. Then he learned how to work with those in authority to get what he needed for effective spiritual ministry. "This Ezra came up from Babylon; and he was a skilled scribe in the Law of Moses, which the LORD God of Israel had given. The king granted him all his request, according to the hand of the LORD his God upon him" (Ezra 7:6). Although Ezra had studied hard and found favor with the king, he understood the importance of securing the blessing of God upon his life. "The good hand of his God [was] upon him" (Ezra 7:9).

Ezra made walking with God and teaching biblical principles to others the priority of his life. "For Ezra had prepared his heart to seek the Law of the LORD, and to do it, and to teach statutes and ordinances in Israel" (Ezra 7:10). This focus enabled him to recognize the role of God in providing all he needed, even when that provision appeared to come from others. In response to resources made available to Ezra by the king, he responded in prayer, saying, "Blessed be the LORD God of our fathers, who has put such a thing as this in the king's heart, to beautify the house of the LORD which is in Jerusalem, and has extended mercy to me before the king and his counselors, and before all the king's mighty princes" (Ezra 7:27–28).

This teaching scribe recognized the importance of team ministry and worked with others to accomplish the work of God. His listing of "the heads of their father's houses" of those who journeyed from Babylon to Jerusalem with him demonstrated his understanding of working with those in authority to gain a maximum impact in his ministry (Ezra 8:1). But he also recognized that his ministry authority came primarily from another source.

Ezra practiced the discipline of fasting and prayer as a means of humbling himself before God when faced with challenges that appeared beyond him and his available resources. "Then I proclaimed a fast there at the river of Ahava, that we might humble ourselves before our God, to seek from Him the right way for us and our little ones and all our possessions" (Ezra 8:21). As a spiritual leader, Ezra knew God was a prayer-hearing and prayer-answering God. "So we fasted and entreated our God for this, and He answered our prayer" (Ezra 8:23).

In addition to fasting, Ezra also practiced "identificational repentance" in his personal prayer life, confessing the sins of Israel's leaders to God. "At the evening sacrifice I arose from my fasting; and having torn my garment and my robe, I fell on my knees and spread out my hands to the LORD my God. And I said: 'O my God, I am too ashamed and humiliated to lift up my face to You, my God; for our iniquities have risen higher than our heads, and our guilt has grown up to the heavens'" (Ezra 9:5–6).

When Israel's leaders later became concerned about their sin, Ezra led them to repent of their sin and make adjustments in their life to bring their personal lifestyle into line with the standards revealed in Scripture.

> Now while Ezra was praying, and while he was con-
> fessing, weeping, and bowing down before the house of
> God, a very large assembly of men, women, and children
> gathered to him from Israel; for the people wept very bit-
> terly. And Shechaniah the son of Jehiel, one of the sons
> of Elam, spoke up and said to Ezra, "We have trespassed
> against our God, and have taken pagan wives from the
> peoples of the land; yet now there is hope in Israel in
> spite of this. Now therefore, let us make a covenant with
> our God to put away all these wives and those who have
> been born to them, according to the advice of my master
> and of those who tremble at the commandment of our

God; and let it be done according to the law. Arise, for
this matter is your responsibility. We also are with you.
Be of good courage, and do it" (Ezra 10:1–4).

Further insight into Ezra's ministry in Jerusalem is recorded in
Nehemiah's record. He and others read and explained the Law of God
to bring the people to repentance. "They read distinctly from the book,
in the Law of God; and they gave the sense, and helped them to understand the reading" (Neh. 8:8). Then they helped the people apply what
they learned in practical ways. As the people came to understand the
necessity for observing the various feasts prescribed in the Jewish cal-
endar, Ezra and the other priests and Levites led the people in the
observance of one of those feasts (Neh. 8:18).

Ezra's purpose was to lead the people to make personal commitments to God so they could continually live by the principles of
Scripture as they understood them. "And because of all this, we make a
sure covenant and write it; our leaders, our Levites, and our priests seal
it" (Neh. 9:38). As the leaders of Israel signed the covenant, they committed themselves and their families to live under the authority of the
Word of God.

Steps to Experiencing God

In recent years, several evangelical leaders have written books calling Christians back to a more intimate relationship with God. One such
book that has had a significant impact on many lives is *Experiencing
God*[1] by Henry Blackaby. In that book, Blackaby outlines several steps
involved in experiencing God through knowing and doing His will.
These steps are illustrated in the lives of various biblical characters
throughout Scripture and serve as a guide for those looking for a deeper
relationship with Christ—a worthy goal for those who would be spiritual leaders.

Blackaby's first step involves recognizing God is always at work around you. Israel may have felt abandoned as slaves in Egypt, but "God heard their groaning, and God remembered His covenant with Abraham, with Isaac, and with Jacob" (Exod. 2:24). As Israelite slaves continued crying out to God, perhaps with little hope of relief, God was already taking steps to resolve the problem.

Throughout the Scripture, there are indications that God pursues a continuing love relationship with you that is real and personal. Long after their initial meeting at the burning bush, "the LORD said to Moses, 'Come up to Me on the mountain and be there; and I will give you tablets of stone, and the law and commandments which I have written, that you may teach them'" (Exod. 24:12).

Blackaby reminds his readers that God speaks by the Holy Spirit through the Bible, prayer, circumstances, and the church to reveal Himself, His purposes, and His ways. "Surely the Lord GOD does nothing, unless He reveals His secret to His servants the prophets" (Amos 3:7). It is God's desire to invite you to become involved with Him in His work. At the burning bush, God explained to Moses, "So I have come down to deliver them out of the hand of the Egyptians, and to bring them up from that land to a good and large land, to a land flowing with milk and honey" (Exod. 3:8). Then He added, "Come now, therefore, and I will send you to Pharaoh that you may bring My people, the children of Israel, out of Egypt" (Exod. 3:10).

God's invitation for you to work with Him always results in a crisis of belief that requires both faith and active obedience. "By faith Moses, when he became of age, refused to be called the son of Pharaoh's daughter, choosing rather to suffer affliction with the people of God than to enjoy the passing pleasures of sin, esteeming the reproach of Christ greater riches than the treasures in Egypt; for he looked to the reward" (Heb. 11:24–26).

Joining God in what He is doing involves making major adjustments in your life. "Now the LORD said to Moses in Midian, 'Go, return to Egypt; for all the men who sought your life are dead.' Then Moses took his wife and his sons and set them on a donkey, and he returned to the land of Egypt. And Moses took the rod of God in his hand" (Exod. 4:19–20).

You come to know God by experience as you obey Him and He accomplishes His work through you. That was certainly Israel's experience. "Thus Israel saw the great work which the LORD had done in Egypt; so the people feared the LORD, and believed the LORD and His servant Moses" (Exod. 14:31).

CHAPTER 17

Nehemiah

The Managerial Leader

The locusts have no king, yet they all advance in ranks.

PROVERBS 30:27

While he may not look like everybody's idea of a great leader, nineteen-year-old Bill Gates began a company with a friend that has grown to become a giant in its field. In the process, his estimated net worth has risen to over forty billion dollars. It has been claimed that Microsoft has produced more millionaires among its employees than any other company in history.

Gates's interest in computers began when his parents transferred him from a local public school to the private Lakeside School in Seattle, Washington, hoping his grades would improve. That was his first exposure to computers, and before long, he had written a program so he could play tic-tac-toe with it. Always something of a math whiz, Gates headed to Harvard after graduation, intending to become a math professor. While there, he realized others were better in math than he. He began pursuing a different career path when friend Paul Allen showed him the January 1975 issue of *Popular Electronics* that featured a new idea—a computer that could fit on a desk. When they spotted a problem in the program, they called the company and sold them a better program, one they had not yet developed. The program worked, and the pair got their start as computer programmers.

Microsoft got its big break when IBM asked the pair to design an operating system for their new personal computers. They bought some software from another Seattle company and adapted it to IBM's needs. The end result, MS-DOS, quickly became the industry standard. But rather than being satisfied with the major success of a single program, the company has continued to expand and develop software to satisfy needs as they arose in the emerging personal computer and Internet market.

Those close to Gates credit much of his success to his effective management of Microsoft. He has been described as fiercely competitive, even ruthless when it comes to dealing with the competition. His brilliant mind soaks up information like a sponge, and his conversations tend to bounce all over the place as he draws analogies to explain his ideas from all over the place. But he also understands his limits. When faced with a topic he has not mastered, he tends to deluge people with questions so he can learn.

Microsoft insiders claim Gates is also fixated with mistakes. When failures do happen, he conducts a thorough "autopsy" to ensure they are never repeated. The company's ability to avoid making the same mistake twice has been identified as one of the biggest factors in its incredible success.

The success of Microsoft is said to have demonstrated to the world that nerds can be cool. But Bill Gates has become more than a nerd. In a *People* magazine interview, Gates claimed, "A nerd couldn't be a good manager and good leader of a company."[1] That is what he has become—a good manager and a good leader. In the work in which he is engaged, there really isn't much difference between the two.

Administration and Leadership

One of the current debates in the field of leadership education centers on the difference between management and leadership. Historically, many schools have thought they were training leaders but produced only managers. This has been in part due to a heavy curriculum emphasis on principles of administration and a tendency to minimize the validity of other leadership styles. The products of that approach tend to maintain or build strong organizations, but fail to make the major leaps forward they might have, had they been led by strong leaders rather than effective managers.

While there is a clear distinction between management and leadership, there are some leaders who might be described as managerial leaders. One such leader, Olan Hendrix, suggests, "It appears to me that management in Christian circles is basically the stewardship of talents of the persons entrusted to our care." Beyond that, leadership motivates followers to accomplish a task together that none could accomplish alone. Nehemiah modeled the principles of managerial leadership necessary for effective project management when he led the remnant to rebuild the walls of Jerusalem in only fifty-two days.

Managerial leadership is the traditional approach to management widely used in both large and small businesses throughout America. Effective businessmen are often enlisted by cultural organizations and major charities to use their skills in planning, organizing, leading, and controlling various efforts to educate students, entertain patrons, and raise financial resources. Church leaders who have been trained in management principles tend to use this approach to organize, implement, and evaluate church stewardship and growth campaigns, missions and other conferences, and ongoing ministries such as Sunday school and small group ministry.

The tasks of managerial leaders are often challenging. Because of their abilities, they may be called in to salvage poorly organized projects just as things begin falling apart. In the process, other more talented members of the organization who lack their managerial abilities may resent their authority. It is not uncommon for creative people within the organization to resent the systems they establish. In some contexts, they may find it difficult to work in environments where established policies tend to hinder their progress as they attempt to communicate to panicky members of the organization how their plans will address the current and likely future problem. They are particularly frustrated when a project approaches completion before new projects are apparent. Sometimes, they may take on a project beyond their ability and not realize it until they are well into the project.

Managerial leaders tend to be well equipped to face these challenges. They lead best when they lead through their gift of administration. They often use the Law of Rewards to recognize the work of their staff. They also rely on the Law of Accountability to ensure work done is accomplished according to mutually agreed upon standards. Managerial leaders are often choleric in temperament.

Skilled managerial leaders may at times appear to be well organized even when they really are not. In addressing the broad picture, they often overlook important smaller details. In their commitment to develop plans, they may appear insensitive to people. This sometimes results in their being accused of being cold, pushy, or using people to build a personal empire. Sometimes, their success in "getting the job done" may be used to justify rather than deal with personal character deficiencies. In a desperate situation, they may resort to manipulating others to ensure the project is completed on time, even using delegation as an excuse for personal laziness.

Because leadership is concerned with leading people to accomplish great projects, all leaders need to learn and incorporate the principles of project management into their personal leadership kaleidoscope. Larger projects tend to overwhelm many people, but when managerial leaders break the project down into achievable tasks, their followers will be motivated rather than discouraged. Because these projects require larger work teams dependent on others to accomplish their work on time, managerial leaders become key to scheduling projects to ensure work is done in an orderly manner.

Problems cry out for answers. Leaders need to know how to develop and implement significant projects that will answer the big problems. They also need to learn how best to manage limited resources to ensure a maximum return on the investment of time, skills, money, and human resources committed to a particular project. No matter how well a project is planned, periodic adjustments need to be made as the project progresses. Leaders need to be able to identify what can be adjusted and how to make those adjustments to ensure the project is completed with excellence.

Nehemiah: The Managerial Leader

The story of Nehemiah and his rebuilding of the walls of Jerusalem has become a classic model in Christian literature dealing with managerial leadership. Several books have been written dealing exclusively with the biblical text from an administrative perspective. While few leaders today may face the challenge of building a city wall, leaders today in the management of the various projects they undertake may successfully apply the principles of managerial leadership illustrated in Nehemiah's example in the management of that project.

The rebuilding of Jerusalem's walls began when Nehemiah first heard about conditions in the city. In a first-hand report from a recent visitor to the city, he learned the walls had fallen and the gates of Jerusalem were charred ruins. He understood such conditions were an embarrassment to any city and demonstrated that city's inability to defend itself. "So it was, when I heard these words, that I sat down and wept, and mourned for many days; I was fasting and praying before the God of heaven" (Neh. 1:4). When he understood the situation, he responded by making it a matter of focused prayer.

Later, Nehemiah seized the moment when a window of opportunity was open to him that held the potential of dealing with the need. In a conference with the king, Nehemiah records, "Then the king said to me, 'What do you request?' So I prayed to the God of heaven. And I said to the king, 'If it pleases the king, and if your servant has found favor in your sight, I ask that you send me to Judah, to the city of my fathers' tombs, that I may rebuild it'" (Neh. 2:4–5). His bold request was granted, and he was soon on his way to Jerusalem with a mission.

When he arrived, Nehemiah researched conditions on site for himself to gain a better understanding of what needed to be done before announcing his intentions and launching the project. "Then I arose in the night, I and a few men with me; I told no one what my God had put in my heart to do at Jerusalem; nor was there any animal with me, except the one on which I rode" (Neh. 2:12).

The next day, Nehemiah gathered others together and began sharing his dream of rebuilding the walls of Jerusalem. First, he identified the problem. "You see the distress that we are in, how Jerusalem lies waste, and its gates are burned with fire" (Neh. 2:17). Then he proposed a specific project that would address that problem. "Come and let us build the wall of Jerusalem," he urged, "that we may no longer be a reproach" (Neh. 2:17). Then he encouraged the people by identifying resources already available to accomplish the project. "And I told them of the hand of my God which had been good upon me, and also of the king's words that he had spoken to me" (Neh. 2:18). He then enlisted their support and secured a commitment to work on the project from the available work team. "So they said, 'Let us rise up and build.' Then they set their hearts to this good work" (Neh. 2:18).

Nehemiah must have known that undertaking a project like this would draw criticism from some quarters. If so, he was not to be disappointed. "But when Sanballat the Horonite, Tobiah the Ammonite official, and Geshem the Arab heard of it, they laughed at us and despised us, and said, 'What is this thing that you are doing? Will you rebel against the king?' So I answered them, and said to them, 'The God of heaven Himself will prosper us; therefore we His servants will arise and build, but you have no heritage or right or memorial in Jerusalem' " (Neh. 2:19–20).

As they undertook the project, Nehemiah divided it into manageable tasks and assigned specific responsibilities to those capable of accomplishing those tasks (Neh. 3:1–32). Then he monitored progress on the project, making adjustments as necessary. Some adjustments needed to be made because of the threats of those opposing the project. "And all of them conspired together to come and attack Jerusalem and create confusion. Nevertheless we made our prayer to God, and because of them we set a watch against them day and night" (Neh. 4:8–9).

Other adjustments were made because of the attitudes of some people involved in the project. "After serious thought, I rebuked the nobles and rulers, and said to them, 'Each of you is exacting usury from his brother.' So I called a great assembly against them. . . . So they said, 'We will restore it, and will require nothing from them; we will do as you say.' Then I called the priests, and required an oath from them that they would do according to this promise" (Neh. 5:7, 12).

Nehemiah stuck to the task until it was completed, not allowing himself to be distracted from the work. "So the wall was finished on the twenty-fifth day of Elul, in fifty-two days" (Neh. 6:15). He then turned the finished project over to responsible leaders in a public celebration. "Then it was, when the wall was built and I had hung the doors, when the gatekeepers, the singers, and the Levites had been appointed, that I gave the charge of Jerusalem to my brother Hanani, and Hananiah the leader of the citadel, for he was a faithful man and feared God more than many. And I said to them, 'Do not let the gates of Jerusalem be opened until the sun is hot; and while they stand guard, let them shut and bar the doors; and appoint guards from among the inhabitants of Jerusalem, one at his watch station and another in front of his own house' " (Neh. 7:1–3).

The Functions of Management

The best ideas usually need to be managed well before they ever become reality. That is one reason why leaders need to study and incorporate the basic functions and activities of management into their personal leadership kaleidoscope. That may appear a daunting challenge to some, but the essential principles of project management may be summarized in four basic functions. Each of these functions involves several activities.

The first function of management is planning. Planning is the work done to predetermine a course of action. This involves seven different activities. Estimating the future is the work done to anticipate the likely future facing your organization. Establishing objectives is the work done to determine organizational goals or targets. Developing policies is the work of formulating standing answers to recurring questions. Programming involves prioritizing a sequence of activities for accomplishing goals and objectives. When you establish procedures, you standardize the methods of work within your organization. Scheduling is the work of putting a time factor into the program. Budgeting is the wise stewardship of financial and other resources to ensure the task is accomplished.

Organizing, the second function of management, is the grouping of people and work so the work can be accomplished with excellence. This function involves three activities. Developing the organizational structure involves grouping and relating the work of people involved in the product. Delegating is the assigning of work to others and transferring the authority they need to get things done. Establishing interpersonal human relationships involves helping people better relate to one another and overcome conflict.

The third function of management is leading. In this context, leading is influencing people to pursue and accomplish the goals of the group. This tends to involve five activities. Decision making is the process of choosing the best answer to resolve a problem.

Communicating is the work of informing others of expectations and accomplishments. Motivating is the work of getting people to want to accomplish the work assigned. Selecting people is the work of finding and enlisting people to accomplish the assigned task. Developing people is the work of adequately training and equipping people for the work assigned.

The final function of management is controlling. This is the work done to ensure results that conform to the plan and involves four activities. Establishing performance standards involves identifying the minimum quality of the work to be done. Performance measuring involves inspecting work to ensure it is being accomplished. Performance evaluating involves valuing the work done to ensure it meets the specifications established by the standard. Performance correcting involves taking steps to correct mistakes and ensure the work is completed correctly.

CHAPTER 18

Daniel

The Subordinate Leader

Then this Daniel distinguished himself above the governors and satraps, because an excellent spirit was in him; and the king gave thought to setting him over the whole realm.

DANIEL 6:3

While it is customary for the wife of the president to take up a noble cause and lobby for it during her husband's term in office, Eleanor Roosevelt's humanitarian efforts on behalf of children, oppressed people, and the poor and hopeless in society went far beyond what one might expect from a woman in her position. But beyond her very public efforts on the part of the underprivileged, her personal support of husband and four-term U.S. President Franklin D. Roosevelt enabled him to pursue his political ambitions in the face of significant barriers.

Eleanor was born into a wealthy New York family who boasted a signer of the Declaration of Independence. Her uncle Teddy was known better to the world as President Theodore Roosevelt. Despite the advantages associated with her birth, she grew up timid with feelings of inadequacy and insecurity. Eleanor was only eight when her mother died. Her father turned to alcohol and died two years later. She grew up in her grandmother's home, educated by private tutors with few friends of her own. At age fifteen, she began her formal education at Allenswood School in England.

Shortly after returning to America three years later, she married a distant cousin who had political ambitions. Perhaps because of the insecurities of her own childhood, Eleanor spent much time in activity on behalf of others. She had six children, one of whom died in infancy. When her husband's promising political career appeared doomed by the effects of polio, she encouraged him to pursue his dreams. Because of her influence, he did go on, first to become governor of New York and then president of the United States.

As America's first lady during the Great Depression, she was an energetic and outspoken representative of the needs of people. She traveled widely, held news conferences, met and corresponded with hundreds of men and women, and communicated the views of the nation to her husband. She had no political authority of her own, but she saw many of her ideas incorporated into the New Deal's social welfare programs.

The nation survived that depression and her husband was still president when the world was thrust into World War II. During that time, Eleanor expanded her activities to the international stage, eventually working with the United Nations in the founding of UNICEF and the passage of the Universal Declaration of Human Rights. She claimed, "You get more joy out of giving joy to others and should put a good deal of thought into the happiness you are able to give."[1] In using her influence for others, she overcame the insecurities of her childhood to influence the most influential world leader of the time and to establish policies that would forever change life in America and throughout the world.

THE GOOD BOOK ON LEADERSHIP

The Challenge of Middle Management

One of the most challenging leadership positions in any organization is that of middle management. Middle managers find themselves both accountable to other leaders and responsible to lead others below them. Some of the world's most effective leaders have served in relative obscurity. They never held the highest office within their organization, yet they were essential to that organization's success. This is the challenge of middle management. Daniel modeled how middle managers can effectively lead through influencing their superiors.

Subordinate leaders are the middle managers in business who implement company policies and help keep the business healthy. Sometimes they serve as executive assistants to college presidents and deans who accept responsibility for implementing the decisions of their superiors. In larger churches, they include members of the pastoral staff who assist the senior pastor in fulfilling God's vision for their church by leading a staff of lay volunteers to accomplish goals in various specific areas of ministry.

Some have described the subordinate leader serving in middle management as "everybody's punching bag." People who resent the subordinate's leader sometimes vent their frustration on the subordinate leader. On the other side of the equation, leaders who are disappointed with the performance of the organization sometimes vent their frustrations on their subordinate leaders. They tend to be the most likely to be blamed for failure and the least likely to be credited for success in any endeavor.

The nature of this position within any organization creates potential problems for those who serve in this capacity. Sometimes, subordinate leaders are called upon to support and implement decisions that they were not involved in making. When those in senior management are insecure in their position, it is not uncommon for subordinate leaders to become the object of jealousy. Even when they have a healthy relationship with their superiors, subordinate leaders may find themselves in rival relationships with other subordinate leaders within the organization.

Subordinate leaders tend to use their gift of ministry to serve others. In doing so, they tend to expand their sphere of influence with no thought of building a personal empire. When they lead, they use the Law of Communication to ensure that their followers understand what their leader expects. They also use the Law of Accountability to ensure that followers accomplish the goals of the leader. Often, subordinate leaders tend to be phlegmatic in temperament.

Middle management may be one of the most dangerous places to be in any organization. Small differences between subordinate leaders and their superiors are always a potential source of conflict. When that relationship sours, subordinate leaders face various unique temptations. Some are tempted to undermine the authority of their leader in hopes of replacing him or her. Others consider leaving the organization to build their own organization with loyal followers. Those who feel that way often accept credit for decisions made by their superiors that work and try to pass off blame for failed ideas to their superiors or those whom they lead.

In contrast, those who have strong company loyalty face a different set of temptations. Some become so blindly loyal to their leader that they fail to confront their superiors when they are wrong. Others, deeply committed to their organization, tend to undermine the authority of other subordinate leaders in their efforts to rise to a higher place of influence within the organization.

Charlie Brown put things in focus when he said, "I love humanity. It is people I can't stand."[2] There are moments in the life of all leaders when they are convinced life would be a whole lot better if they did not have to deal with people. But learning how to work as part of the leadership team is a skill all leaders need to incorporate into their personal leadership kaleidoscope. Team leadership uses the gifts and expertise of many to meet challenges no one person could handle well. It provides leaders with the emotional and psychological support of other leaders they need. It often results in better decision making and problem solving as leaders share insights together. It helps ensure the survival of everyone on the leadership team as they share the burden of leading in situations likely to overwhelm any individual member of the team. Also, team leadership allows leaders to grow and mature in leadership as they serve under and with the assistance of more mature leaders.

Daniel: The Subordinate Leader

Daniel knew much about the dangers and potential that subordinate leaders face. As one of Judah's princes, he would have been trained to lead from early childhood. But before he came of age, he was among the first captives taken to a foreign land. Although it seemed his destiny crumbled as the Babylonian captivity began, he went on to rise to positions of significant political authority in the dynasties of two of history's greatest empires. The lessons of his life illustrate the principles of subordinate leadership.

Daniel's potential for leadership was recognized early in his life by Babylonian authorities. As a result, he was among those chosen as a candidate for leadership training. "Then the king instructed Ashpenaz, the master of his eunuchs, to bring some of the children of Israel and some of the king's descendants and some of the nobles, young men in whom there was no blemish, but good-looking, gifted in all wisdom, possessing knowledge and quick to understand, who had ability to serve in the king's palace, and whom they might teach the language and literature of the Chaldeans" (Dan. 1:3–4).

Conditions in Babylon were significantly different from those in Daniel's native Judah. While some of those differences were matters of cultural distinction, others challenged the values he had been taught in his younger years. Others in his situation decided compromises were necessary for survival in this new world, "but Daniel purposed in his heart that he would not defile himself with the portion of the king's delicacies, nor with the wine which he drank; therefore he requested of the chief of the eunuchs that he might not defile himself" (Dan. 1:8). He made a conscious decision not to compromise his character and values as he prepared for leadership.

Daniel learned to appeal to those in authority over him to effect desirable changes. When faced with this initial challenge in Babylon, he and three companions appealed to the chief steward responsible for their care. When they understood his reluctance to make changes to diet, they suggested, "Please test your servants for ten days, and let them give us vegetables to eat and water to drink. Then let our appearance be examined before you, and the appearance of the young men who eat the portion of the king's delicacies; and as you see fit, so deal with your servants" (Dan. 1:12–13). When approached with this reasonable proposal, the authorities "consented with them in this matter, and tested them ten days" (Dan. 1:14). That interim proposal became the basis of a later decision concerning their diet throughout their training period.

Throughout that training period, Daniel and his companions prepared well to become the best-qualified persons they could be for the challenges that they would later face. "As for these four young men, God gave them knowledge and skill in all literature and wisdom; and Daniel had understanding in all visions and dreams" (Dan. 1:17). "And in all matters of wisdom and understanding about which the king examined them, he found them ten times better than all the magicians and astrologers who were in all his realm" (Dan. 1:20).

As a junior member of the team responsible for advising the Babylonian king, Daniel learned to identify the needs of his leader and to satisfy them. When others were unable to interpret the dreams Nebuchadnezzar himself had forgotten, "Daniel went in and asked the king to give him time, that he might tell the king the interpretation" (Dan. 2:16). The next day, Daniel stood before the king and announced, "There is a God in heaven who reveals secrets, and He has made known to King Nebuchadnezzar what will be in the latter days" (Dan. 2:28).

As Daniel's influence and authority within the kingdom grew, he used that influence for the benefit of other subordinate leaders on the team. "Then the king promoted Daniel and gave him many great gifts; and he made him ruler over the whole province of Babylon, and chief administrator over all the wise men of Babylon. Also Daniel petitioned the king, and he set Shadrach, Meshach, and Abed-Nego over the affairs of the province of Babylon; but Daniel sat in the gate of the king" (Dan. 2:48–49).

Often, a change in leadership within an organization results in the resignation or termination of subordinate leaders who have been loyal to the former leader. Few it seems are capable of transferring that loyalty to the new leader. Daniel was certainly among those few. He continued serving faithfully in a subordinate leadership role even after the transition from Babylonian authority to that of the Medes and Persians. "It pleased Darius to set over the kingdom one hundred and twenty satraps, to be over the whole kingdom; and over these, three governors, of whom Daniel was one, that the satraps might give account to them, so that the king would suffer no loss. Then this Daniel distinguished himself above the governors and satraps, because an excellent spirit was in him; and the king gave thought to setting him over the whole realm" (Dan. 6:1–3).

When subordinate leaders experience that kind of success, they often become targets of attack by jealous colleagues within an organization. That proved to be Daniel's experience. Yet despite being falsely accused and thrust into a trial by ordeal, Daniel remained loyal to his leader. After a night in a pit with hungry lions, Daniel told the king, "My God sent His angel and shut the lions' mouths, so that they have not hurt me, because I was found innocent before Him; and also, O king, I have done no wrong before you" (Dan. 6:22). Daniel's rivals were dealt with and destroyed in the same manner by which they had sought to destroy Daniel (Dan. 6:24). "So this Daniel prospered in the reign of Darius and in the reign of Cyrus the Persian" (Dan. 6:28).

Finding Your Place on the Leadership Team

At some point, all successful leaders need to find their place on the leadership team. There can only be one number one in any organization. That means many others will serve as subordinate leaders if they choose to continue within that organization. Even those who ultimately rise to the top need others to help them. Regardless of one's ultimate aspiration, all effective leaders need to understand their role and be the best they can be within that context. There are at least six considerations involved in that process.

As you look for your unique role on the leadership team, begin by identifying your passion for ministry. If you could do anything at all for God, and there were no limitations on you, what would you choose to do? As you look back over your ministry experience to date, is there some recurring emphasis that develops in your ministry? The answers to these questions and others like them will help you determine where you would be most comfortable in ministry.

Next, identify your spiritual giftedness and begin developing your dominant gifts for maximum effectiveness in ministry. God gives spiritual gifts as He wills. They are His way of equipping you for the kind of ministry in which you will do best and in which you will find the greatest fulfillment. Serving out of the strength of your gifting will produce maximum results with minimal effort. If you have not already done so, take a spiritual gifts inventory to determine how God has equipped you for ministry.

Be sure to consider other personal factors that may influence the kind of ministry you feel most comfortable doing. Age is one of those factors. There are some things that can be done while you are young whereas other ministry opportunities require the maturity that comes with age. Also, men and women can have unique ministries, especially with members of their own sex. Sometimes one's ethnic or linguistic background may open doors for ministry. Previous experience and learned abilities and skills are additional factors to consider in making this decision.

Sometimes it is helpful to identify ways you can assist other leaders to accomplish their vision or mission from God. It may be you can help other leaders expand their influence by accepting a supporting role as a subordinate leader. On other occasions, you may be able to help other potential leaders find a place of ministry and develop their leadership skills by appointing them as subordinate leaders on your leadership team.

Regardless of your role on the leadership team, recognize the valid role others have as part of the team. This also applies to those whose ministry emphasis differs from your own. Remember God "gave some to be apostles, some prophets, some evangelists, and some pastors and teachers, for the equipping of the saints for the work of the ministry, for the edifying of the body of Christ" (Eph. 4:11, 12). Support others God has called as part of the team in the work to which God has called them.

One of the greatest challenges in any organization is to maintain a good work environment. Therefore, work hard to establish and maintain healthy relationships with others on the leadership team. "With all lowliness and gentleness, with long-suffering, bearing with one another in love, endeavoring to keep the unity of the Spirit in the bond of peace" (Eph. 4:2, 3).

CHAPTER 19

Esther

The Interventional Leader

And Mordecai told them to answer Esther: "Do not think in your heart that you will escape in the king's palace any more than all the other Jews. For if you remain completely silent at this time, relief and deliverance will arise for the Jews from another place, but you and your father's house will perish. Yet who knows whether you have come to the kingdom for such a time as this?"

ESTHER 4:13–14

Born into a poor family in the Siberian village of Butka, Boris Yeltsin did not have a promising future. Outspoken in his opinions even as child, Yeltsin was once expelled from school for arguing with a teacher. But Yeltsin was determined to make a better future for himself and in 1955 graduated with a degree in civil construction engineering. He married Naina Girina, also an engineering graduate, and together they began raising a family.

After several years working as a manufacturing foreman and superintendent, Yeltsin began taking a more active interest in politics. In 1968, he became the secretary of the Communist Party in the

Sverdlovsk region. He continued his political involvement even after moving to Moscow in the mid-1980s and was elected to the Congress of People's Deputies by March 1989. Just over a year later, he became the speaker of the Congress.

Russia was in the midst of transition following the break-up of the former Soviet Union. President Gorbachev was negotiating a slow and cautious economic transition toward a free market system. As speaker of the Congress, Yeltsin urged the nation to move forward and institute reforms at a quicker pace. Unfortunately, there were many within the government who opposed the reforms. In August 1991, conservative elements within the Russian government and military staged a coup.

What happened next raised Yeltsin's profile not only in Russia but also in the rest of the world. He later explained, "It is especially important to encourage unorthodox thinking when the situation is critical. At such moments, every new word and fresh thought is more precious than gold. Indeed, people must not be deprived of the right to think their own thoughts." Yeltsin led the resistance to the short-lived coup from the Russian White House. In a bold step, he climbed on a Russian tank to address the crowds in Moscow. That picture said more than a thousand words. To the West, Yeltsin looked like the kind of reformer within Russia whom the West could deal with. Within Russia itself, the picture was reminiscent of one of Lenin's classic poses. Russians began thinking of Yeltsin as a true Russian leader.

Although the coup quickly ended, ongoing political infighting frustrated Yeltsin, leading him to renounce the party. His actions in the coup together with his renunciation of the party made him extremely popular among those looking for reform. Riding that wave of populist support, Yeltsin became Russia's first democratically elected president in 1991. Despite serious personal health problems, continued strong opposition from more conservative elements in the government, an unpopular war in Chechnya, and the significant economic challenges associated with a transition from communism to capitalism, Yeltsin used the strength of his personality and political insights to maintain a strong grip on power.

By the end of his first term, the Russian population seemed increasingly nostalgic for the former glory days of the Soviet Union. Gennady Zyuganov, the popular leader of the Communist party, challenged him for the presidency. Yeltsin campaigned vigorously and won reelection, but the campaign took its toll. He collapsed in July 1996 and vanished from the public eye until a coronary bypass surgery later that year. His political foes claimed his political career was over, but after a robust recovery, he returned to completely overhaul his cabinet in March 1997 and to continue down the path of reform. When he abruptly resigned at the end of 1999, Yeltsin claimed, "I understand that I have done the main joy of my life. Russia will never return to the past. Russia will now always be moving forward."[1]

Interventional Leadership

Interventional leaders rise to the challenge of the darkest hour and bring hope and enthusiasm to their followers to pay the price, endure the pain, and pass through a crisis to the victory side. In this respect, an interventional leader is a type of crisis leader. In this book, the authors are distinguishing between these two very similar leadership styles in that interventional leadership tends to be more proactive in dealing with a crisis whereas effective crises leaders tend to manage through the crisis as opportunity presents itself. Just as Hezekiah is described as the model of crisis leadership in an earlier chapter, so Esther is the biblical illustration of the more proactive interventional leader.

Interventional leaders are essential throughout society, especially in contexts where groups are struggling. They include the businessman called to turn a failing business around and restore it so that it becomes a contender in a competitive market. Coaches who assume control of a losing team and lead it to a winning season are also in this group.

Pastors of churches with a significant debt who help that church restructure and adopt a workable strategy to become debt-free and those who pastor divided churches but work with various factions within the church to achieve reconciliation and establish spiritual unity within the body also demonstrate this leadership style. Their success in resolving a major ministry crisis often results in establishing a foundation for effective ministry in the community they serve.

The task of interventional leaders is not an easy one. They tend to lead people who feel threatened and organizations at risk in an uncertain context with significant time and resource pressures. They are called on to provide leadership without the benefit of a strong support network to provide them and their followers with the emotional support needed in a crisis. If they fail in this task, they are often blamed for the demise of the organization. In contrast, if they are successful, they are seldom valued once the crisis is past.

Those who lead groups through a significant crisis must do so from their strength. These leaders tend to use their giftedness in prophecy to discern the cause of the crisis and attack that directly. They rely heavily on the Law of Problem Solving to resolve the crisis they face. It is not uncommon for them to be choleric in temperament.

Interventional leaders practice the fine art of brinkmanship. They run the risk of suffering the losses feared most when they encounter the crisis. In the midst of the pressure cooker, it is easy for them to become irritated with people who resist the changes they perceive to be necessary for survival. The lack of resources needed to achieve what needs to be done serves as a constant source of frustration. If the crisis lasts too long or the solution appears too distant, they may become discouraged in their work. That discouragement can quickly become depression, especially if the group rejects them when the crisis is past.

The very nature of this leadership style and context suggests a high potential for personal burnout. Leaders who use this leadership style with success may even be tempted to create new crises so they can continue leading the group.

If there is one thing that distinguishes the interventional leader from other leaders who manage crisis well, it is courage. That is one of the essential character traits all leaders need to incorporate into their personal leadership kaleidoscope. Without courage, few leaders would ever amount to much. There is no success in leadership without the risk of failure. Because problems tend to thrive on fear, if a leader is not courageous in addressing a crisis, the crisis will continue growing larger. Interventional leaders tend to acquire a higher profile and become targets for those who would cause harm. B. R. Lakin claimed, "The greatness of a man is not measured by what he does, but by what it takes to stop him."[2] The challenge of interventional leadership is always bigger than the leader. Leaders need courage to begin walking down the path to the unknown.

Esther's Act of Intervention

Interventional leadership is sometimes viewed as opportunistic in that it depends on the existence of a crisis over which the leader has no control. Former President Bill Clinton was said to have lamented there had been no great international conflict during his tenure that would enable him to be recognized in the history books as a great leader. Those who are thrust into crisis usually do not find them attractive, especially if they believe there was a way to prevent the crisis in the first place.

Esther's rise as an interventional leader began when she first learned from Mordecai of a major crisis facing her race. When she sent a servant to find out what the problem was, "Mordecai told him all that had happened to him, and the sum of money that Haman had promised to pay into the king's treasuries to destroy the Jews. He also gave him a copy of the written decree for their destruction, which was given at Shushan, that he might show it to Esther and explain it to her, and that he might command her to go in to the king to make supplication to him and plead before him for her people" (Esth. 4:7–8).

The threatened genocide of the Jews was indeed a crisis for the nation, even if Esther thought she might somehow escape because of her position in the palace. Still, there were also significant risks associated with becoming involved in this crisis. Before making a final decision on the matter, she took time to calculate the risks. She told Mordecai, "All the king's servants and the people of the king's provinces know that any man or woman who goes into the inner court to the king, who has not been called, he has but one law: put all to death, except the one to whom the king holds out the golden scepter, that he may live. Yet I myself have not been called to go in to the king these thirty days" (Esth. 4:11).

Esther called a fast to seek God and prepare spiritually for the challenge she faced. Because her actions could potentially affect all the Jews, she asked them to participate in the fast with her. "Go, gather all the Jews who are present in Shushan, and fast for me; neither eat nor drink for three days, night or day. My maids and I will fast likewise. And so I will go to the king, which is against the law; and if I perish, I perish!" (Esth. 4:16).

When the fast was complete, Esther took significant risks to deal with the crisis and rescue her people. "Now it happened on the third day that Esther put on her royal robes and stood in the inner court of the king's palace, across from the king's house, while the king sat on his royal throne in the royal house, facing the entrance of the house. So it was, when the king saw Queen Esther standing in the court, that she found favor in his sight, and the king held out to Esther the golden scepter that was in his hand. Then Esther went near and touched the top of the scepter" (Esth. 5:1–2).

Esther patiently addressed the crisis by giving the situation time to become manageable rather than acting quickly and rashly. "So Esther answered, 'If it pleases the king, let the king and Haman come today to the banquet that I have prepared for him'" (Esth. 5:4). At that dinner, Esther made a second request. "If I have found favor in the sight of the king, and if it pleases the king to grant my petition and fulfill my request, then let the king and Haman come to the banquet which I will prepare for them, and tomorrow I will do as the king has said" (Esth. 5:8).

When the timing was right, Esther appealed directly to King Ahasuerus, who had the authority to preserve the lives of the Jews. "Then Queen Esther answered and said, 'If I have found favor in your sight, O king, and if it pleases the king, let my life be given me at my petition, and my people at my request. For we have been sold, my people and I, to be destroyed, to be killed, and to be annihilated. Had we been sold as male and female slaves, I would have held my tongue, although the enemy could never compensate for the king's loss'" (Esth. 7:3–4).

Esther identified Haman as the source of the problem so he could be dealt with directly. "And Esther said, 'The adversary and enemy is this wicked Haman!' So Haman was terrified before the king and queen" (Esth. 7:6). Once he had been dealt with, the queen proposed a strategy to address the consequences of Haman's prior actions in arranging for the genocide of the Jews. "If it pleases the king, and if I have found favor in his sight and the thing seems right to the king and I am pleasing in his eyes, let it be written to revoke the letters devised by Haman, the son of Hammedatha the Agagite, which he wrote to annihilate the Jews who are in all the king's provinces" (Esth. 8:5).

Together, Esther and Mordecai drew up letters to communicate the solution to the crisis to the Jews throughout the kingdom. "By these letters the king permitted the Jews who were in every city to gather together and protect their lives—to destroy, kill, and annihilate all the forces of any people or province that would assault them, both little children and women, and to plunder their possessions" (Esth. 8:11). What appeared destined to be a day of mourning turned into a day of celebration as the people celebrated the resolution to the crisis that had threatened them. "And in every province and city, wherever the king's command and decree came, the Jews had joy and gladness, a feast and a holiday. Then many of the people of the land became Jews, because fear of the Jews fell upon them" (Esth. 8:17).

The plan of Esther and Mordecai was implemented in defense of the Jews to eliminate any future danger. "Thus the Jews defeated all their enemies with the stroke of the sword, with slaughter and destruction, and did what they pleased with those who hated them" (Esth. 9:5). Knowing people have a tendency to forget the great things God does for them, measures were taken to memorialize this event as an annual reminder of their deliverance from this crisis and encouragement to Jews who might face a similar crisis in the years to come. "And Mordecai wrote these things and sent letters to all the Jews, near and far, who were in all the provinces of King Ahasuerus, to establish among them that they should celebrate yearly the fourteenth and fifteenth days of the month of Adar, as the days on which the Jews had rest from their enemies, as the month which was turned from sorrow to joy for them, and from mourning to a holiday; that they should make them days of feasting and joy, of sending presents to one another and gifts to the poor" (Esth. 9:20–22).

Responding to Your Next Crisis

In the midst of his suffering, Job declared, "Yet man is born to trouble, as the sparks fly upward" (Job 5:7). Problems are inevitable for leaders, and among those problems are some severe enough to be considered a crisis. As you develop your personal leadership kaleidoscope, be sure to learn how you will respond to your next crisis.

An important first step in the midst of a crisis is to take inventory and recognize the real danger you face. Some leaders get into the habit of spinning situations, describing them in the best possible light, to encourage followers. Leaders who begin believing their positive spin on a bad situation are leaders in trouble. Leaders who fail to recognize a real and present danger will fall to it because they will not prepare for it.

Once you understand your situation well, calculate all the risks that lie before you. There are always significant risks involved in addressing a crisis situation. Usually, the larger the crisis, the greater the risks. But there are also greater risks involved in refusing to address a crisis situation.

Step three involves taking time to fast and pray about your situation. Both Esther and Ezra are described in Scripture as fasting for wisdom and protection. The discipline of fasting is a prayer discipline that will help you gain spiritual insight as you develop a problem-solving strategy to apply to the crisis you face.

Your goal in this situation is to develop and implement the strategy that holds the greatest potential to turn the crisis into a celebration. It is often beneficial to consult a few key people in the development of the crisis-solving strategy. Do not advertise the strategy widely before implementing it. Rather, take care to implement the strategy with the right timing, neither rushing ahead nor lagging behind.

Always attempt to address the root cause of the problem before treating the symptoms. If the symptoms alone are treated, they will return, often stronger and in a more significant manifestation. But when the source is removed, the problem begins to die. Even when the root cause is addressed, there may be some symptoms left over that need to be addressed.

As you lead your people out of a crisis, celebrate the successful resolution of that crisis. The celebration will allow your people a legitimate emotional release from the tension with which they have been living. As part of the celebration, memorialize the event as an encouragement to yourself and others. You will face another crisis in the future. Remembering how God brought you through a previous crisis will encourage you as you work through your next crisis.

CHAPTER 20

Shepherd

The Servant Leader

*And He sat down, called the twelve, and said to them, "If anyone
desires to be first, he shall be last of all and servant of all."*

MARK 9:35

W illiam and Charles Mayo never knew of a life that did not put
others first. Their father was a doctor for the Union Army who
settled his family near the end of the war near the district recruiting
station in Rochester, Minnesota. When the war came to an end, Mayo
Sr. continued practicing medicine and teaching all he knew to his sons.
At age 52, he left his remote practice to update his knowledge and skills
at New York's Bellevue Hospital. He was determined that both he and
his boys would grow with the medicine they practiced. Some biogra-
phers claim he was among the first American doctors to use a micro-
scope in his practice.

Both William and Charles shared their father's commitment to
helping people in need. William graduated from the University of
Michigan Medical School in 1883. His younger brother Charles graduated from Chicago Medical School in 1888. When St. Mary's Hospital
opened in their hometown of Rochester, Minnesota, a year later, there

were three Dr. Mayos on staff. They established a medical practice near the hospital that eventually became known as the Mayo Clinic.

The Mayo brothers were driven in their practice of medicine by a deep concern for people. They organized their practice to ensure they could help as many people as possible, regardless of their socioeconomic status in life. No one was ever charged more than ten percent of his or her annual income regardless of the actual cost of the procedure. They made it their practice to apply every dollar over one thousand dollars collected on a medical bill to help others who normally could not afford their services. It is estimated about 30 percent of those treated by the brothers received their bills with the words "Paid in Full" handwritten across them.

Providing economic assistance to patients was not the only way these brothers helped those in need. Like their father before them, they continued studying medicine and looking for new and improved ways to treat disease. When they discovered effective treatments, they were eager to share them with others so more people could be helped. In the course of their practice, they published over one thousand scientific papers about their work in medical journals.

Though highly successful as both humanitarians and scientists, it has been suggested their real success was as brothers. For over seventy years they remained close, working together to serve others. Neither brother seemed to have any desire for recognition for all they did. Whenever a medical society, university, or government chose to honor one of the brothers for his work, that brother always began his acceptance speech with four words, "My brother and I . . ." Their commitment to serving others placed them in an awkward position when others chose to serve and honor them.

Servant Leadership

Servant leaders are those who recognize that the real secret of leadership is found in identifying the needs of others and ministering to them. This leader believes people will follow if their leader is meeting their needs. In this respect, Christian leadership differs significantly from the Machiavellian leadership practiced by many political rulers. Christian leadership finds its credibility in ministry to others. Jesus both taught and modeled the principles of servant leadership throughout His public ministry and private mentoring.

There are many places where servant leaders are serving effectively. They include the business leaders who ensure that their employees work in a healthy environment and have the tools and other resources they need to complete their assigned tasks. Teachers who stay after classes are done to coach the school team and shape the character of young athletes are among this group. So also are pastors who define their life as an opportunity to meet the needs of others.

Because of their others-orientation, servant leaders always have things to do. The job of serving others is never done. This puts them in high demand. Most people would rather be served than serve. These leaders tend to work with people who demand more of their time than others. Also, it is not uncommon for servant leaders to assume a personal burden for the welfare of those they serve. They are always giving of themselves and rarely have the opportunity to receive from others. They provide the emotional support others need, but may not have the strong support network that will uphold them. They are often the subjects of abuse by those who make extreme and unreasonable demands on them.

Servant leaders are most effective when they use the strength of their spiritual giftedness. They use their gift of empathy (being able to put yourself in someone else's circumstances) in meeting the needs of the stressed and distressed people with whom they work. In group settings, they use their gift of shepherding in caring for the needs of their flock. They also use their gift of ministry in helping others in any way they can. This leadership style relies heavily on using the Law of Problem Solving to help people deal with the situation and find answers. Many servant leaders tend to be sanguine in temperament.

Many servant leaders struggle with time management because they try to do too much for others. They may also become problem-focused and discouraged because so many people they know and work with seem to be struggling. When they fail to see progress in the lives of others, they may become increasingly frustrated. The stressful nature of shepherding and serving others causes a constant emotional strain, which can make them physically tired. Tired leaders tend to make mistakes and may be candidates for burnout. Others may be abusive toward servant leaders, taking advantage of their willingness to serve without regard for their own needs. In a worst-case scenario, servant leaders on the edge may themselves become abusers of others.

Despite the risks, leaders need to incorporate shepherding skills into their personal leadership kaleidoscope if they intend to become all the leader God wants them to be. People need the kind of help only shepherds can provide because they are like harassed sheep without leadership. When Jesus "saw the multitudes, He was moved with compassion for them, because they were weary and scattered, like sheep having no shepherd" (Matt. 9:36). That is why God has entrusted the spiritual care of His flock to pastors and calls them to "shepherd the flock of God which is among you, serving as overseers, not by compulsion but willingly" (1 Pet. 5:2). Those who are faithful in this task will be evaluated and rewarded for their labors. "And when the Chief Shepherd appears, you will receive the crown of glory that does not fade away" (1 Pet. 5:4).

Shepherding the flock as pastors is an evidence of our love for Christ. When Jesus called Peter into a shepherding ministry, each challenge was given in the context of his affirmation of affection for the Lord (John 21:15–17). When we shepherd others, we model the character of Christ toward others. Jesus said, "I am the good shepherd. The good shepherd gives His life for the sheep" (John 10:11).

Jesus: The Good Shepherd

Even before He was born, Jesus was described as a shepherd. "But you, Bethlehem, in the land of Judah, are not the least among the rulers of Judah; for out of you shall come a Ruler who will shepherd My people Israel" (Matt. 2:6; see Mic. 5:2). Throughout His ministry on earth, Jesus modeled servant leadership through a shepherding ministry. Various biblical descriptions of shepherds reveal something of the character and nature of Jesus' shepherding ministry.

One of the first descriptions of shepherds in Scripture describes their willingness to suffer the reproach of others for the welfare of the sheep. When Joseph's family joined him in Egypt, he warned them not to talk about their occupation with the Egyptians "for every shepherd is an abomination to the Egyptians" (Gen. 46:34). In some urban communities today, many professionals have the same attitude toward farmers.

Shepherds tend to be willing to place themselves at risk to ensure the security of the sheep. In seeking to assure Saul he was capable and could do battle with Goliath, David recalled, "Your servant used to keep his father's sheep, and when a lion or a bear came and took a lamb out of the flock, I went out after it and struck it, and delivered the lamb from its mouth; and when it arose against me, I caught it by its beard, and struck and killed it" (1 Sam. 17:34–35).

The Twenty-third Psalm may well be the best-known chapter of Scripture. While the psalm describes many aspects of the Christian life in the context of a shepherding metaphor, it begins with the overarching statement, "The LORD is my shepherd; I shall not want" (Ps. 23:1). As David thought about God in the context of shepherding, he began by noting the nature of a shepherd to identify and provide for all the needs of the flock.

Shepherds are strong enough to be gentle with the sheep. Describing the shepherding ministry of Jesus hundreds of years before He was born, the prophet Isaiah wrote, "He will feed His flock like a shepherd; He will gather the lambs with His arm, and carry them in His bosom, and gently lead those who are with young" (Isa. 40:11). Shepherds not only feed and lead the flock; they also carry the young lambs that are unable to keep up with the flock.

TO HELP AND NOT HURT

Hippocrates, the father of medicine, lived four hundred years before the birth of Christ at a time when physicians believed disease was caused by the four fluids of the body and healing could be found only in the Temple of Aesculapius, the god of medicine. In his desire to be more effective in healing the sick, he studied his patients carefully and trained his students to look for symptoms as they sought to diagnose disease. In his writings, Hippocrates described many illnesses, including pneumonia, tetanus, tuberculosis, arthritis, mumps, and malaria.

He urged patients to eat and exercise moderately for better health. He developed remedies for the management of pain and encouraged the body in its own healing process. When surgery was necessary, he insisted that the operating room be well lit and cheerful. He believed patients in bright and cheerful environments would heal faster.

Perhaps Hippocrates's greatest contribution to medicine was his insistence that physicians be men of honor. In an era when bribery was common within the medical profession, Hippocrates urged doctors to put the welfare of their patients first. It was not uncommon for a patient's enemy to bribe a doctor to kill rather than heal the patient. A key phrase in the Hippocratic Oath named in his honor and still taken by doctors today calls on doctors "to heal and do no harm."

Jesus told a parable about a shepherd that illustrated his willingness to accept the responsibility for each member of the flock. "What man of you, having a hundred sheep, if he loses one of them, does not leave the ninety-nine in the wilderness, and go after the one which is lost until he finds it?" (Luke 15:4). It is the nature of shepherds to expend great effort in the care of even one wandering sheep. Sunday school teachers who continue praying for and reaching out to former class members long after they quit attending demonstrate they have a shepherd's heart.

Shepherds differ from others hired to care for the flocks in that they are willing to make a more significant sacrifice for the sheep. Jesus said, "I am the good shepherd. The good shepherd gives His life for the sheep. But a hireling, he who is not the shepherd, one who does not own the sheep, sees the wolf coming and leaves the sheep and flees; and the wolf catches the sheep and scatters them" (John 10:11–12).

Over time, shepherds develop significant relationships with their sheep as they care for their needs. "The sheep hear his voice; and he calls his own sheep by name and leads them out. And when he brings out his own sheep, he goes before them; and the sheep follow him, for they know his voice. Yet they will by no means follow a stranger, but will flee from him, for they do not know the voice of strangers" (John 10:3–5). In light of this description of shepherds, Jesus added, "I am the good shepherd; and I know My sheep, and am known by My own" (John 10:14).

Developing a Servant's Heart

Ministry to others was one of the primary goals of Jesus' life. He told all who would listen, "For even the Son of Man did not come to be served, but to serve, and to give His life a ransom for many" (Mark 10:45). As soon as He had accomplished that goal and had risen from the dead, He met with His disciples and told them, "As the Father has sent Me, I also send you" (John 20:21). He who had modeled servant leadership among them now expected them to do the same among others.

Although recently popularized in business and management literature, the concept of servant leadership has always been at the core of effective ministry. Regardless of personal gifting, temperament, or preferred leadership style, God has always expected Christian leaders to have an others-orientation in life. As you develop your personal leadership kaleidoscope, a servant's heart is indispensable. It is an essential aspect of the character and attitude that brings balance and focus to ensure that other elements in the kaleidoscope function correctly.

Those who would have a servant's heart begin by becoming others-oriented in their leadership. As they make decisions, they focus more on the needs of those being led than personal ambitions. Sometimes, progress toward achieving the goals of the organization needs to be slowed to take time to minister to the needs of the people within that organization. One pastor understood this principle when he led his people to build a new church campus. Throughout the entire process, he hung a four-word banner in the church auditorium reminding him and his congregation their primary business was "building people, not buildings."

An others-oriented pastor will take time to identify the needs of his congregation and begin developing strategies to ensure those needs are being adequately met. A frustrated woman confided in her pastor, "You are always telling us to take the gospel message to others, but there is so much wrong in my life I find it hard to tell others about Jesus." When the pastor realized that feeling was widespread within the congregation, he began preaching on how to resolve some of the issues with which his people were struggling. In the process, he discovered unsaved people in the community began attending to hear him preach, and those who had been helped within the congregation began sharing what God was doing in their lives with their unsaved friends and family.

Servant leaders need to be gentle with people, especially those who repeatedly fail them and tend to be sources of irritation and frustration. A pastor going through a particularly difficult time in his ministry was discussing the situation with an older, more experienced pastor. It was clear to the older pastor that the younger man was in an abusive situation. His church was making unreasonable demands and failing to honor their pastor as they should. The younger man responded, "But that's the way sheep are. If they did not have problems, they would not need shepherds." His attitude enabled him to endure a difficult situation and help his people grow.

Servant leaders need to accept the awesome responsibility of spiritual oversight. Refuse to blame others for their backsliding when you know you have not done all you could have done to restore them to Christ. Don't give up on your people too quickly.

The key to this approach to leadership is relationships. Build strong, warm, and caring relationships with your followers. Get to know them not only by name, but also by nature. Become a friend and much more. As your relationship grows, they should come to think of you as the first person they would call in time of need.

CHAPTER 21

Jesus

The Mentoring Leader

And He went up on the mountain and called to Him those He Himself wanted. And they came to Him. Then He appointed twelve, that they might be with Him and that He might send them out to preach.

MARK 3:13–14

Born into the home of Missouri slaves, George Washington Carver, it seemed, was destined to live in poverty and obscurity. He contracted whooping cough as a baby, and though he recovered it left him sickly. Unable to do work in the fields as other slaves, he learned to cook and sew and tend the garden. But even as a child, Carver was consumed with a desire to learn. He taught himself how to read and write, but his family was so poor they could not afford a pencil. Carver developed a pencil holder, his first of many later inventions, that enabled him to use a pencil only one-quarter of an inch long.

At age twelve, he attended a one-room school with seventy-five African-American children and one teacher. Despite the poor learning environment, he studied hard both in class and during his free time at recess and after doing his chores. He did well and decided to pursue a college education. He wrote to a college and was accepted, until they found out he was black. It was not until he was thirty that he was finally accepted at an Iowa college. Later, he continued his studies in botany at Iowa State College, earning the reputation of being the best botany student on campus.

Upon graduation, Carver was invited to teach biology to first-year students. Later, he returned to the South to teach at the Tuskegee Institute in Alabama. Shortly after his work in Alabama began, local farmers struggled with the failure of the cotton crop due to an insect infestation. Carver urged farmers to begin growing crops that insects tended to avoid, including peanuts and sweet potatoes. When they switched crops, their harvest improved significantly. But that created another problem for the farmers. The increased crops created a glut on the market, driving down product prices.

In an effort to help farmers with this new problem, he and his students returned to the lab to discover new uses for these crops. As a poor struggling student, he had insisted that nothing be thrown out and that everything could be used again. That attitude, which had resulted in notebooks made from old wrapping paper during his student years, now drove him in his new quest. Eventually, he developed more than 300 products from peanuts, including bath soap and ink. Flour and candy were among the 118 products he developed from sweet potatoes. He developed an additional 75 products from pecans.

Carver's work at Tuskegee gave him greater credibility as a teacher. Students flocked to his classes to study under one of the leading scientists of his age, even though he earned a reputation of being very demanding as a teacher. When students told him they had done something "about right," he responded, "Don't tell me it's about right. If it's about right, then it's wrong."[1] That he had risen from slavery to such a prominent position made him a role model for several generations of African-American students.

Carver's ingenuity did not escape the notice of other notables of his age. Thomas Edison offered him $100,000 a year to come and work for him, but he turned down the offer, believing he could accomplish much more teaching at Tuskegee. His influence extended far beyond his life as his students applied his lessons in various spheres of service.

Leaders Who Make Disciples

According to Walter Lippman, "The final test of a leader is that he leaves behind in others the conviction and will to carry on." Mentoring leaders are the teachers who make disciples, training others who will someday continue the work they began. These leaders believe their work will be better accomplished if several people are trained to lead rather than relying on only one person to do all the work. While vast crowds followed Jesus throughout much of His public ministry, Jesus chose to devote most of his time and energy in the training of the Twelve. That effort resulted in eleven equipped leaders who reached the world with His message and gave birth to a movement that has survived two millennia.

Mentoring leaders exist in significant roles in various organizations and institutions even though they are not always the leaders with the highest profile. They include personnel directors who train workers for increased effectiveness and productivity in business. They are also the teachers who share knowledge, insights, and skills in their area of expertise and reproduce themselves in the lives of their students. Among their number are the pastors who devote significant resources to the training of strong lay leaders in the church who impact the lives of others.

The task of mentoring new leaders is not without its difficulties. Many of these difficulties are tied directly to our culture. The transient nature of urban life hinders the development of long-term mentoring relationships. The development of those relationships is also hindered by the sociological phenomenon of "cocooning" in urban centers. Also, the failure of Western civilization to recognize the wisdom of elders further erodes the credibility of the mentoring process. Beyond this, television has conditioned Baby Boomers, Generation Xers, and every generation since to think in terms of instant gratification rather than long-term commitments.

The success orientation of many leaders today is also a barrier to be overcome by those who would mentor others. The larger demands of ministry to a larger group erode the time available for individual and small-group mentoring. The value expressed in the phrase, "bigger is better," also tends to discourage leaders from investing significant resources in an individual or small group. As in any project undertaken by leaders, the risk of failure sometimes discourages leaders from engaging in this work. The failure of potential leadership candidates to develop in the mentoring process discourages one's commitment to this ministry. This prospect was even faced by Jesus, who devoted much time and energy mentoring Judas Iscariot.

Those who are effective in mentoring other leaders tend to use their giftedness in teaching to communicate the principles of leadership to others. They also use their giftedness in exhortation to demonstrate the principles of leadership to others and motivate them to apply those principles to their own leadership style. Mentoring leaders use the Law of Communication to share the principles of leadership with a new generation of leaders. It is not uncommon for mentoring leaders to be phlegmatic in temperament.

Mentoring new leaders can be a discouraging process, especially when leaders expect rapid results on the part of their leadership trainees. In frustration, they may short-change the learning experience of others by doing themselves what could and should be delegated as part of the mentoring process. If the pool of potential leaders is small, they may hesitate to demand the high degree of commitment required from their protégés. Of course, because the ministry of mentoring requires leaders to pour themselves into the lives of others, there is always the risk of burnout, which happens when leaders have nothing left for themselves.

One common struggle of mentoring leaders is their tendency to isolate themselves from their leadership trainees. They may be effective in communicating principles but when they fail to share their life, they hinder the learning of the leaders they are mentoring. In contrast, some mentoring leaders become so committed to the mentoring process that they neglect other leadership responsibilities. In a local setting, pastors who focus on mentoring leaders are often misunderstood as having favorites in the church because of the time they spend together.

Despite the risks, knowing how to equip others for ministry needs to be the part of the leadership kaleidoscope of growing leaders desiring to have an influence on others that outlive them. Most Christians would like to be trained for significant ministry, but they will be reluctant to minister if they believe they are inadequately prepared for the task. While this approach to leadership initially involves a significant time investment with limited results, its long-term benefits produce value for the initial investment. Equipping others for ministry frees up time that would normally be spent doing that ministry.

Also when you train others, you multiply your effectiveness and extend your influence. Equipping others for ministry is the only way the task of making disciples of all nations can be accomplished within our generation. After all, according to Ralph Nader, "The function of leadership is to produce more leaders, not more followers."

Jesus: The Mentoring Leader

Jesus has been described as the most influential leader of all time. A close study of His life demonstrates He incorporated many approaches to leadership within His personal leadership kaleidoscope. Jesus modeled the principles of mentoring leadership in His training of the twelve. In his book *The Master Plan of Evangelism*,[2] Robert Coleman identifies the eight steps Jesus took in training His disciples.

According to Harvey S. Firestone, "The growth and development of people is the highest calling of leadership." Jesus recognized potential in twelve men and selected them from among His followers to be His apostles. "And when it was day, He called His disciples to Himself; and from them He chose twelve whom He also named apostles" (Luke 6:13).

Jesus chose the Twelve primarily "that they might be with Him" (Mark 3:14). He devoted significant time to His personal relationship with those He had chosen. He understood some things are better "caught than taught" and used His life as a teaching tool in the mentoring of His disciples. Someone noted, "Children have more need of models than of critics." That is also true within the family of God.

Jesus expected His apostles to obey Him and challenged them to be fully committed to Him and His cause. His expectations of the disciples were high. He taught them, "If anyone desires to come after Me, let him deny himself, and take up his cross daily, and follow Me" (Luke 9:23). Anything less than full devotion fell short of what was required.

The commitment Jesus demanded of His followers was based on His own commitment to God's call on His life. Jesus demonstrated His love for the disciples by giving Himself to them and for them. During His final session of instruction prior to His betrayal and crucifixion, Jesus taught, "Greater love has no one than this, than to lay down one's life for his friends" (John 15:13). Within twenty-four hours of making that statement, Jesus demonstrated the ultimate expression of His love for them by laying down His life. It is easier to be committed to a leader who is committed to you.

Jesus trained His disciples by example. When all His teaching about humility failed to change their attitude, He modeled humility before them in a vivid way they would never forget. After enjoying a meal with His disciples, Jesus humbled Himself, took on the role of a servant, and washed His disciples' feet. When He had completed the task, He explained, "I have given you an example, that you should do as I have done to you" (John 13:15). In their study of *The Leadership Challenge*,[3]

James M. Kouzes and Barry Z. Posner emphasized the importance of communicating to others as a role model. Based on their research, they conclude, "Being a role model means paying attention to what you believe is important. It means showing others through your behavior that you live your values."[4]

Jesus gave His disciples the opportunity to apply the lessons they were learning by delegating responsibility and authority to them in short-term ministry projects. Someone said well, "No man will make a great leader who wants to do it all himself, or to get all the credit for doing it." Shortly after selecting and beginning the training of the Twelve, "Jesus sent out and commanded them" (Matt. 10:5). Throughout His ministry with the disciples, He assigned various tasks and responsibilities to help them gain confidence as leaders.

These ministry projects were part of a larger training strategy. Jesus supervised His disciples by debriefing them following their ministry tours. "And the apostles, when they had returned, told Him all that they had done. Then He took them and went aside privately into a deserted place belonging to the city called Bethsaida" (Luke 9:10). During these times apart from the crowds, Jesus provided further training for His disciples that would improve their ministry skills and help them realize their leadership potential. This process was not without risk. According to Kouzes and Posner, "While managers appraise their subordinates, subordinates also appraise their managers. The test they use is a simple one: Does my leader practice what he or she preaches?"

When His disciples were adequately trained as leaders, Jesus challenged them with the responsibility of reproducing themselves and multiplying their influence by making disciples of all nations. In a statement that has become known as the Great Commission, Jesus said, "Go therefore and make disciples of all the nations, baptizing them in the name of the Father and of the Son and of the Holy Spirit, teaching them to observe all things that I have commanded you; and lo, I am with you always, even to the end of the age" (Matt. 28:19–20).

Mentoring Others to Lead

The mentoring ministry of Jesus suggests a model by which leaders can be developed today. Indeed, as disciples of Christ it is only logical that Christian leaders would follow His practice in mentoring new leaders today. When you begin developing leaders in your ministry, the following eight steps will guide you through that process toward success.

Begin by identifying and selecting those who could be trained to be effective leaders. Most often, those who already have an influence on others are already demonstrating their leadership potential. Don't overlook those whose influence on others is primarily negative. As they grow in their Christian life and develop Christian values, that negative influence will change. Historically, God has raised up godly leaders from those who have a checkered past to demonstrate what He Himself is able to do in a life.

Once leadership candidates have been identified, begin spending quality time with them so they can recognize the leadership incarnate in your life. Some pastors establish a formal schedule of meeting with those they are mentoring and develop a mentoring curriculum to be covered in those sessions. While this is effective in many cases, some potential leaders are better equipped through conversations in fishing boats or over a meal together.

As you meet individually or corporately with your trainees, challenge them to a high degree of personal commitment to you as their mentor and the cause to which you are committed. When students asked a wise teacher what they could expect to get out of their course, the teacher responded, "You will get out of this whatever you put into it." The mentoring process works best when both teachers and students are highly committed to the process.

Pour your life into those you are training. Share your knowledge, experience, and wisdom as a foundation on which they can build. Take time to show your leadership trainees how to lead by leading them.

Model the principles of leadership so they can see how they work in practice. View time spent in this mentoring process as important because it is the most important investment leaders will ever make.

While your trainees will learn some from what you teach them, the more involved they become in the learning process, the better they will learn the lessons you are trying to teach them and the more effective they will be when they assume their leadership responsibilities. Help them build their personal confidence by delegating limited responsibilities and authority, as they are able to assume it. As you supervise the assigned work of your trainees, assist them as necessary and use those experiences as part of their training to become all the leader they can be.

Always remember you are training leaders who will reproduce themselves in the lives of other potential leaders. Remind your trainees of this responsibility often. As they struggle to learn new skills, this will give them hope that someday they will be able to pass these skills on to others. Also, when you mentor leaders who mentor others, you extend your own influence as a mentoring leader on to generations you may never see.

CHAPTER 22

Peter

The Self-Correcting Leader

---

*For a righteous man may fall seven times and rise again, but
the wicked shall fall by calamity.*

PROVERBS 24:16

Some people struggle all their lives to achieve something worthwhile, but despite their best efforts success seems just beyond their
grasp. To his friends and family, it certainly seemed that was destined
to be the fate of a young Illinois lawyer. It seemed everything he tried
failed. On the few occasions when he seemed to achieve some success,
that success quickly proved short-lived.

At age twenty-two, he recorded his first business failure.
Unsuccessful in business, he thought he would try his hand at politics.
At age twenty-three, he ran for the state legislature and was defeated.
He returned to business again, and at age twenty-four, he failed in
business again. At age twenty-five, he ran for public office again and
was elected to the legislature.

226

He never really had an opportunity to enjoy his political success. At age twenty-six, the woman he loved dearly and hoped to marry died. At age twenty-seven, he suffered a nervous breakdown. When he ran for speaker of the house at age twenty-nine, he was defeated. At age thirty-one, he was defeated in his attempt to become an elector.

Turning to national politics, he ran for Congress at age thirty-four, only to be defeated at the polls. At age thirty-seven, he was elected to Congress for a single term. When he sought reelection two years later, he was once again defeated. At age forty-six, he was defeated in his bid for a Senate seat. At age forty-seven he was defeated in his bid to become vice president. Two years later, he was defeated again in his bid for a Senate seat. As he marked the half-century mark of his life, there was a lot of failure and limited success to look back on.

But at age fifty-one, Abraham Lincoln was elected president of the United States of America.

Before he assumed office, seven southern states seceded from the Union in protest of Lincoln's widely known opposition to slavery. For all but the last five days of his life, he served as president of a divided country. But on September 22, 1862, the man who did not seem to succeed at much issued his Emancipation Proclamation, which declared all slaves in Confederate states free. That action eventually led to the *Thirteenth Amendment to the U.S. Constitution* that abolished slavery in America.

Lincoln understood it is always too soon to quit.

Failing Forward

Failure need never be final. Every leader makes mistakes or fails from time to time. Self-correcting leaders rise from their failures to achieve ultimate success. When they stumble, they do not fall. When they fall, they get back up. They may not succeed every time, but they stay on the path to success. They understand real success is a journey, not a destination.

The key to avoiding failure is to be nothing, say nothing, and do nothing. But being nothing was not good enough for Peter. In his attempt to serve Christ, he often failed. Despite a pattern of failure, his commitment to Christ did not allow him the luxury of quitting. He rose again repeatedly to become the leader God called him to be.

Self-correcting leaders are evident wherever leaders accomplish significant achievements despite prior failures. They are the business-men who come back from a series of financial setbacks to establish a thriving business in the community. They are the motion picture directors who direct a highly profitable picture that wins an Oscar even though several of his previous pictures did poorly. They are the pastors who learn from their mistakes, resolve the problems they caused, and lead their churches to make an impact on their communities.

In a leadership culture "in pursuit of excellence," some leaders for-get that excellence is only a worthy goal when something is already happening. It should never be an excuse for not attempting something significant because someone else may be able to do it with greater finesse. According to Robert Schuller, "It's better to do something imperfectly than to do nothing perfectly." Emphasizing the need to act even when you don't have everything you would like to have in place before launching a project, Stuart Briscoe declares, "If something is worth doing, it is worth doing poorly."

Self-correcting leaders often find themselves living with problems of their own making. They live with the consequences of their previous mistakes and the reputation they have earned of having had significant errors in judgment in the past. It is not uncommon for them to encounter people who are cautious about following their leadership. Self-correcting leaders tend to make poor decisions based on poor information. As a result, they tend to lack credibility when they announce a new project following a significant failure. They may not be taken seriously even when they announce new and good ideas.

Ultimately, they tend to limit the size of their following as people desert the cause during setbacks.

Self-correcting leaders may be gifted in any area, but it is unlikely they use the strength of their gifting in their leadership style. They do use the Law of Problem Solving to resolve problems—problems that are often the consequence of previous actions. They use the Law of Decision Making when correcting previous actions. They may also use the Law of Dreams to keep themselves and their followers motivated. Many self-correcting leaders are sanguine in temperament.

Self-correcting leaders face many personal challenges. They may struggle with self-esteem, especially if they identify themselves in the context of personal progress made on a particular project. They may also become frustrated with the hesitancy of followers to believe them "this time." As Will Rogers noted, "People's minds are changed through observation and not argument." They may have a tendency to blame others rather than assume personal responsibility for their own decisions. Good leaders take a little more than their share of the blame and a little less than their share of the credit.

It is not uncommon for a self-correcting leader to identify failure too soon and abandon a project that could be successful during a minor setback. They may short-circuit the decision-making process, leading to more bad decisions in the future. They may develop a loser attitude and begin anticipating failure rather than working toward success. After experiencing a series of failures, they may expect the worst and fall victim to self-fulfilling prophecies of failure. In a worst-case scenario, self-correcting leaders may choose to stop correcting themselves.

Frank J. Ruck once observed, "When people don't make mistakes, I'm uncomfortable. They're not reaching out and growing." At some point, every growing leader will fail while attempting to do something worthwhile. The leader who has incorporated the skills of the self-correcting leader into his personal leadership kaleidoscope will be able to rebound out of that failure into success.

Failure can be an important tool to gain significant insight into a problem or situation. Understanding how and why a project fails may suggest principles and practices to determine the success of future projects. Even a series of failures is not an accurate predictor of one's likely ultimate success or lack of success. Just ask Lincoln. Even defining failure itself can be very subjective. Given time, apparent failures often prove to be the key to ultimate success. Christian leaders understand God uses all things, even failure, to accomplish His purposes in our lives. "And we know that all things work together for good to those who love God, to those who are the called according to His purpose" (Rom. 8:28).

Peter: The Self-Correcting Leader

Despite his best intentions, Peter often found himself desiring to do one thing but practicing something different. He could easily identify with Paul's testimony, "For I know that in me (that is, in my flesh) nothing good dwells; for to will is present with me, but how to perform what is good I do not find. For the good that I will to do, I do not do; but the evil I will not to do, that I practice" (Rom. 7:18–19). Peter's moments of glory were often overshadowed by significant failure.

While it is doubtful anyone else saw much potential in Peter, Jesus recognized it as soon as they met. "Now when Jesus looked at him, He said, 'You are Simon the son of Jonah. You shall be called Cephas' (which is translated, A Stone)" (John 1:42). The Greek word translated "looked" suggests the idea of a penetrating look that looks through the exterior of a person to discover the real self. Jesus realized Peter was not very good at listening (the name Simon means "hearing one"), but that he had the potential of becoming a solid rock upon which He could build a significant ministry. Sometimes, the only way to live happily with people is to overlook their faults and admire their virtues.

In one of Peter's greatest moments, "he walked on the water to go to Jesus" (Matt. 14:29). There were eleven other disciples who preferred the security of the boat, because of the storm on the Sea of Galilee, but Peter stepped out on faith at the Lord's invitation. But that moment was short-lived. "When he saw that the wind was boisterous, he was afraid; and beginning to sink he cried out, saying, 'Lord, save me!'" (Matt. 14:30). According to Olle Bovin, "You have to be brave enough to fail as a leader."

In another moment of glory, it was Peter who confessed, "You are the Christ, the Son of the living God" (Matt. 16:16). This was the most profound statement ever made by a disciple in the Gospels and would become the heart of the apostolic message throughout the Acts. Still, in the context of that statement, he resisted Jesus' plan when he first learned about the cross. "Then Peter took Him aside and began to rebuke Him, saying, 'Far be it from You, Lord; this shall not happen to You!'" (Matt. 16:22).

Approximately a week later, Peter was among those who saw Jesus transfigured before him. As Jesus was praying, He was transformed as He stood between Moses and Elijah. Together the three discussed the cross, but Peter failed to recognize the uniqueness of Jesus in their midst. "Then it happened, as they were parting from Him, that Peter said to Jesus, 'Master, it is good for us to be here; and let us make three tabernacles: one for You, one for Moses, and one for Elijah'—not knowing what he said" (Luke 9:33). Peter would have been better off considering the wisdom of Zeno of Citium: "We have been given two ears but a single mouth in order that we may hear more and talk less."

As the disciples gathered for their last Passover dinner with Jesus, Peter had still not learned to "hear more and talk less." Initially, he refused to let Jesus wash his feet, then insisted on a bath. "Peter said to Him, 'You shall never wash my feet!' Jesus answered him, 'If I do not wash you, you have no part with Me.' Simon Peter said to Him, 'Lord, not my feet only, but also my hands and my head!'" (John 13:8–9).

Later at the same meal, Peter swore allegiance to Christ, even to the point of death. But before the sun rose the next morning, he had denied Christ three times. In a conversation in the upper room, Jesus warned Peter what would happen. "Peter said to Him, 'Lord, why can I not follow You now? I will lay down my life for Your sake.' Jesus answered him, 'Will you lay down your life for My sake? Most assuredly, I say to you, the rooster shall not crow till you have denied Me three times'" (John 13:37–38). According to Joubert, while "genius begins great works; labor alone finishes them."

When the enemies of Jesus came for Him later that evening, Peter did rise to Jesus' defense with a sword. "Then Simon Peter, having a sword, drew it and struck the high priest's servant, and cut off his right ear. The servant's name was Malchus" (John 18:10). Peter's attitude at that moment may be best expressed in what has been called the ten most powerful two-letter words. "If it is to be, it is up to me." But once again, despite his best intentions, Peter found himself doing things contrary to the agenda Jesus had set. As Peter attempted to prevent the arrest, Jesus was beginning the process of willingly laying down His life for our sins. "So Jesus said to Peter, 'Put your sword into the sheath. Shall I not drink the cup which My Father has given Me?'" (John 18:11).

In describing various attitudes in difficult circumstances, John C. Maxwell notes, "The pessimist complains about the wind. The optimist expects it to change. The leader adjusts the sails."[1] Throughout their three-to-four-year relationship, Jesus was adjusting the sails in Peter's life to catch the winds that would shape him into who he needed to become. And despite his failings, God chose Peter as His chief spokesman on the day of Pentecost (Acts 2:14–40). Thomas Edison once said, "If we all did the things we are capable of doing, we would literally astound ourselves." As Peter looked back on his life, there must have been moments of astonishment.

According to Donald McGavran, "Leadership is action, not position." Peter became the primary leader of the early church not because of his office but because of his willingness to act. When he made mistakes, he learned from them and moved on. After being mentored by Jesus for several years, he made fewer mistakes and achieved greater success. He did not spend a great deal of time trying to defend himself or explain his actions. He simply did what he believed was right at the moment. He practiced the advice of Henry J. Kaiser long before it was offered: "When your work speaks for itself, don't interrupt."

Starting over Following Failure

Between Peter's night of failure—the night when he both defended and denied Christ—and the day of Pentecost, there was a significant meeting that changed things for Peter. Jesus' meeting with Peter on the shore of Lake Galilee involved a process of restoration and recommissioning. The biblical account of that meeting identifies the four steps we need to take to return to the Lord when we find ourselves drifting from Him.

First, we need to identify our need to make a correction in our lives. Good leaders must face the truth. There are several ways we may come to that point of realization in our life. We may need to exhaust our personal resources before we are responsive to the Lord. In the case of the disciples, "They went out and immediately got into the boat, and that night they caught nothing" (John 21:3). On other occasions, we may need to fail to recognize the futility of our own efforts. Jesus helped the disciples come to that point when He asked, "Children, have you any food?" (John 21:5). Often, we are not willing to listen to the Lord until all else has failed. In the case of the disciples, Jesus said, "Cast the net on the right side of the boat, and you will find some" (John 21:6). When they did so, the net was so full of fish they had difficulty drawing it into the boat. Sometimes, the best way to get the last word in is to apologize.

A second step in the process of restoration involves acknowledging the Lord at work around us and in our lives. The response of the disciples to Jesus illustrates how various people respond to the Lord today. Some, like John, see God at work around us and quickly recognize His presence. "Therefore that disciple whom Jesus loved said to Peter, 'It is the Lord!' " (John 21:7). Others are like Peter; they need to have events interpreted to them before they recognize God's presence.

There is also a great variety in the manner in which some people return to the Lord. Peter's response was zealous even to the point of being irrational. "Now when Simon Peter heard that it was the Lord, he put on his outer garment (for he had removed it), and plunged into the sea" (John 21:7). His outer garment would only add weight as it absorbed water while Peter swam to shore. Most would remove their outer garment before diving in. In contrast, the other disciples returned to shore in a more logical manner—by boat (John 21:8).

The third step in the restoration process involves renewing our relationship with Christ in both words and actions. The disciples renewed fellowship with Jesus by enjoying what had been prepared. "Then, as soon as they had come to land, they saw a fire of coals there, and fish laid on it, and bread" (John 21:9). They also contributed to the cause by bringing to the fire some of the fish they had just caught (John 21:10). But actions were not enough to restore the relationship that had been broken between Jesus and Peter. Just as Peter had denied Jesus three times during his night of failure, Jesus walked Peter through a process that enabled him to confess his love for Jesus three times (John 21:15–17). Peter did not make excuses for his previous actions, but confessed his commitment. According to Ben Franklin, "He that is good for making excuses is seldom good for anything else." As Peter declared his affection for Jesus, Jesus entrusted him with increased ministry responsibility.

Ultimately, the restoration process involves settling the commitment question up front. Failure in the face of difficulty is never an excuse that others will accept. Leaders need to count the cost of pursuing God's call upon their lives. Jesus told Peter, "Most assuredly, I say to you, when you were younger, you girded yourself and walked where you wished; but when you are old, you will stretch out your hands, and another will gird you and carry you where you do not wish" (John 21:18).

Leaders need to rise to the challenge of being the leader God has called them to be. Peter understood Jesus was describing the death he would experience at the end of his life of service. According to the reliable tradition of the early church, Peter was crucified upside down during the Roman persecution of the church. Still Jesus said, "Follow me" (John 21:19).

God's calling to be a leader means the leader must be prepared to stand alone, leading regardless of what others may do. Peter's first instinct when he understood what following Jesus would cost was to ask about his friend and fellow disciple, John. Jesus responded, "If I will that he remain till I come, what is that to you? You follow Me" (John 21:22).

Being a leader involves being a person of integrity whose credibility stands without question. As the Gospel of John concludes, it includes a verse some Bible teachers believe reflects the attitude of the Ephesian church toward John, who was their pastor when he wrote his Gospel. "This is the disciple who testifies of these things, and wrote these things, and we know that his testimony is true" (John 21:24).

Finally, restored leaders need to remain focused on the task before them rather than becoming involved in other incidentals. John understood that in the process of writing his Gospel. He concludes with the words, "And there are also many other things that Jesus did, which if they were written one by one, I suppose that even the world itself could not contain the books that would be written" (John 21:25). In his Gospel, he sifted through the many things Jesus did to highlight those that best helped illustrate the message he wanted to communicate, that Jesus was indeed "the Christ, the Son of God" (John 20:31).

CHAPTER 23

Paul

The Visionary Leader

*If a man hasn't discovered something he will die for,
he is not fit to live.*

MARTIN LUTHER KING, JR.

B orn into the home of a Baptist minister during the Great
Depression, young Michael (later renamed Martin) did not seem
to have a bright future. Beyond that, he was born into an African-
American home in America's deep South at a time when that race was
still subject to racial discrimination enshrined in law. But his parents
had great dreams for their son, and despite the hardships they faced,
they ensured that their son received a good education. In 1948, Martin
Luther King Jr. graduated from Morehouse College in Atlanta, Georgia,
with a Bachelor of Arts degree.

That was a significant accomplishment for a young black
American, but King dreamed of following in his father's footsteps
and serving his people as a Baptist minister. Knowing that opportunities for young African-American men were greater in the northern
United States than the South, he enrolled in the Bachelor of Divinity
program at Crozer Theological Seminary in Chester, Pennsylvania,

and graduated in 1951. Four years later, he completed his Doctor of Philosophy degree in systematic theology. By that time, he was married and had begun his first pastorate at Dexter Avenue Baptist Church in Montgomery, Alabama.

Racial tensions were high in the mid-fifties. Laws were enforced to attempt to keep the growing African-American population under control. Various fringe elements on both sides of the racial dispute were resorting to violence to make their point. By the end of January 1956, King's home had been bombed. A year later, a group of Black ministers formed what became known as the Southern Christian Leadership Conference. Recognizing his growing influence within the civil rights movement, his peers named King as their first president. That year, King traveled 780,000 miles and made 208 speeches, a pattern that would become typical of his efforts in the years to come.

As his influence grew within the civil rights movement, he increasingly became a target for those content with the status quo. In 1958, he published his first book, *Stride Toward Freedom* (New York: Harper and Brothers, 1958), an account of the Montgomery bus boycott he had helped organize earlier. While promoting his book in a Harlem bookstore, he was stabbed by an African-American woman. Five years later, he was arrested in Birmingham for demonstrating in defiance of a court order. While there, he wrote *Letter from Birmingham Jail*,[1] which became a classic of the movement. In 1965, James George Robinson of Birmingham assaulted King when he registered to vote in Selma, Alabama. His success ultimately made him the target of an assassin's bullet on April 4, 1968.

But despite the opposition, people who had the power to make the changes he wanted made recognized King's influence. In 1962, he met with President John F. Kennedy to win his support for civil rights. Three years later he met with President Lyndon B. Johnson and other American leaders to urge equal voting rights for African-Americans. He had audiences with leaders in India and West Germany. Even Pope Paul VI met with King in 1964. In December of that year, his efforts were recognized internationally when he won the Nobel Peace Prize.

But King had not endured the opposition and fought the struggle for international recognition. On August 28, 1963, King delivered what would become his most remembered address at the foot of the Lincoln Memorial. That day, a quarter million people gathered for the March on Washington, and millions of others watching television reports of the event heard King outline his vision of the future. He described a country where children could grow up without discrimination on the basis of race or religion. In that speech, he used the familiar phrase, "I have a dream." That phrase is what the life of Martin Luther King Jr. was all about. He had a dream, and he devoted all his energies in pursuit of that dream.

People of the Dream

While the nature of leadership presupposes vision, there are some leaders who can only be described as "people of the dream." They not only know what they want and where they are going, but they have also mastered the ability to popularize their dream and communicate that vision effectively for others. That dream energizes a movement that accomplishes more than it would otherwise. It realizes the dream.

Visionary leaders are those who define the task of leadership not by what could be done but by what should be done. They look beyond their own abilities or the immediate needs to recognize a larger goal. Then they develop effective strategies to accomplish that vision. In the process, they accomplish much more than they might have originally thought possible.

Paul was one of those people of the dream. He also understood some ways of doing ministry were more effective than others. He realized much more could be accomplished not by working harder, but by working smarter. Therefore, he developed a series of strategies to effectively accomplish his ministry goals. In the two millennia since, church leaders have not been able to improve upon the Pauline strategy for ministry.

Visionary leaders are growth-oriented leaders in every context in which they lead. They are the entrepreneurs in business who see the potential in a new product and build a profitable industry around it. They are college deans who recognize emerging trends in society and are among the first to implement study programs to train students to service new needs. They are the pioneer church planters who go to a new community and establish a church that reaches people for Christ formerly thought of as unreachable. They are the visionary pastors who assume responsibility for a church in decline and lead that church to dream again and adopt a strategy that turns a dying church into a dynamic church.

In a world content with the *status quo,* visionary leaders face unique challenges. They are almost always slightly ahead of their time. The dreams they dream are usually bigger than most people think possible, and the tasks required to realize them often require a greater commitment than many people are willing to make. They live and work in a culture that is, at least initially, resistant to their new ideas and proposals. Initially, they find themselves standing alone in their optimistic outlook toward the future. As they pursue their dream, they have a tendency to draw a following of uncontrolled dreamers and those who cannot dream their own dreams. Because they are forward-looking, it is not uncommon for visionary leaders to see the answer before most people even understand the question. They tend to begin thinking of solutions while others are beginning to recognize the existence of a problem.

Many visionary church leaders are gifted in evangelism and use their gift to declare a message of hope to those who have begun to lose hope. Because much of this leadership style is built around the dream, they use the Law of Dreams to encourage others with a brighter vision of the future. Visionary leaders are often sanguine or phlegmatic in temperament.

While visionary leaders have a difficult time seeing the downside to any situation, there are significant dangers tied to this approach to leadership. Visionary leaders may take on a task beyond their ability and flounder in their leadership as the project fails. It is not uncommon for a visionary leader to dream too far ahead of his followers and cause them to become overwhelmed and/or discouraged. Sometimes, visionary leaders struggle in their attitude toward their followers. They may become frustrated with the initial negative response to their ideas. On other occasions, they may move too fast and become irritated waiting for followers to be ready to follow. They may even become impractical in their expectations when they attempt too much. When that happens, the task of convincing those without vision becomes even more difficult. Perhaps the greatest danger they face is the tendency to go off in pursuit of their dream without an effective strategy to make that dream a reality.

The Italian economist Pareto postulated the highest rate of production comes from the smallest segment of society. In what has been coined, "the Pareto Principle," John C. Maxwell explains, "Twenty percent of your priorities will give you eighty percent of your production, if you spend your time, energy, money, and personnel on the top twenty percent of your priorities."[2] Someone once said, "You can lead a horse to water, but you can't make him drink." Effective visionary leaders invest their resources in leading thirsty horses to water so they will drink when they get there. When you invest the best you have to get the best you can, the rest will eventually follow.

As important as dreams are, it takes more than dreams to be effective in leadership. Visionary leaders need to learn how to develop effective strategies to make their dreams reality. Working harder is not nearly as effective as working smarter. Strategy identifies the means by which specific goals can be achieved. Most people can only follow their leader when clear action steps have been outlined for them. Also, practice wise stewardship of all resources by making sure every action builds toward the desired end. Strategy is what we do as humans; then we let God do what only He can do. According to A. L. Williams, "All you can do is all you can do, but all you can do is enough."[3]

The Strategic Ministry of Paul

Paul has been described as the greatest Christian leader of all time. As a pioneer missionary to unreached people groups, Paul used a strategy still used by effective mission agencies and national churches today with great success. Paul developed and used strategy in several ways to accomplish the various ministry goals that grew out of his vision.

The development of strategy to accomplish goals is often the missing link among leaders with great vision but limited success in achieving that vision. According to James M. Kouzes and Barry Z. Posner, "Every organization, every social movement begins with a dream. The dream or vision is the force that invents the future." In order for that future to be realized, leaders need to develop a plan to take them and their followers from where they are to where they want to be. Often, that plan turns out to be a series of plans or strategies that accomplish various goals on the way to realizing the vision.

Paul developed an ethnic strategy to reach his fellow Jews. Paul expressed this strategy in two ways. First, he believed the gospel was "the power of God to salvation for everyone who believes, for the Jew first and also for the Greek" (Rom. 1:16). Therefore, Paul usually began his ministry in a community by preaching first to the Jewish population within that community. Second, he developed his unique ministry to Gentiles. "Inasmuch as I am an apostle to the Gentiles, I magnify my ministry, if by any means I may provoke to jealousy those who are my flesh and save some of them" (Rom. 11:13–14).

Depending upon the particular audience he was addressing, Paul also developed a unique preaching strategy. In a predominantly Jewish context, this involved disputing the Scriptures with a view of demonstrating that Jesus was the Messiah. He used this strategy in Thessalonica when he "reasoned with them from the Scriptures, explaining and demonstrating that the Christ had to suffer and rise again from the dead, and saying, 'This Jesus whom I preach to you is the Christ'" (Acts 17:2–3). This approach to ministry was effective among the Jews because Paul and his audience shared a common understanding of the Old Testament Scriptures. When preaching to a predominantly pagan audience, Paul found common ground in creation. In Athens, he began his message with "God, who made the world and everything in it" (Acts 17:24). In both cases, his preaching goal was to call people to personal faith in Christ, but the unique character of his audience dictated the way in which he chose to communicate that message.

Paul also understood the unique infrastructure of his society and developed a sociological strategy that involved reaching leaders as the key to reaching communities. This was part of God's purpose for Paul right from his conversion. God described Paul to Ananias as "a chosen vessel of Mine to bear My name before Gentiles, kings, and the children of Israel" (Acts 9:15a).

His understanding of social networks led him also to develop a networking strategy. This involved reaching the heads of households who in turn reached others in their sphere of influence with the gospel. This aspect of his ministry is especially evident in Philippi in the conversion of the households of Lydia (Acts 16:15) and the Philippian jailer (Acts 16:33).

One key to Paul's ministry success was the geographic strategy he developed that involved reaching large centers as the base of a broader regional ministry. The cities in which Paul established new churches were regional centers with an influence beyond their city boundaries. This was especially true of Ephesus, the city in which Paul ministered the longest. There Paul "continued for two years, so that all who dwelt in Asia heard the word of the Lord Jesus, both Jews and Greeks" (Acts 19:10).

Paul also had a bridge-building strategy that involved identifying with those he tried to reach so he could reach them more effectively. He outlined this approach when he told the Corinthians, "For though

I am free from all men, I have made myself a servant to all, that I might win the more; and to the Jews I became as a Jew, that I might win Jews; to those who are under the law, as under the law, that I might win those who are under the law; to those who are without law, as without law (not being without law toward God, but under law toward Christ), that I might win those who are without law; to the weak I became as weak, that I might win the weak. I have become all things to all men, that I might by all means save some" (1 Cor. 9:19–22).

Paul also developed a pastoral strategy to ensure that all who were under his spiritual watchcare were taught the Scriptures and warned appropriately. He reminded the Ephesian elders of how he had implemented that strategy during his ministry in that city. "I kept back nothing that was helpful, but proclaimed it to you, and taught you publicly and from house to house, testifying to Jews, and also to Greeks, repentance toward God and faith toward our Lord Jesus Christ" (Acts 20:20–21). Then he urged the elders in that church to do the same. "Therefore watch, and remember that for three years I did not cease to warn everyone night and day with tears" (Acts 20:31).

Despite his commitment to developing ministry strategies, Paul never allowed his strategy to change or alter his message in any way. He reminded the Corinthians, "And I, brethren, when I came to you, did not come with excellence of speech or of wisdom declaring to you the testimony of God. For I determined not to know anything among you except Jesus Christ and Him crucified" (1 Cor. 2:1–2).

Building a Strategic Plan

Effecting change in a stable organization is one of the most difficult tasks leaders may face. Even when people know the way things are is not right, they are still more comfortable with what they know. When an established church calls a pastor with a vision to revitalize the church so it can become more effective at reaching people for Christ, a tension already exists. A wise pastor understands it takes hard work and a carefully developed strategic plan to effect a slow transition in the church from where it is to where it needs to be. Growing a church is a process of continuous improvement just as in growing businesses and other institutions.

Effective long-term leaders know how to develop and implement a strategic plan. Indeed, strategic planning is a tool that needs to be a part of every leader's personal leadership kaleidoscope. While the actual planning process varies to some degree in every organization, there are essentially seven steps involved in building a strategic plan.

First, identify the goal you hope to achieve in a clearly written goal statement. David George once observed, "There is nothing so fatal to character as a half-finished task." When you know where you are going, you can keep on going until you get there. Great leaders are always enthusiastic because they can visualize the desired future in the midst of a dismal process. While it is great to dream, sooner or later reality must set in.

The second step in the planning process involves identifying those things that may help you achieve your goal. Many great dreams are never attempted because the dreamer doesn't think there is much chance of success. But something is always better than nothing. According to Sydney Smith, "It is the greatest of all mistakes to do nothing because you can only do a little. Do what you can."

Once you have identified things that can help you achieve your goal, *take time to identify those things that are likely to hinder you in the pursuit of that goal.* While these forces need to be taken into account, the key to success in any venture involves building on your strengths. Former U.S. President Calvin Coolidge correctly observed, "Little progress can be made by merely attempting to repress what is evil. Our great hope lies in developing what is good."

Next, list the steps that need to be taken to realize that goal. According to Zig Ziglar, "Success is a cinch by the inch."[4] When a large project is broken down into smaller manageable steps, the project becomes achievable one step at a time. The more you do, the more you can do.

Once the steps have been identified, prioritize the steps by listing them in the order in which they need to be achieved. In the construction of a new building, the carpenter needs to frame the wall before the painter can paint it. Between these two workers, those responsible for wiring the wall for power, insulating the wall for energy efficiency, and for dry walling and mudding the wall, all have to do their work. Leaders lead by asking, delegating, guiding, encouraging, and risking. Therefore, a good leader will ask questions to understand what needs to be done, delegate responsibility and give authority to those who will oversee various aspects of the project, guide his followers in the right direction so the project can be accomplished, and encourage those working together so they will take risks to effect a significant change.

Many leaders find it helpful to transfer those steps to a PERT chart or similar tool to identify a logical scheduling sequence. The acronym PERT stands for Program Evaluation and Review Technique. A PERT chart looks like a series of connected boxes in which each step involved in a project is identified. Each step is listed in a time sequence so the project manager can quickly see if the project is on schedule. Also, you realize each step that is dependent on a previous step being completed before you can take another step. The PERT chart helps the project manager identify quickly other parts of the project likely to be delayed if one step is not completed on time.

Finally, once the plan has been developed, implement it. Use your PERT chart to monitor progress and make periodic adjustments as necessary. Careful planning normally helps move the project along at a more efficient rate than might be expected. But sometimes it is not until the work actually begins that problems in the plan become apparent. Leaders need to be flexible enough with their plans to make the necessary adjustments to achieve the goal for which the plan was developed.

CHAPTER 24

Paul

The Training Leader

*And the things that you have heard from me among
many witnesses, commit these to faithful men who will be
able to teach others also.*

2 TIMOTHY 2:2

In every generation, Christianity risks extinction. If the present generation of Christians fails to reproduce itself in the next generation, the evangelical faith will fade out of existence with the death of the last Christian. The challenge to maintain our faith is the challenge of our heritage, if we do not pass on our faith to successive generations, and it could have a disastrous effect (Judg. 2:10). That is why the Great Commission is at the very heart of the mission of the church. Every generation is called to "make disciples of all the nations" (Matt. 28:19).

As a young man, Dawson Trotman sure didn't look like a respected evangelical leader. By his own admission, he embezzled funds from both his employer and the student council funds for which he, as student council president, was responsible. In an effort to reform, he got involved in a church youth group, eventually becoming president of the young people's society. But nothing changed for Dawson on the inside. Eventually he concluded he didn't have what it takes to be a good leader. At that point, he gave up trying and began drinking alcohol.

The alcohol didn't help matters at all. His health deteriorated, and he was soon in trouble with local law enforcement officials. While under the influence one Friday night, he was arrested and was on his way to jail. In desperation he cried out to God, "If You will get me out of this mess tonight, I'll do whatever You want me to." When the police officer accompanying him to the jail saw him crying, he asked, "Do you like this kind of life?" When Dawson responded, "Sir, I hate it," the officer took him to a park, made him sit there for three hours to sober up, and let him go when Dawson promised to reform.

Two nights later he attended a local church which was beginning a Scripture memory contest. Dawson began memorizing ten verses a week, and the verses had a profound impact on his life. After two weeks of memorizing Scripture, one of them came to mind as he walked to work one morning. Intrigued with the promise of eternal life it offered, he checked his New Testament to be sure he was remembering it right. That day he was converted to Christ, and his life began changing from the inside out.

Dawson continued memorizing Scripture, a verse a day for the first three years of his Christian life. He was so excited about the change God had made in his life that he took advantage of every opportunity he could to witness for Christ and led many people to Christ. While he rejoiced in many people coming to faith in Christ, he was discouraged that so few experienced the kind of change he had experienced in his own life. That's when he realized the importance of discipling new believers in the Christian life. With a renewed zeal for not just "getting decisions" but "making disciples," he began spending more time following up those he led to Christ. The principles he learned in the process were eventually incorporated into a new ministry that he called the Navigators.

HOW TO REACH THE WORLD IN THIRTY-THREE YEARS

According to an ancient legend, the chessboard was originally invented in India. The wealthy ruler was so appreciative of the new game that he offered to reward the inventor and asked him what he wanted. His answer was simple. He asked for a single grain of rice to be placed on the first square of the board. Then he asked for twice as much on the second square, and that the ruler would continue doubling the rice on each square until the board was filled. It doesn't sound like a lot for a new game, but when you do the math it takes over 4.8 billion metric tons of rice to fill the last square. That is more than eight times the current worldwide annual production of rice.

When the principle of compounding is applied to disciple making, it is theoretically possible for one Christian to reach the entire world in just thirty years. If one Christian led someone to Christ and invested a year into that person's life, equipping him to lead another person to Christ and disciple him or her, then there would be two doing the work of evangelism at the end of a year. If both did the same thing the next year, there would be four at the end of year two. In year three, that number would increase to eight; sixteen in year four and thirty-two in year five. That may seem like a lot of effort with

It was not long before other evangelical ministries also recognized the value of following up on their converts. Dawson Trotman helped many ministries develop follow-up materials that are still being used fifty years later. When Evangelist Billy Graham invited Trotman to join his staff as follow-up director, he declined because that commitment would not leave him enough time to adequately follow up individuals he was personally leading to Christ. He believed strongly in following up new Christians one-on-one. His life ended June 18, 1956, in a drowning accident, but his influence as a leader continues into the twenty-first century through the ministry he founded.

minimal results, especially when you are trying to reach over six billion people. But don't despair.

In year six, the thirty-two become sixty-four. In year seven, the sixty-four become 128. In year eight, 128 become 256. In year nine, 256 become 512. In year ten, 512 become 1,024. In year eleven, 1,024 become 2,048. In year twelve, 2,048 become 4,096. In year thirteen, 4,096 become 8,192. In year fourteen, 8,192 become 16,384. In year fifteen, 16,384 become 32,768. In year sixteen, 32,768 become 65,536. In year seventeen, 65,536 become 131,072. In year eighteen, 131,072 become 262,144. In year nineteen, 262,144 become 524,288. In year twenty, 524,288 become 1,048,576. In year twenty-one, 1,048,576 become 2,097,152. In year twenty-two, 2,097,152 become 4,194,304. In year twenty-three, 4,194,304 become 8,388,608. In year twenty-four, 8,338,608 become 16,777,216. In year twenty-five, 16,777,216 become 33,554,432. In year twenty-six, 33,554,432 become 67,108,864. In year twenty-seven, 67,108,864 become 134,217,728. In year twenty-eight, 134,217,728 become 268,435,456. In year twenty-nine, 268,435,456 become 536,870,912. In year thirty, 536,870,912 become 1,073,741,824. In year thirty-one, 1,073,741,824 become 2,147,483,648. In year thirty-two, 2,147,483,648 become 4,294,967,296. And in year thirty-three, we will run out of people to reach.

And it all began with one person making one disciple!

Reproducing Reproducers

Though his life was tragically cut short, Trotman had the right idea. The leader who reproduces himself in others ultimately has the greatest influence in the world. If leadership is influence, then the greatest leaders are those who reproduce themselves in others.

This approach to leadership seems to be what Jesus had in mind when He left His followers the Great Commission (Matt. 28:18–20). The principal verb in that commission is "make disciples" (Matt. 28:19). Just as Jesus had invested Himself in the training of the Twelve, so He expected them along with His other followers to invest themselves not only to reach people with the gospel, but to disciple them so they would "observe all things that I (Jesus) have commanded you" (Matt. 28:20). A *disciple-making leader* is one who takes seriously the Great Commission and reproduces himself in the lives of others to multiply his effectiveness as a leader.

Disciple-making leadership is illustrated throughout the Scriptures. Moses mentored Joshua, equipping him to accomplish God's vision for his life. Elijah discipled Elisha and others in the school of the prophets. Some Bible teachers believe that Samuel first established a school and that David may have been among its alumni. The Old Testament Book of Proverbs, especially the first nine chapters, appears to have been a text used in the training of the princes (future kings) of Judah. In the New Testament, Jesus trained the Twelve, Barnabas mentored Saul of Tarsus, and Paul trained a new generation of leadership that included Timothy, Titus, and a host of others.

Great leadership outlives the leaders. These leaders multiply and extend their influence through the development of leaders who share their vision and commitment. Paul modeled effective leadership training strategies by making disciples who not only assisted him in his ministry; they also became the effective leaders of the next generation.

Disciple-making leaders have an impact in every area of life. They are the personnel directors who train workers for increased effectiveness and productivity in business. They include teachers who share their knowledge, insights, and skills in their area of expertise, reproducing something of themselves in others. They are the mechanics who take on young apprentices and pass on years of experience and knowledge to help them develop the skills they need to be mechanics. And they include the pastors who preserve the results of evangelistic efforts by training new converts and helping them find their fit in ministry.

Of course, a "disciple making" approach to leadership is not without its problems. Disciple-making usually involves a longer term commitment than other approaches to evangelism. It tends not to have the dramatic initial results other evangelistic strategies produce. Making

TWO APPROACHES TO DISCIPLESHIP TRAINING

When Dawson Trotman founded The Navigators, he advocated following up new Christians one-on-one. Ideally, Trotman hoped the person God used to lead an individual to faith in Christ would also be the one to follow up the new convert. That approach remains the primary focus of the Navigators and has been widely adopted by many evangelical churches and ministries.

Among churches that have adopted Trotman's one-on-one approach to discipleship training, most incorporate it into their broader evangelistic ministry. Using a team approach to ministry, these churches recognize some Christians tend to be more effective in evangelism whereas others appear better equipped to disciple new believers. In some ministries, the person who begins discipling a new believer may not be the one who continues later as the believer matures in Christ.

A second approach to discipleship training recognizes everyone has his blind spots that he may reproduce in others through the discipling process. To minimize this effect, many ministries have adopted a small group approach to discipleship training. In this approach, new converts are incorporated into small groups to grow in the Christian life. Sometimes, these groups are primarily composed of new Christians who work through a curriculum designed to introduce them to the basic disciplines of the Christian life. In other contexts, they may be existing Sunday school classes or small groups meeting in homes throughout the week.

The advantage of this second approach to discipleship training is twofold. First, it allows the church to disciple more new converts faster because several people are being discipled in a meeting rather than just one. Second, advocates argue new Christians are being discipled better because several Christians in the group rather than a single discipler are influencing them. In the process, new converts form relationships with more church members. Research suggests the more people a new convert forms relationships with in the church, the longer they are likely to stay in that church.

disciples involves training people in spiritual disciplines which may seem foreign to new converts. Even those who have been Christians for some time may struggle in the growth process of discipleship.

In our hurry-up world, discipleship training challenges the very core values of our age. It is not surprising that other ministry demands often cut into the time and resources available for making disciples. Since its arrival in 1940, television has conditioned every generation since the Baby Boomers to think in terms of instant gratification rather than long-term commitments. Even among Christians, there are apparently few who recognize the long-term benefits of a disciple-making ministry. Contemporary evangelicalism is more inclined to practice "decision making" than "disciple making."

Disciple-making leaders are uniquely gifted for success in this approach to leadership. They use their gift of teaching to effectively communicate biblical principles to others. Beyond that, they use their gift of exhortation to help people understand how to practice various spiritual disciplines and to accomplish ministry. Disciple-making leaders depend heavily on the Law of Communication to share biblical principles with new converts. Often, they tend to be somewhat phlegmatic in temperament.

Disciple-making leaders face their own unique challenges and dangers. It is not uncommon for them to become discouraged with the progress of their disciples, especially when they struggle over minor issues. Sometimes, the problem is of their own making. They may slow the progress of their disciples by failing to disciple adequately. Sometimes, they transfer their own blind spots and shortcomings as they reproduce themselves in others. On occasion, they may waver in calling new converts to a complete commitment to Christ because they fear new converts may be scared off.

Pastors who lead their churches through disciple making are often criticized, sometimes for good reasons. They may spend too much time with newer people who are growing in Christ and neglect the older members of the church. Disciple making is a time-consuming process. Pastors committed to this process may find less time to fulfill their other ministry responsibilities. They may even invest so much time encouraging growth in others that they neglect their own personal walk with God and hinder their spiritual growth in Christ.

In spite of the problems, leaders need to learn disciple-making skills and blend this approach to leadership into their personal leadership kaleidoscope. Reproducing yourself in even one other person effectively doubles your ministry potential. If Christians could catch the vision of reproducing themselves at a rate of even one disciple per year, the entire world population would be Christian in just over three decades.

Because a former generation reproduced itself in us, we have a moral obligation to do the same for the next generation. The Great Commission makes us responsible to transfer our Christian faith to others through the process of disciple making (Matt. 28:19).

Paul: Leading through Disciple Making

The apostle Paul modeled disciple-making leadership in his commitment to train a new generation of leaders for the churches he was establishing throughout the Gentile world. Paul trained many disciples throughout his ministry. At least thirty-eight associates of Paul are identified by name within the pages of the New Testament. While the Scriptures record details about many people whom Paul discipled, we know more about Timothy's training than others'. Paul's unique relationship with Timothy illustrates both the influence of the apostle on his younger protégé and the varied means by which he mentored Timothy.

Someone once noted, "If we work marble it will perish. If we work upon brass, time will efface it. If we rear temples, they will crumble into dust. But if we work upon immortal minds and instill into them principles, we are then engraving upon tablets which no time will efface, but will brighten and influence all eternity."

Paul began discipling Timothy by example. Although he is first mentioned early in the account of Paul's second missions tour (Acts 16:1), many Bible teachers believe he was among the Galatian converts on Paul's previous visit to that region (Acts 13:14–14:23). Paul's own

THE TRAINING OF TIMOTHY

Timothy's association with Paul is described in various New Testament books. When compiled together, the training of Timothy through his association with Paul becomes clearer.

Timothy was apparently converted to Christ through Paul's initial visit to Galatia (Acts 13:14–14:23; 2 Tim. 3:10–11). When Paul passed through the same area on his second missions tour, he invited Timothy to join the team (Acts 16:1). When he was forced to leave Berea prematurely, Paul left Timothy and Silas behind to continue the ministry there (Acts 17:14). They later rejoined Paul in Corinth, perhaps bringing financial aid with them from Macedonia (Acts 18:5; Phil. 4:15).

Paul later sent Timothy back to Macedonia (Thessalonica) with an epistle and to minister to the young church in that region (Acts 19:22; 1 Thess. 3:2). Having fulfilled that responsibility, Timothy returned to Paul with a full and positive report on the work in Thessalonica (1 Thess. 3:6). He continued to travel with Paul until the apostle himself returned to Macedonia (Acts 20:4).

Timothy traveled to at least three additional cities to minister at Paul's request. First, he was sent to Corinth (1 Cor. 4:17; 16:10). Later, Paul sent Timothy to Philippi (Phil. 2:19). Ultimately, Paul urged Timothy to remain in Ephesus where, according to an early church tradition, he became the church's first bishop (1 Tim. 1:3).

Timothy was still in Ephesus when Paul contacted him again and asked him to come to Rome (2 Tim. 4:9, 13). This occurred during Nero's reign, a time of intense persecution directed against the Christians. Timothy was apparently arrested in Rome, but later released. Upon his release, he was once more sent to a struggling church, a predominantly Jewish congregation in Jerusalem or Alexandria (Heb. 13:23).

writing seems to support this view. Much later, he wrote an epistle to Timothy in which he reminded him, "But you have carefully followed my doctrine, manner of life, purpose, faith, long-suffering, love, perseverance, persecutions, afflictions, which happened to me at Antioch, at Iconium, at Lystra; what persecutions I endured. And out of them all the Lord delivered me" (2 Tim. 3:10–11). Even before a more formal discipleship training process was launched, Timothy learned from Paul as he watched Paul.

There is no substitute for leadership by example. People are more likely to see what we do than to hear what we say. According to Albert Schweitzer, "Example is not the main thing in influencing others. It is the only thing." When Frank J. Ruck Jr. wanted to change his organization, he began with himself. "I began by becoming a role model that exemplifies the organizational and management values I believe are important," he explained. Sooner or later, every institution becomes the length and shadow of its leader.

Timothy also learned from Paul through association. Recognizing the potential in this young man, Paul invited Timothy to become a part of his ministry team (Acts 16:2–3). That began a relationship that grew deeper over the years. In his final years of ministry, Paul expressed the depth of that relationship in describing Timothy as his "true son in the faith" (1 Tim. 1:2) and "a beloved son" (2 Tim. 1:2).

Paul also discipled Timothy by assignment. As a member of the ministry team, Timothy was given periodic assignments that helped the apostle in his ministry to the churches and encouraged Timothy's personal growth as a disciple. Corinth (1 Cor. 4:17), Macedonia (Acts 19:22), Philippi (Phil. 2:19–23), and Thessalonica (1 Thess. 3:1–2) are among the places Paul sent Timothy. There may have been many other assignments of which we have no record today.

Public instruction was no doubt part of Timothy's training. As part of Paul's ministry team, he would have heard Paul teaching publicly in synagogues, homes, and public forums. In calling Timothy to follow his example as a disciple-making leader, Paul urged him to teach "the things that you have heard from me among many witnesses" (2 Tim. 2:2). One particular public forum of which Timothy may have been a part was the School of Tryannus (Acts 19:9). Early in Paul's Ephesian ministry, Paul chose to leave the synagogue rather than continue dealing with the hostility there and taught a more receptive audience in a school probably established by a man named Tryannus. Those trained in that forum traveled throughout the region establishing churches so that within two years, "all who dwelt in Asia heard the word of the Lord Jesus, both Jews and Greeks" (Acts 19:10).

The disciple-making leader also uses private counsel in the mentoring process. We will never know the details of conversations between Paul and Timothy as they traveled together between cities. We can make reasonable assumptions about the contents of those conversations based on two personal epistles to Timothy that are part of the New Testament canon. Each illustrates the kind of advice Paul must have shared with Timothy on other occasions throughout their years of association.

Paul discipled Timothy by promotion. In his epistles, Paul promoted Timothy as a full partner in ministry. Sometimes, Paul listed Timothy's name alongside his in the opening verses of an epistle (2 Cor. 1:1; Phil. 1:1; Col. 1:1; 1 Thess. 1:1; 2 Thess. 1:1; Philem. 1:1). On other occasions, Paul described Timothy in terms that express deep appreciation for Timothy (1 Cor. 4:17). Sometimes Paul simply described Timothy as his "fellow worker" or "brother," meaning, a full partner in ministry (Rom. 16:21; Heb. 13:23). He told the Corinthians, "he does the work of the Lord, as I also do" (1 Cor. 16:10). When writing to the Philippians, Paul's endorsement of Timothy's ministry was even stronger. "For I have no one like-minded, who will sincerely care for your state" (Phil. 2:20).

Part of Paul's discipling of Timothy involved prodding. Even though Timothy had been taught well, he still needed to be motivated periodically to apply the principles of growth in his life. This need is evident in several encouragements written into Paul's final epistle to Timothy. "Therefore I remind you to stir up the gift of God which is in you through the laying on of my hands. For God has not given us a spirit of fear, but of power and of love and of a sound mind" (2 Tim. 1:6, 7). "You therefore, my son, be strong in the grace that is in Christ Jesus" (2 Tim. 2:1). "But you must continue in the things which you have learned and been assured of, knowing from whom you have learned them" (2 Tim. 3:14). "Preach the word! Be ready in season and out of season. Convince, rebuke, exhort, with all long-suffering and teaching. . . . But you be watchful in all things, endure afflictions, do the work of an evangelist, fulfill your ministry" (2 Tim. 4:2, 5).

The test of being a disciple-making leader is successfully mentoring children who mentor grandchildren who mentor great grandchildren. In the Old Testament, the blessing of God was passed on to the third and fourth generations. A disciple-making leader has not completed his task until his disciple can reproduce into someone else the ability to be a reproducer (2 Tim. 2:2).

What Does a Disciple Look Like?

The disciple-making leader makes himself necessary to someone else. He becomes the mentor of a protégé who needs his input to grow. But the process of disciple making will not work if the leader is unclear about what he is trying to accomplish. According to Kouzes and Posner, "In order to lead by example, leaders must first be clear about their business beliefs. Managers may speak eloquently about vision and values, but if their behavior is not consistent with their stated beliefs, people ultimately will lose respect for them." Lachlan McLean got it right when he said, "You can only lead others where you yourself are willing to go."

The goal of the disciple-making leader is to *produce a disciple.* That involves helping Christians develop the six basic disciplines of the Christian life taught by Jesus. Just as Paul discipled Timothy by both example and explanation, it is necessary for the disciple-making leader to master these disciplines in his own life before teaching them

SECRETS OF THE VINE

In his book, *Secrets of the Vine: Breaking Through to Abundance,*[1] Bruce Wilkinson describes four kinds of Christians based on Jesus' teaching on the vine in John 15. He distinguishes each group based on their level of "fruit production," i.e., those who bear no fruit, those who bear fruit, those who bear more fruit, and those who bear much fruit. Although many Christians find themselves in the first category, God's ultimate goal is that we bear "much fruit."

The process of moving from bearing no fruit to bearing fruit is a process of discipline. Because He loves us, God is prepared to discipline us much as a father disciplines the children he loves. The use of words like "rebuke," "chasten" and "scourge" to describe this discipline process suggests God disciplines by degree and will use whatever it takes to bring His children back into line (Heb. 12:5–6).

Those who bear fruit move to a higher level of fruit bearing through a process of pruning. In many respects, the pruning experience may feel a lot like the discipline experience, but there are a couple of significant differences. Christians are disciplined because they are doing something wrong whereas they are pruned because they are doing something right. Also, while discipline addresses the problem of sin in one's life, pruning deals with the problem of self.

The final stage of growth in the vineyard involves moving from more fruit to much fruit. The key to success in this phase of growth is abiding in Christ, that is, nurturing our personal relationship with God. Wilkerson suggests two key principles that, when consistently applied, can help make that happen. First, we need to deepen the quality of our time devoted to God. This usually involves making our time with God a priority rather than something we fit into our schedule. Second, we need to begin seeing our time with God in a broader context, not just the designated "devotional time" in our schedule, but a realization that we constantly live in His presence.

to others. Becoming a disciple is the first step in becoming a disciple maker.

When Jesus called people to discipleship, He called them to a *radical commitment*. He described the nature of that commitment when He said, "If anyone desires to come after Me, let him deny himself, and take up his cross daily, and follow Me" (Luke 9:23). Becoming a disciple begins with giving Christ first place in your life. That commitment is ultimately expressed in the development of six spiritual disciplines.

The first discipline involves *abiding in Christ.* In describing the relationship He desired with His disciples, Jesus said, "I am the vine, you are the branches. He who abides in Me, and I in him, bears much fruit; for without Me you can do nothing" (John 15:5). Jesus described a union between Himself and His disciples that became the basis for our communion with Him. Later He added, "If you keep My commandments, you will abide in My love, just as I have kept My Father's commandments and abide in His love" (John 15:10).

The second mark of discipleship is *abiding in the Word of God.* On another occasion, Jesus said, "If you abide in My word, you are My disciples indeed. And you shall know the truth, and the truth shall make you free" (John 8:31–32). The Scriptures, which are also called "the word of Christ" (Col. 3:16), are Christ's primary means of communicating His will to us. It is impossible to develop the kind of intimacy described in the vine metaphor without communication.

Communicating with Christ in prayer is the third discipline of the Christian life. Jesus promised His disciples, "If you abide in Me, and My words abide in you, you will ask what you desire, and it shall be done for you" (John 15:7). Indeed, one of the evidences that Christ had chosen them as disciples was "that whatever you ask the Father in My name He may give you" (John 15:16).

Developing bonds of fellowship with other believers is another distinguishing mark of discipleship. Jesus told His disciples, "A new commandment I give to you, that you love one another; as I have loved you, that you also love one another. By this all will know that you are My disciples, if you have love for one another" (John 13:34–35). While Christians use various acronyms and symbols today to express their faith publicly, the most powerful witness of evangelical Christianity is the spirit of unity between believers because it gives credibility to the gospel. When Jesus prayed for us in the Garden of Gethsemane, He prayed, "that they all may be one, as You, Father, are in Me, and I in You; that they also may be one in Us, that the world may believe that You sent Me" (John 17:21).

Bearing faithful witness to Christ is the fifth discipline of the Christian life. "By this My Father is glorified, that you bear much fruit; so you will be My disciples" (John 15:8). When Jesus delivered a demon-possessed man in the country of the Gadarenes, he wanted to become one of Jesus' disciples. Jesus instructed him, "Go home to your friends, and tell them what great things the Lord has done for you, and how He has had compassion on you" (Mark 5:19). Jesus expected His disciples to talk about Him when they talked to others.

Ultimately, discipleship is expressed in ministry to others. Jesus said, "Greater love has no one than this, than to lay down one's life for his friends" (John 15:13). Ministry involves using the gifts and abilities God has given us to meet needs in the lives of others. Therefore, "If anyone speaks, let him speak as the oracles of God. If anyone ministers, let him do it as with the ability which God supplies, that in all things God may be glorified through Jesus Christ, to whom belong the glory and the dominion forever and ever" (1 Pet. 4:11).

Endnotes

Chapter 1

1. Lee Roberson, cited by Jerry Falwell, "Foreword" to *How to Develop Leadership: Becoming a Leader* by Elmer L. Towns (Lynchburg, VA: Church Leadership Institute, 1986), 4.

2. Mary Higgins Clark, *Daddy's Little Girl* (New York: Simon & Schuster, 2002).

3. Henry Cloud and John Townsend, *The Mom Factor: Dealing with the Mother You Had, Didn't Have, or Still Contend With* (Grand Rapids: Zondervan Publishing House, 1996).

4. Gary Smalley and John T. Trent, *The Blessing* (New York: Pocket Books, 1990).

5. "Famous Quotes, Love Quotes, Motivational Quotes, Cool Quotes and Quotations," <www.indianchild.com/Quotes/confidence_quotes.htm> (August 17, 2004).

6. Management House, "Thoughts on Leadership," <http: //www.man-agementhouse.com/ProductsArchivesPages/ArchivePages/A%20LeadQuotes.html> (August 17, 2004).

7. Ordway Tead, *The Art of Leadership* (New York: McGraw Hill Book Company, 1963).

8. DM Review, *"The CRM-Ready Data Warehouse: Top 10 Characteristics of a BI/CRM Leader, Part 1,"* <http: //www.dmreview.com/article_sub.cfm?articleId=5668> (August 17, 2004).

9. Management House, "Thoughts on Leadership,"<http: //www.manage-menthouse.com/ProductsArchivesPages/ArchivePages/A%20LeadQuotes.html > (August 17, 2004).

10. Bring Them In, *"Starting a Bus Ministry,"* <http: //bringthemin.com/generic8.html> (August 17, 2004).

11. Tim LaHaye, *Spirit-Controlled Temperament* (Wheaton, Ill.: Tyndale House Publishers, September, 1993).

12. The Quotations Page, <http: //www.quotationspage.com/subjects/leadership/> (August 17, 2004).

13. Mary Barrett, "You Are the Leaders of Tomorrow," *NextStep Magazine*, <http: //www.nextstepmagazine.com/NSMPages/articledetails.aspx?articleid=893> (August 17, 2004).

14. Career Summit 2004 Newsletter, <http: //portal.sfusd.edu/data/news/pdf/ACF3044.pdf> (August 17, 2004).

Chapter 2

1. Eric Goldfarb, "The CIO As Coach," *CIO*, 15 July 2000, <http: //www.cio.com/archive/071500/re.html> (August 17, 2004).

2. The Vision Thing, <http: //www.tompkinsinc.com/think/Revolution_Ch_5.pdf> (August 17, 2004).

Chapter 4

1. Bill Bright, *Have You Heard of the Four Spiritual Laws?* (Orlando, FL: Campus Crusade for Christ International, 1965-1995).

2. Michael Richardson, *Amazing Faith* (Colorado Springs, CO: Waterbrook Press, 2001), 243.

3. Ibid., 247.

4. Ibid.

5. Richard M. Nixon, posted at <http: //www.jespinal.com/leadership.htm> August 31, 2004.

6. Gilbert Keith Chesterton, cited by John Maxwell, *Developing the Leader Within You* (Nashville: Thomas Nelson Publishers, 1993), 59.

7. John C. Maxwell, *Developing the Leader Within You* (Nashville: Thomas Nelson Publishers, 1993), 55.

Chapter 6

1. John F. Kennedy, *Profiles in Courage* (New York: Harper and Row, 1964).

2. John F. Kennedy, *Inaugural Address* (January 20, 1961) posted at <http: //www.bartleby.com/124/pres56.html> August 30, 2004.

3. Douglas Porter, "An Analysis of the Nature of Charismatic Leadership and Its Role in Sectarian Fundamentalist Churches with Suggestions Concerning the Development of Personal Charisma" (MA Thesis, Liberty Baptist Seminary, 1982), 1.

4. Elmer L. Towns, *The Successful Sunday School and Teacher's Guidebook* (Carol Stream, IL: Creation House, 1980), 210.

Chapter 7

1. Spencer Johnson, *The Value of Kindness: The Story of Elizabeth Fry* (La Jolla, CA: Value Communications Inc., 1976), 61.

2. John C. Maxwell, *Developing the Leaders Around You* (Nashville: Thomas Nelson Publishers, 1995), 2.

3. Andrew Carnegie, cited by John Maxwell, *Developing the Leader Within You,* 158.

4. David Jackson, cited by John C. Maxwell, *Developing the Leader Within You*, 158.

5. Konrad Adenauer, cited by John C. Maxwell, *Developing the Leader Within You*, 127.

6. Niccolo Machiavelli, cited by John C. Maxwell, *Developing the Leader Within You*, 158.

7. V. Gilbert Beers, cited by John C. Maxwell, *Developing the Leader Within You,* 32.

8. Socrates, cited by John C. Maxwell, *Developing the Leader Within You,* 32.

9. Ann Landers, cited by John C. Maxwell, *Developing the Leader Within You,* 39.

10. Billy Graham, cited by John C. Maxwell, *Developing the Leader Within You,* 40.

11. Dwight D. Eisenhower, *Great Quotes From Great Leaders*, ed. Peggy Anderson (Franklin Lakes, NJ: Career Press, 1997), cited by Rich King, "Leading with Integrity" posted at <http: //www.leadingtoday.org/Onmag/may02/rk-may02.html> August 31, 2004.

12. Peter Drucker, cited by John C. Maxwell, *Developing the Leader Within You,* 39.

13. Maxwell, *Developing the Leader Within You,* 33.

14. Richard Kerr for United Technologies Corp., *Bits and Pieces*, March 1990.

15. Stephen Covey, *The Seven Habits of Highly Effective People* (New York, NY: Simon & Schuster, 1989), cited by John C. Maxwell, *Developing the Leader Within You*, 56.

Chapter 8

1. Vince Lombardi, "Number One Speech" posted at http://www.vincelombardi.com/about/speech.html> August 30, 2004.

Chapter 9

1. Abraham Lincoln, cited by John C. Maxwell, *Developing the Leader Within You*, 145.

Chapter 10

1. Jerry Falwell, "And the Brook Dried Up: Why Do Troubles Come?" (Recorded message based on 1 Kings 17: 7).

2. Helmut Thielicke, *Encounter with Spurgeon* (Philadelphia, PA: Fortress Press, 1963), chapter 15, "The Blind Eye and the Deaf Ear," 203-213.

Chapter 11

1. John C. Maxwell, *The Winning Attitude: Your Key to Personal Success* (Nashville: Thomas Nelson Publishers, 1993).

Chapter 12

1. Adolph Hitler, cited by Michael Lee Lanning, *The Military 100: A Ranking of the Most Influential Military Leaders of All Time* (Secaucus, N.J.: Citadel Press, 1996), 57.

2. http: //www.hitler.org/writings/Mein_Kampf/, accessed August 26, 2004.

Chapter 13

1. This page created and maintained by Ed Allen, allen@sequence.stanford.edu, <http: //tetrad.stanford.edu/Frederick.html, accessed August 26, 2004.

2. Laurence J. Peter, *The Peter Principle* (Cutchogue, NY: Buccaneer Books, 1996).

Chapter 16

1. Henry T. Blackaby and Claude V. King, *Experiencing God: Knowing and Doing the Will of God* (Nashville: LifeWay Press, 1990).

Chapter 17

1. Bill Gates, *People*, August 20, 1990.

Chapter 18

1. Ann Donegan Johnson, *The Value of Caring: The Story of Eleanor Roosevelt* (La Jolla, CA: Value Communication Inc., 1977), p. 63.

2. Charles Munroe Shulz, "Peanuts Cartoon" posted at <http: //en.wiki-iquote.org/wiki/Charles_Schulz> August 31, 2004.

Chapter 19

1. Boris Yeltzin, *Resignation Statement of December 31, 1999* posted at <http: //www.i-resign.com/uk/halloffame/viewHOF_21.asp> August 30, 2004.

2. Jerry Falwell, *Convocation Message to Liberty University Students* (Lynchburg, VA: Liberty University, August 25, 2004).

Chapter 21

1. George Washington Carver, posted at <http: //www.gardenofpraise.com/ibdcarve.htm> August 31, 2004.

2. Robert Coleman, *The Master Plan of Evangelism* (Grand Rapids: Fleming H. Revell Company), 1986.

3. James M. Kouzes and Barry Z. Posner, *The Leadership Challenge,* 3rd ed. (San Francisco: Jossey-Bass, 1996).

4. Ibid.

Chapter 22

1. John C. Maxwell, *Developing the Leader Within You* (Nashville: Thomas Nelson Publishers, 1993), 92.

Chapter 23

1. Martin Luther King, Jr., "Letter from Birmingham Jail," April 16, 1963, http: //almaz.com/nobel/peace/MLK-jail.html (January 2, 2003).

2. John C. Maxwell, *Developing the Leader Within You* (Nashville: Thomas Nelson Publishers, 1993), 17.

3. A. L. Williams, *All You Can Do Is All You Can Do but All You Can Do Is Enough* (Nashville: Thomas Nelson, 1988).

4. Zig Ziglar, *See You at the Top* (Gretna, LA: Pelican Publishing Company, 1979).

Chapter 24

1. Bruce Wilkinson, *Secrets of the Vine: Breaking Through to Abundance* (Sisters, Oreg.: Multnomah Publishers, 2001).